ADVENTURES ON THE PAN AMERICAN HIGHWAY
OF SOUTH AMERICA

Map kept by the Donnells of their adventures.

ADVENTURES ON THE PAN AMERICAN HIGHWAY OF SOUTH AMERICA

June 4, 1953 to November 20, 1953

Lucretia Ayres Donnell and Earl Roe Donnell, Sr.
with
Illustrations by Lucretia Donnell Newman Coke

SUNSTONE PRESS
SANTA FE

© 2018 by Bonnie Newman Pohl and Carilane Newman Vieregg
All Rights Reserved
No part of this book may be reproduced in any form or by any electronic or mechanical means including information storage and retrieval systems without permission in writing from the publisher, except by a reviewer who may quote brief passages in a review.

Sunstone books may be purchased for educational, business, or sales promotional use. For information please write: Special Markets Department, Sunstone Press, P.O. Box 2321, Santa Fe, New Mexico 87504-2321.

Illustrations by Lucretia Donnell Newman Coke

Book and cover design › Vicki Ahl
Body typeface › Adobe Caslon Pro
Printed on acid-free paper

Library of Congress Cataloging-in-Publication Data

Names: Donnell, Lucretia Ayres, 1893-1988, author. | Donnell, Earl Roe, Sr., 1889-1960.
Title: Adventures on the Pan American Highway of South America : June 4, 1953 to November 20, 1953 / by Lucretia Ayres Donnell and Earl Roe Donnell, Sr. ; with Illustrations by Lucretia Donnell Newman Coke.
Description: Santa Fe : Sunstone Press, 2018.
Identifiers: LCCN 2018005946| ISBN 9781632932228 (softcover : alk. paper) | ISBN 9781632932235 (hardcover : alk. paper)
Subjects: LCSH: South America--Description and travel. | Donnell, Lucretia Ayres, 1893-1988--Travel--South America. | Donnell, Earl Roe, Sr., 1889-1960--Travel--South America. | Pan American Highway System--South America.
Classification: LCC F2224 .D66 2018 | DDC 918.04--dc23
LC record available at https://lccn.loc.gov/2018005946

WWW.SUNSTONEPRESS.COM
SUNSTONE PRESS / POST OFFICE BOX 2321 / SANTA FE, NM 87504-2321 /USA
(505) 988-4418 / ORDERS ONLY (800) 243-5644 / FAX (505) 988-1025

Lucretia Ayers Donnell and Earl Roe Donnell.

The Donnells Board a Freighter in Galveston, Texas for South America, 1953.

Contents

Foreword / 9

Sailed from Galveston on the Steamship *Jean Lykes*, no later than June 4, 1953

    1. Puerto Rico: June 11, 1953 _____ 11
    2. Caracas, Venezuela: Around June 16, 1953 ____ 14
    3. Colombia: June 28, 1953 _____ 23
    4. Ecuador: July 7, 1953 _____ 36
    5. Peru: July/August, 1953 _____ 54

Travel Sketches / 85—106

    6. Chile: August/September, 1953 _____ 107
    7. Argentina: October, 1953 _____ 144
    8. Brazil: October, 1953 _____ 161
    9. Uruguay: October 26, 1953 _____ 166
    10. Brazil, November, 1953 _____ 170

Biographies / 183

Sailed from Rio de Janeiro on the Freighter, *Mormacdale*, November 18, 1953
Destination first US Port.

Foreword

This seems the best possible way to acquaint you with our experiences on a trip over the Pan American Highway of South America.

We landed at Caracas, Venezuela, and made it to Rio de Janeiro, covering 15,692 miles, which included many side trips. A whale of a good time was had—going, seeing, and doing things we never dreamed we would have the privilege of seeing and doing, and it will take a lifetime to record all of the human interest experiences of this trip.

These pages are filled with the highlights of the adventure. Though we wouldn't go over this route again, with road conditions such as we found them, we would not have missed some of the experiences for anything in the world.

Things that stand out in memory are the spectacular mountains and the magnificent valleys of VENEZUELA; the panorama of colorful, flower filled and cultivated lands of COLOMBIA; the friendly people, the rare plants, the high volcanoes, the wild bird life of the jungles of ECUADOR; the millions of Indians in native surroundings, the Chan Chan, Phenares, pre-Inca and Inca ruins, the desolation, queer formations of mountains of sand in PERU; the volcanoes, glaciers, mountains, lakes, streams, the unusual flowers, the luxurious hotels, the hospitality of the people of CHILE; the bleak Pampa, the lush field, the secret police phoning ahead and keeping track of our every move for fear we might trespass on forbidden territory, the colorful, friendly gaucho, his customs and mode of living, the prosperity and modern development of the country of ARGENTINA; the well kept, fully developed modern country of URUGUAY; the tremendous size of the country; the true-to-type peoples of the

Southern section, the polyglot types of the broiling, seething, larger cities in the Northern section of the land of BRAZIL.

This all made a profound impression on us and to have been able to follow through and not give up—to complete our venture—we had to learn the meaning of three important Spanish words: *DIPLOMACIA, CORAJE, PACIENCIA.*

DIPLOMACIA (de-plo-mah-sea) – At the border of each and every country entered, diplomacy played an important part in getting through. This had to be learned the hard way, through trial and error. The Latin mind is critical and slow of comprehension. They would ask why an American couple would want to drive through their country, over rough, impossible roads, and stand the chance of losing or ruining a good car, when there were airplanes to take one quickly through the dangerous and difficult parts of the country; but when it was explained to them it's just for fun and adventure and that there were no political or business connections involved, they would literally pat you on the back and motion you on. If one would exuberantly say, "*Hermoso, Bonita*" and sweep the hand toward the horizon, which is to admire the beauty of their country and their people, they will beam with the greatest satisfaction and will be very kind and shower upon you unbelievably kind attentions and gifts, regardless of whether they are of your color or creed.

CORAJE (ko-ray-hay) – When one says it took courage to do some of the things we did, it's putting it mildly. "Fools go where angels fear to tread," could be aptly applied. At times it took "gall"—some would say "guts"—to continue on over such terrible roads, with the odds against our getting through safely.

PACIENCIA (pah-the-en-the-ah) – Last, but not least, patience was what we had to learn the "mostest." It took patience to get us through the gumbo mud, the quick sands, the deep streams, the obliterated sand roads of the deserts, the long waits while roads were being made, the extreme cold and the deep 15-foot snows of the Andean mountains.

Without the constant putting into practice of these three words, diplomacy, courage, and patience, *DIPLOMACIA, CORAJE, PACIENCIA* we would not have been.

LUCKY US.

1

Puerto Rico: June 11, 1953

Monday, off the coast of Cuba! It's been smooth sailing so far. The cows, 200 strong, mooed in relays the first two nights, but seem to have adjusted themselves to the rocking boat, as have the humans—they look content, the humans act contented.

Little "Jean Lykes" was born the first night out—she's bound to be the cutest little calf ever born on the Gulf of Mexico. Cows and cars—some cargo!

They drained the gasoline out of the cars, so there's no bother with the cars; but the dung and urinous smells from the cows makes it impossible to stay on lower decks very long at a time; though there seems to be plenty of nursemen watering, feeding, cleaning, scraping, and spraying the cows.

The Captain seems pretty glum—all the other officers and crew men are very cheerful and are striving to please. The food is fairly good, but nothing to compare with French cargo ship cooking to be found on ships going to and from Europe.

The berths are cool and comfortable; everything would be the berries if they weren't so high—one passenger fell out of bed the first night out. You should see her now! A black cheek and a blacker eye, and a definite injury to the floating ribs. There is no doctor on ship, so they found the First Mate—a young, good looking, but embarrassed first-aider, who took over and taped her up.

With two wonderful days to see Puerto Rico, the ship entered San Juan Harbor about 8 o'clock in the evening, the lights of the city reflecting an iridescent glow in the Bay. As the ship glided past Moro Castle and San Cristobal Fortress, the dark outlines of the ancient fortresses cast a black, magical effect on an otherwise brilliant setting.

As soon as the gangwalk was down, the passengers rushed off to see the sights. A driver of a station wagon was hired to show the visitors the city at night. Going up and down all the main business districts, the sea front, and into some spooky slums, the squalor and stench, with bleary, wild eyed, tattered clothed natives staggering around, brought about a desire to get away from that spot as fast as possible, as there was an unsafe feeling.

Then on to the Caribe Hotel, one of the most beautiful of the Hilton chain—built in a tropical setting overlooking the Bay—where letters were mailed and magazines and papers were bought to take back to the boat. There could be no reason for staying overnight in an expensive hotel when the ship was moored in the most attractive spot in the harbor, away from the noise of most of the dock working.

The driver of the night before drove the party over the island the next morning, through the sun-drenched mountains on narrow winding roads, where there was thick, lush vegetation to be seen from every bend of the highway.

The Puerto Rican oak trees, rising tall and majestic, were in full bloom—a bloom similar in color and shape to the wild rose. The red flamboyant tree was a riot of color, overhanging fences, bordering roads, and dotting the distant mountains and valleys. All the flowers and many more that grow in the USA were growing wild—the hibiscus in many colors—then a large purple flowering tree, similar to the catalpa, gave a cool, contrasting effect to the brighter warmer colors.

The people in wayside shops were selling gardenias, orchids, and camellias for a few nickels, fruits, such as red raspberries, papayas, bananas, pineapples, and mangoes were very reasonable, while avocados were twelve for a dime.

On a mountain road, looking down upon one village with each home built on different levels, as in Taxco, Mexico, was to be found every color conceived by man on the tile roofs of the homes.

The people were well-dressed and mostly of a brown skin texture; yet every so often there was to be seen a perfectly white child sucking at the breast, or toddling along with a dark-skinned mother. The question arose as to whether the babies were fair-skinned when born and later turning dark, or if the father perchance was a white sailor on a leave.

Ponce-Puerto Rico, southernmost tip of the island—last stop before sailing due south through the Caribbean to Venezuela. Oh! this Ponce—it's the hottest, stickiest place on earth.

Twenty dogs rushed to greet the boat as it came into the harbor, their faces turned up toward the ship, and they, like an off-key orchestra, howled in mournful tones for something to eat. One old bitch, dragging herself, looks as if she would give birth to an even dozen pups at any moment.

There were human beings more pitiful than the dogs; no shoes, torsos bare with gunny sacks tied around the waist, kinky, thick matted, unkempt hair. Some of these dockhands were seen eating garbage out of buckets—garbage which is usually thrown overboard. Such wretchedness is hard to believe unless seen.

There is some talk about giving up seeing Angel Falls because a fellow passenger from Del Rio, Texas, now a store manager in Caracas, says the only way to see the Falls is to go by airplane and, at that, an overhanging mist might hide the view. Others have made three or four trips before they have had a peek at it.

Angel Falls, which plunge over the northern rim of Auyen-Tepui mountain in Venezuela, are the highest falls in the world and from all that's being said about them, they should be worth a great deal of effort to see.

The man also says prices in Venezuela are staggering on all imported goods, and nearly all foods must be brought in. If this is so, there's no reason to stay very long in Venezuela land. Think of butter being $2.50 a pound, oleo at $1.00 a pound, and coffee 25 cents a cup!

There are also many stories to be heard about the natives of Venezuela—how the sailors from other countries are not allowed to leave the ships for fear of riots, fights and waylaying. The seaman, if allowed to go ashore, sometimes disappears, or they return with severe injuries, and there is danger of the ship not having a full crew.

Last minute packing, preparing necessary papers, penciling memoranda for important provisions, bidding farewells to newmade friends, together with the excitement and anticipation of soon arriving in port and getting off the ship, kept us awake most of the night hours.

Suddenly awakening from a short, exhausted sleep, we realized that the boat had stopped moving and the anchor chains could be felt sliding to the bottom of the sea.

2

Caracas, Venezuela: Around June 16, 1953

Out of the porthole could be seen one of the most beautiful harbors in the world—that of La Guaira. The stars in the heavens were shining in competition with the lights of the city; one light looked like a star, it was so high up, yet a star could not shine so brightly without twinkling.

When dawn penetrated the darkness, there was a backdrop of overpowering mountains, with a light pole perched on the topmost peak—the star of the night before!

This was it! The beginning of a long-anticipated automobile trip over the Pan American Highway of South America. We received so much kidding, ribbings and half-truths at the hands of our fellow passengers and ship personnel, regarding our venture, that there was a feeling of apprehension mixed with the pleasure of anticipation.

Though the Esso maps had been studied very carefully, and though most countries showed bright red lines indicating good highways, there was never a doubt that they were different from the North American roads. A good red line on a South American road map may indicate you can get through at one given time of the year, but not during the winter season, or the rainy season; and as each country entered knew so little of the next country, all of this had to be learned the hard way.

But this is getting ahead of the story, so back to the ship personnel, who liked to tease us about the head hunters of southern Venezuela, and they said that they would be back this time next year to see our heads all shrunk up and on exhibit.

They said one should not carry much money as there were men on every corner, who would resort to killing to get money. Some said there was a fine of $100 for honking an automobile horn in Venezuela.

They said there were possibilities of landslides which could hem a car in the mountains and isolate people for days. They told of roving bands of men who followed people and held them for ransom. They said there was a specie of bug that got under the skin and kept eating out the flesh until they killed their victim.

They said if one ever reached Colombia, not to risk walking around after dark, even in the cities, as someone might take a pot shot at them. Most every one of the crewmen wanted to wager it would be impossible to ever make it all the way around the continent of South America to Rio de Janeiro—in a jeep maybe, but not a low slung car.

The passengers were hours topside watching a native pilot the ship into the harbor; then they started unloading the cows first—these fine cows are to help increase the milk requirements of Venezuela.

After a long wait, two officials came aboard to explain about taking the car off the ship. One of the men, a Lykes representative and interpreter, said a bond would be required—one-fourth the value of the car—which was preposterous, and foolish to think of doing.

The American AAA officials had given instructions that the Captain of the ship would give clearance papers to proceed through Venezuela, and that that was all that was necessary until arriving at the Colombian border. But the Captain refused to fix the papers!

Getting off the ship and walking for what seemed hours, from one official place to another, in the sticky, tropical heat, the question of how to go through the country without having to post bond, was finally solved.

When other ruses failed, the Lykes man offered to drive to Caracas to get the newly established American Automobile Association Club office to help fix the papers, asking one percent of the value of the car, plus taxi fare, which would have amounted to approximately $100.

Finding there had been established, just the week previous, in Caracas, a AAA organization—was wonderful news as the talk before leaving the States had been of hopes of just such a club. The AAA in the US had been trying for years to establish a club in Venezuela, but had not succeeded, and cars and people would be out of the club jurisdiction until arriving in Colombia.

Asking a colored man, standing by his car across the street, how much he would charge to drive to Caracas and back, he replied, in the softest and gentlest of voices, "$25." This man had been born in Port of Spain; had been reared by English people; but spoke Spanish fluently. As an interpreter and driver, he was all that was needed and a good man.

The La Guaira to Caracas one-way highway was spectacular with its many winding turns, its magnificent views, its colorful, copperas looking peaks, and its lavish new tunneled highway under construction below; but trying to find the right procedure to follow had wasted so much of the morning, that it was twenty minutes before siesta time upon arrival in Caracas.

The city and the AAA officials had already prepared the papers as the reports on them had been sent from home, which was something to be thankful for; but the clerk of the AAA said the manager wanted to wait until the following day—just to sign the papers! Mañana!

An English insurance salesman in an adjoining office acted as interpreter and tried to explain to the AAA clerk that it was absolutely necessary to get the papers signed that day, as the car could not be taken from the dock without these signed papers, and another expensive taxi trip would have to be made over to Caracas, as all personal luggage was in La Guaira with the car.

When it was suggested that the manager would be reported to the national organization and that he might lose his franchise if he did not get the papers fixed up that day, he was quickly called by the clerk, and he signed immediately.

Returning to La Guaira and to the docks there was much more red tape to be hurdled. Clearance papers were required for the cars to leave port; *Aduana* (police) okay and stamps were a necessity on these official papers before it was possible to proceed through the country.

The docks closed at 4 o'clock, so there was nothing to do but wait until the following morning (another experience of mañana, in Mañana Land) to get the papers signed and get the car released.

Taking a bus ride over the city, to the east of town was found a most attractive seaside playground with a wide avenue of trees bordering the waterfront. Many children were playing games in the park and older people were lolling on benches and getting full advantage of the sea breeze.

A quaint, antiquated hotel with outdoor gardens, flower-decked fences, and restful views of the sea, was seen nearby—and inquiry was made regarding a room for the night. Their service, including breakfast for two, was $36. Walking away, they must have been surprised from their looks, as the average Americans who come to these hotels just accept the prices and pay.

Strolling along, watching the people returning home from work, the children playing in the parks, also seeing the fishing craft off the point, there was this sign "Ponceon Buena Vista" in front of an attractive home overlooking the sea.

Here was acquired a cool, double room with bath. In the yard were banana, orange, lemon and lime trees, and beautiful flowering plants; the yard was just as lovely, but not as large as the hotel patio.

Here instead of $36, the night's lodging had cost about $4—it was easy to learn that even in Venezuela, the country reputed to be the most expensive in the whole world, living costs could be lowered if one would go to the trouble to look for reasonable places.

Next morning, while waiting for a bus, a coffee vendor stationed near the bus stop supplied people with a very dark and bitter mixture. Boiling water poured into a cup, with a few drops of this mixture from the glass containers, was similar to the condensed liquid coffee found in the USA.

On arriving back in the city, the first thing on the agenda was to get the car papers fixed. While waiting through this procedure in the offices of Doctors Romero & Pizzi in the newly-constructed modern office building, the time was spent looking out the windows at the magnificent view of the bay and jutting point of land.

A large French liner was seen being tugged into the docks. Upon inquiry it was learned that the ship was loaded with displaced persons and immigrants from all of the wartorn countries of Europe, seeking new homes in a new world.

Later, watching these people going through customs, there could be seen tragedy, bewilderment, and relief written on their faces. Some had a studied, faraway look; there were some grouped together in happy, friendly companionship; while others—mostly younger ones—had a curious, sizing-up look, as if they could hardly wait for this great adventure.

Many were carrying their most cherished possessions in their hands; oriental rugs, clocks, vases, chairs, chimes, linens, and laces. Some were well-groomed; others flashily dressed as if for parties—probably the only clothes they had; while others were shabbily dressed, cringing to one side, as if to shrink up, and showing pale, emaciated haunted looks. There were some older couples who seemed to cling together in trembling fear with memories, written on their faces, of losing much and suffering more.

Officials say there is no restriction in these migration ventures into Venezuela other than that these people must give the country six months' work in agricultural development, before they can become citizens and go into work of their own choosing. It seems that learning to grow foods would be a good thing for any country to require of its new immigrants.

Many of these people are said to be artists and will line the highways trying to sell their pictures, carvings, linens, laces, and other handcraft, after they have finished their six months' work for the government.

Finally arriving back at the docks with the necessary papers, a man got gasoline, connected the battery, and brought the car around to check for possible scratches, dents, and breaks. The front grill was bent, right door bottom slightly bent, and the back left taillight was broken.

Customs was gone through very quickly, with the help of a young Venezuelan who had received his education at A & M College Station at Bryan, Texas. But when the officials opened the trunk of the car to put the luggage in, they started arguing with the colored man who was assisting with the luggage.

Asking what they were talking about, the helper kept saying, "*Momenteto, Señora.*" Finally, after much deliberation, it was found they were arguing about the oil canvas boards which were wrapped up in brown paper and stacked together. The officials must have thought these were carton of cigarettes, or something of great importance, from the way they stood carefully on guard, surrounding the car, as they were taken out and opened up. The big, husky leader, wearing a gun [grin?] and carrying a club, looked rather silly when he saw they were just canvas boards; however, it took another hour to put them through [page 10 cut off at bottom?]

Caracas has many points of interest; there were several beautiful parks lined with trees and contrasting floral arrangement in their best blooms at this time of year; one park with a statue of Simon Bolivar, who was the liberator of the country, was especially lovely and well worth seeing.

The Government Palace, the cathedral, universities, theatres, apartments, hotels and the wide, shady avenues and double lane boulevards descending from the beautiful mountain homes to the lovely valley homes, showed the city to be one of great progress and prosperity. And the majority of the populace looked surprisingly well fed and well groomed for the country to be so expensive to live in.

Leaving the city, the countryside of Venezuela was most attractive and much cheaper prices prevailed after leaving Caracas. At Valencia a hotel room with shower bath cost only $4.50 for two. Boiled ham with poached eggs seemed the safest thing on the menu for dinner, and was $2 each.

The hotel was a big, sprawling, tile-floored place, tiles all loose, and a klinkety klink sound seemed to echo through the halls regardless of whether the walking was hard or light, and uneasiness followed each step as if walking on broken glass.

The room was without screens and on awakening in the morning what looked to be mosquito bites had left large, peppery red spots on legs. While driving along in the heat of the day, these spots itched as no mosquito bite had ever itched before; and after clawing and scratching for several hours, and with legs covered with what looked like smallpox, a cold mountain stream brought immediate welcome relief to feverish, stinging feet and legs. Mentholatum was the only remedy that could be found to cover the spots with and give a degree of comfort for a time.

The second day out the dry roads turned into the most smothering white chalky dust and penetrated into every cranny and nook of the car. A scarf tied over the hair helped some, but what was needed most was a gas mask!

The stinging, itchy legs, the unbearable dust entering eyes, ears, nose and mouth and seeming to settle in every cavity of the lungs, the sweltering heat and the glare of the sun on the eyes, brought out this question many times that day—why in the devil was this hell-hole picked for a summer trip, anyway?

The first deep tropical jungle area driven through was like going over a precipice at night—there always seemed to be a hill to climb which could not be seen over. It was thrilling to slowly go through and look at the dense foliage of the trees and bushes, with orchids and other terrestrial plants clinging where limbs join on to the tree trunks, and hanging from craggy points.

The eke, eke, eke, and light bark or chatter of monkeys could be heard in relays, and the locust bugs kept up a continuous buzz which would gradually develop into a shrill tone beyond the reach of human ears. Then the call of birds, loud and ferocious at times, would cause a commotion; then things would subside for a time; then this would start all over again.

The strangeness and the aloneness of the situation was overpowering, but as long as the car was perking, and there would be sunshine ahead, all seemed well.

Another day, another miserably hot desert region near Barquisimeto and, with the dust and heat together, the logical thing seemed to be to just give up and quit, but how could one quit in a spot like that!

This South American trip had been planned to get away from the heat—but there had never been anything experienced at home as stifling as this!

Beyond Valera, as the road improved and started climbing into the mountains, the weather became cooler as the road climbed higher. The car made the 14,294-foot pass near Paramo de Mucuchies without the least effort, although several men had said there might be trouble due to the car being a high-compression motor, and having to use the low and only grade of gas sold in South American countries.

This Pass, newly revamped by an American construction company, but forming a zig zag pattern in its climb to the top, was spectacular all along the way, being able to look down thousands of feet to many levels of the road.

Wild forget-me-nots, yellow and pink wild running roses, and blue lupine-like flowers were blended into the foreground—at the timber line snow-on-the-mountain flowers of great size and beauty looked like their name—while the distances seemed to go on and on forever in a maze of fog and sunshine playing loop-the-loop over the vast domain. It was bitter cold on top; it was nice to be in a cold spot again—but not that cold!

Making a very careful descent down this first, but highest pass, with a sigh of relief, the thought was brought out that if all these high mountains heard about were like this, there was nothing to be afraid of. In a short time, however, that sigh of relief turned to a chill of panic.

An extremely narrow, winding road, which ran along high ledges, steep slopes, hairpin turns, and blocked-off areas, was encountered with many small, but dangerous landslides. The large rocks would bring the car to a standstill, and one would get out of the car and, by hand or foot, push these rocks from the path—or cow trail would be a better name for the road.

Some of these rocks, larger than water buckets, would be rolled over the cliff and be heard when they hit bottom hundreds of feet below. Then the car would be put in motion again and, by gunning the motor, make it through the loose sandslide.

There was no turning back on this road, and very few places wide enough for another car to pass, which was found out the hard way. It was wise, on rounding every curve, to honk loud and long with the hope that if a truck or car heard the honk, they would wait in a good spot until the car got by.

One hair-raising experience was when a high off the ground Ford jitney bus of 1930 vintage, with six older people and two children aboard, whizzed right up on the car, touching the front bumper. The cocky driver of the jitney insisted the car with the fewest number of people in it, counting them out on his fingers and making other motions, had to do the backing. Getting out of the car and surveying the situation, it was plain to see several hundred feet had to be backed over to let them by.

Can anyone think of a more nerve-racking thing to have to do 10,000 feet up, with the road just a ledge straight down and more or less a cow trail—it would have been dangerous on a horse or donkey, much less a car. A few more experiences of that kind and who wouldn't want to call this whole thing off? There was always the thought, if one could get through this jam, they would be more careful the next time.

All the way up to La Grita were encountered many steep grades, fast flowing ravines to drive the car through, constant turns, rocky roads—the road beds where trucks are driven develop a high arch of rocks and rubbish in the center, caused from friction of fast-moving tires striking the large round rocks and throwing them toward center, as they used rocks instead of fine gravel for roads.

This ridge in the center made it necessary for a low-slung passenger car to ride the ridges to one side of the road to keep from pounding the gas tank, universal joint, brakes, and oil pan below the motor; but often, in spite of being careful with the car, and driving slow, this loud ping noise could be heard against the metal underneath and, with a good imagination, one could believe the car was being torn to pieces.

There were many stops along this highway to view the magnificent vistas of snow in the distant Andes, and see the closer, cultivated areas of mountain, from top to bottom, in colors of the yellows of golden wheat, browns, leaf green to deepest green, with hedgerow effect borders of flowering trees and plants marking each individual field of a few acres—this all giving the effect of the silk embroidery edges on a grandmother's patchwork velvet quilt.

The building of bamboo huts attracted much attention, the bamboo growing in abundance, rising straight and tall along the roadways, from tiny poles to trunks eight inches in diameter. This bamboo serves many purposes in these South American countries—it makes attractive fences, drainage pipes, and is used in all kinds of irrigation projects.

Often drinking water from springs a mile away is carried through these hollow troughs of bamboo, and the stilts which hold up and support these troughs are also of bamboo. There is no shortage of this material, as it does not rot out and deteriorate in these countries.

The natives in their lackadaisical way, wearing filthy rags, were singing, dancing, and prancing around barefooted at their tasks—seemingly happy in their squalid surroundings where many children, up to twelve years of age, were stark naked and absolutely unashamed of their nakedness, showing no inhibition or restraint whatsoever, as they would line up by the car to sell fruit, avocados, melons, or just beg for pesos (money). There were many more naked boys than girls. It was a common thing to see a man excreting on the highway without so much as turning his back. Women are scarce on these highways; if seen, they were trudging along the side of the highway, a baby strapped to shoulders.

Very few good cars, trucks old and dilapidated, and jitneys could be seen going along, or jacked up by the side of the road with natives fixing tires or motors.

There were many dangerous landslides after leaving Merido. Just the week before a whole mountain decided to bury a small village. Rebuilding a road through such a place looked to be a colossal task for the inadequate building machinery of Venezuela.

The roadmen would cut out a new high road, then lose it in a new landslide. Getting through this new road of deep rutted sand, and detouring every which way, with a low-slung car and a high compression motor, was a difficult and uneasy task. There were times when it was possible to lose car and occupants in a slide, the sand was so unpredictable.

Many times, it was necessary to stop to rest the driver as well as the car, and size up the situation, in this nerve-racking job of getting through. Other cars, mostly trucks, were making it, which was reassuring when arriving at some temporary rocked-up spots barely wide enough to get over and nothing but sand holding up the spot.

Reaching the summit of an adjoining mountain, and while having a picnic lunch, it was a spectacular sight to look back and see the unusual winding road being traveled, and the magnitude of damage done by landslide to roads and towns.

Having finished the food and folded the leftovers into a bag to throw away, there appeared from out of space, it seemed, under some trees, not four feet from the car, a group of small, stocky, sweaty brown Indians with dirty cloths tied around their middles, eyes crossed staring at the car or the food, it was hard to tell which. Throwing the bag toward them and saying "Buenos Dias," a rush into the car and a quick getaway was the best quick thinking done that day, as it was found out later.

Entering the small village of La Grita with a slowly leaking tire dashed all hopes of making San Cristobal that night. As the plaza was driven around, in search of a station, dozens of dirty, half-clad boys from every direction came running toward the car, piling and picking over it.

Trying to find a regular place to have the tire changed was impossible, but a filling station man suggested, by patting one of the older boys, who had been following the car, on the arm, that he could fix the tire.

Finding a cut place on the tire, it was decided to use a boot to make it stronger. Then the boy put the repaired tire back on the car.

In the meantime, the manager had cashed a travelers' check, taking out pay for gasoline and boot. Giving the boy who fixed the tire a generous tip, and preparing to drive on, the boys crowded around the car yelling, and by literally holding fenders, door knobs, and standing in from of the bumper, the car could not be moved an inch without hurting someone.

Getting out the conversation book and taking word by word, they were asked why they were holding the car. The boy did not think the boot had been paid for. Insisting that it had been, and gunning the car as though to leave, several of the ragamuffins pulled out long knives and showed by hand motion, that if the car was moved another inch, they would slash up the occupants and the car tires.

Realizing the desperate situation, a twenty-peso note was about to change hands, when up walked a lovely, blue-eyed, blonde lady into this mob, leading two small, fair-haired girls by the hand, and in English she asked, "May I help you?"

After explaining the situation to her, she said, "Let's go up to the mission and get my husband to help you." "But these boys will not let the car go." "Oh, yes, they will when I explain."

As she talked to them, they put knives back in pockets and stood back to let the car go, then followed at a safe distance. At the mission school the husband came out and, after his wife explained the situation, went along to the filling station where he asked the manager to explain to the boys that the boot had been paid for at the same time the gasoline was bought—which he did.

Had not Mr. and Mrs. Richard A. Gray, missionaries, appeared on the scene at the time they did, it's doubtful what the outcome might have been with those boys.

The lengthening shadows of late evening were casting their spell over this small village. It was impossible to make it on into San Cristobal and a good hotel. Tired and weary from the commotion, but no matter how tired one got, the car had to be put in a safe place for the night—safe from that same bunch of boys—or else there might not be pieces of a car in the morning.

The springless beds of the hotel, a washbowl and pitcher of water, took care of the immediate needs and, with the aid of a candle, the makeshift toilet was found out in the alleyway, which served as a chicken roost, also.

3

Colombia: June 28, 1953

To enter Colombia, Venezuela officials made it a high-jacking deal. The official literally took a 100 Bolivar note and tucked it under his desk pad without giving back any change. Thinking the job was finished, and getting in the car to leave, other officials, rushing toward the car, whistled it and the passengers back to sign more papers, and asked for more money. Then the last bit of change that could be found was dumped on the desk, and they were told that was all. But they kept asking for American dollars. Showing them the uncashed travelers' checks finally satisfied their belief that was all they could get and, by patiently standing by for what seemed an hour, the exit was made.

It was hard to understand what the trouble was as no one on this border could speak English, and the Spanish conversation book proved inadequate for that problem and many other times to come.

They must have been trying to explain that a visa could be had in the city of Urena, a small town nearby. The Colombian Consulate in Houston, Texas, on June 3, had refused to prepare visas to enter Colombia, when trying to get clearance papers from them, saying it wasn't necessary for anyone who was going through Venezuela first, to have visas.

Arriving at the Colombian border at siesta time, and with head officials at lunch, it was impossible to get the men in charge to prepare the necessary papers needed to proceed on through Colombia—they insisted we go back into Venezuela and get visas. Waiting, waiting, waiting two hours, they just kept saying we had to go back to get visas.

Refusing to go back and be bribed again—just sitting there talking, and talking, with the aid of the Spanish conversation book, trying and trying to explain what the Colombian

Consulate at Houston had said; but *no comprend* was the most that could be gotten out of them.

Almost giving up, at last a fine-looking officer came up and asked, in good English, what was the trouble. Explaining the problems of going back into Venezuela, he said that he would get the proper clearance visas and, since it was Saturday and everything was closed, he would send a man along to Cucuta to help the AAA officials fix these papers.

Luckily, by driving hurriedly into the city, the AAA official just finishing his bath, was contacted just in time as he was preparing to leave the city for a few days.

While waiting and chatting with a small girl next door about their patio flower garden—*bonita flores*—she started plucking a bouquet of the choicest large blooms. When the mother came to the door, there was doubt that she would approve of what the child was doing, but she helped gather an armful. Giving them gum and candy brought from the ship seemed a happy exchange to them.

The night was spent at the International Hotel in Cucuta. It was unique in that the large patio was completely covered with vines, which gave a cool and rested feeling after a week of difficult and nerve-racking driving.

An American from Bakersfield, California, helped get money exchanged 3.16 pesos to 1 American dollar, at the Petroleum Club. Another nice fellow, a native who traveled for a New York concern, helped as interpreter.

It's hard to believe that such an elegant little town like Cucuta has the danger of wild tribes of Indians near and surrounding it. Having been warned again and again when starting south to stay in the car and not picnic by the side of the road, as had been done the last hundred miles before arriving in Cucuta, from descriptions it's easy to believe the silent people seen under the trees must have been of the tribe of Montilone Indians.

It is said that when American oil companies are drilling down in this section of the country, they build large metal fences covering an area of several blocks or more, to protect their workers from these Indians.

This tribe of Indians is made up of short stunted people of broad hip development, slender ankles, long feet, big toes, beady eyes, and matted hair.

The bow staves they use for shooting are very heavy—too heavy for the average man to use—and it is believed they are drawn with the feet of these savages, as it must take a terrific force to shoot an arrow completely through a man.

The Indians have only a sign language, as far as anyone knows; they group themselves into small tribes and live in mud huts; they leave no tracks when stalking; they are not robbers; they seem to have only a lust for killing.

One incident worth retelling came direct from an oil field worker. This particular time the solid metal fence of the oil company had accidentally been left with a small crack or opening, just wide enough for an arrow to be forced through. Two of the workmen, in range at this small opening, had been shot and killed by these arrows, the arrows going completely through them. A third man, who was up on the bulldozer at the time, survived an arrow which went through his arm and protruded a foot at the shoulders.

Later, the oil officials had an opportunity to examine these hard but delicately carved instruments of death, and found them to be of remarkable workmanship for a tribe of Indians to produce without any modern tools, in the depths of the jungle.

Leaving on Sunday afternoon over a difficult, rough, narrow road for Pomplona, many natives in flashy clothes were to be seen on the highway and grouped together in huts, as is to be found on a Sunday in the USA. All along the highway there were coffee plantations with row upon row of plants, many were red with berries—the soil freshly softened by workmen with crude hand tools lying near, had brought about an exceptionally rich green coloring to the plants.

The clean condition of the land and the many foot trails leading over the mountainous region, indicated this was a busy, thickly populated area—this area looked safe enough. Wild cacao trees near the roads and in the forest part of this section were of great interest, and a desire to examine some of the pods growing on the trees was intriguing, but better judgment overcame curiosity after remembering the warning about the Montilone Indians.

Hotel Pomplona! From three hotels, this one was selected because it looked the cleanest. The people must have thought these are crazy Americans the way they ask to see the *cocina* (ko-thee-nah) and then go back in the kitchens and look it over before deciding to stay at a place.

A cute little native lady, with at least ten children, was the manager of the hotel and was thrilled at getting to ride in the car to show the garage. She must not have ever been in a car before, surely not a Cadillac; you could tell by the way she reared back and waved to her friends as she passed.

Not one word of English could she say, but she kept motioning with signs that someone would break the glass if the car was left outside. It was many blocks to the garage and weary from the day's journey, the logical thing was to take a taxi back to the hotel, the taxi a model A Ford about 25 years old, but clean and in good running order.

But first, before returning to the hotel, the lady wanted to show the way to get out of town the next morning, or she was getting in some extra riding—maybe both. On the way back into the village the car was stopped on a high hill to view mountains with clouds literally dipping down and kissing the hillsides with moisture, then raising up to dip down again.

Having overbought a lot of food two days before in San Cristobal, such as tamales baked in banana leaves, ham, cheese, and delicious fried pie goodies of chicken, rice and cumin seed, a happy solution was to share this food. It was easy to overbuy, when so many natives were coming into this London Bar and buying up large sacks of this food. A French waitress, who spoke English, said the food was absolutely safe at this place.

Sharing this food with all the hotel family, including an uncle and an aunt, they ate as if they were starved, and to show their appreciation, a dance was started with old American records being played in loud crescendo, getting out each record carefully and lovingly and sometimes kissing it.

This kept up for hours and hours and sleep was long in coming. It seems the common thing down here, when Americans show up, the people get out their American records and blare them loud and long. It does give a nostalgic touch to the weary traveler and they promise themselves, if they ever get out of these dangerous situations, they'll stay at home.

This Monday was a horrible day—sometimes less than 15 miles an hour was made. One time water from a swift mountain stream came over the floor of the car as the car, coughing and spitting, barely made it through. The car was going so fast, very little water had time to seep in and damage the luggage. The brakes got wet and were a nightmare of worry as the car started climbing a muddy and slick red clay road, with many turns, steep ascents and descents, all of the high sections unguarded.

Reaching the summit of the Paramo del Almorzadero (12,754 feet high) after an extremely difficult and, what looked like a 45-degree climb, it was a perfectly gorgeous morning to view the panorama of mountains and villages for hundreds of miles from this height.

On the outskirts of Milaga, when approaching a chain barricade, a group of civilian dressed men, wearing holsters with mean looking guns strapped to their waists, stopped the car.

Before realizing what was happening, these men had the luggage out of the car and were going over it with a fine-tooth comb. They must have been looking for firearms as there had been a change in government just a few days before.

They dumped some costume jewelry on the ground and examined certain pieces minutely, as though looking for diamonds. It was upsetting, but diplomacy is the best thing to strive for under a new government. When one of the men picked up a package of six nylon stockings, counted them out and started dancing around and then commenced to put them in his shirt, he was told to put them back in the bag and it looked as though he had done that.

Another fellow opened a box containing several colored tam hats and put them on his head. There's a limit to what one can stand; that was just too much for a grown man to do, and he was told in no uncertain terms that he would be reported to "*Americanos Embaja.*"

They are bound to have understood what was being said; at least they must have understood "*Telephona Americana Embaja*" as it was repeated several times and the leader, a well-dressed guy, got very red in the face and motioned for the others to come away.

The bags had been left for the travelers to straighten up, so with hot tempers, dirty looks, and tired nerves, the bags were put in the car and the journey resumed. Opening the bags the next morning, the nylons could not be found anywhere, so the Colombian government should be charged up with six pairs of hose, that some wench, perhaps, had the pleasure of wearing.

Milaga seemed a tough spot—in the center of the town dozens of wild looking goofs clambered over the car as it moved along. To get out of the confusion and not wanting to stay in the filthy hotel, which had been inspected, the best thing was to try to make it on to Soata. But it was destined that we stay in that hotel and suffer the misery of chinch bugs all night.

A tire was found slowly going down, and it took the Esso station man such a long time to find the leak and fix it that it was unsafe to risk leaving so late, for fear of having to drive at night over a reported dangerous mountain pass. That pass was one continuous turn on a narrow ledge and a dangerous risk in the daytime, much less at night.

Through Susacon, on through Belen, the country was breathtaking with beauty. Creeping at a snail's progress over this unguarded, rocky road, it was possible to take in and study the scenery.

The poinsettia trees were towering fifteen feet and had the largest blooms imaginable; there were geranium trees in full bloom, a foot in diameter, and as tall as the homes; the fragrant lilac grew in massed array along the road, and made one heady with its odor; the bougainvillea trees, in purple, pink and white, could be seen climbing on every little hut dotting the mountainous terrain; the flamboyant tree, though thinly scattered, made up for its sparseness in tremendous size and color.

There were hedgerows of wild yellow Scotch broom weed; there were lupine flowers much larger than the bluebonnets at home; there were masses of flaming red, trumpet-like flowers overhanging the road and dangling down in their mad climb from tree trunks to limbs; and last, but not least, the most exotic blooms of all—a deep, purple-red fuchsia, with a velvety look, which grew in clusters of eight or ten blooms, close together, similar to the oleander bush.

In the small village of Duitama, a narrow patch of pavement continued for about ten miles. It was heavenly to once again know what it feels like to be on good smooth road.

There was another low tire before reaching Tunja. Continuing on and trying to make it to station, the rim of the tire had been cut. A boot was put in, thinking that the tire would stand lots of punishment yet, since there were to be better roads. Glory be! There were better roads! The fifty miles of pavement on into Bogota was worth kissing.

Bogota, capitol of Colombia, nearly 8,000 feet above sea level, with its old-world charm, is a city of contrasts. Beautiful old colonial buildings stand side by side with the most modern of architecture.

The hotel, Tequendama, is ultra-New Yorkish. The comforts of this swank place were most enjoyable after the physical as well as mental anguish of the past weeks. It's absolutely luxuriating to take two or more baths in one day, as it's been possible to do here. If this comfort could last forever, is the feeling at the moment.

No amount of money would entice us to go back over these roads, yet the natives say the most dangerous roads are still ahead!

Since June 13, 1953, the Colombians have had a new president, Teniente General Gustavo Rojas Pinilla. Everyone seems to be happy over the brilliant stratagem he pulled off. They are relieved that it was a bloodless coup.

With such an admirable leader, as the majority of the natives seem to think of the new president, there couldn't be a better time for Marion Eisenhower to come to this country than today. This morning a welcoming committee of hundreds of cars met him at the airport. Tonight they are having a reception for him in the hotel; everyone of importance is on hand wearing their best bib and tucker. My! Such magnificent jewels the women are wearing, some of the diamonds and emeralds look like the headlights on the Santa Fe.

The women, some a little dark in skin tones, were wearing lovely trim, black dresses. There was to be seen one blonde in an aqua dress, with a pony-tail hairdo. She looks American—could be? All of these people are coiffured and gowned in as good taste as anyone at home.

Another parade was seen this afternoon, a funeral procession led by a large, ornately trimmed black hearse, drawn by prancing black horses, all tasseled and in shiny silver and gold harness; the drivers resplendent in top hats and cutaway suits sat stiffly in seats, looking straight ahead. It was a splendid sight to see. Flowers were beautifully arranged on top of every car in the line. This seems to be such a lovely custom for so saddening an occasion.

There is much to see in and around Bogota, and there is pleasure in seeing things in a cool altitude, 8,500 feet high. The salt mines at Zipaquira are most impressive and can be driven into in a car. The million-dollar bullfight ring is the pride of the city. The chapel of El Sagrario and the San Carlos Palace are something to remember. One should take the funicular railroad up to Manserrate to get a beautiful view of the city and the surrounding country. Also, the Tequendama Falls are a must on the list for visitors.

Leaving the city in the late morning gave a better chance to see the Falls in the middle of the day when the fog usually lifted. Driving south, over a good paved road, through deeply wooded sections, there was a feeling of rushing to some great event while following the swift and noisy river Funga to an amphitheatre-like place surrounded by a grove of magnificent trees. The fog was very dense upon arrival but the ten-minute wait was rewarded—there was this sheer drop—460 feet of falling water churning into a misty white froth.

An unmarked road from the Falls, a road which the truck drivers were going over, was taken on a hunch to El Colegio, Viota, and Tocima, and saved backtracking through the city again. The scenery was spellbinding. The weather was perfect for seeing the distances.

Very few tourists go this way and have not spoiled the natives, so prices were low on fruits, vegetables, and handmade gewgaws. There was pavement all the way into Girardot, but south to Espinal was one of the dirtiest, roughest, and vilest roads for humans to travel. Giving up for the day at Gualanday was easy when there was found a clean but antiquated hotel.

Light rain in the night settled the dust on the roads and much better progress was made the next day. All along the highway was to be seen beautiful twelve-foot tall cotton, thick with bloom and boll, banana groves with rich yellow and pink fruit, avocadoes in deep foliage, mangoes in red and yellow fruit, coffee trees with waxy leaves and half-ripe green and red berries; all were growing right near the cotton. It looked kind of funny to Texans who are used to such large fields of just cotton.

In all the little villages, sections of streets were roped off and tons of coffee were being dried right on the ground, near the homes and business houses.

Dogs, monkeys, chickens, ducks, geese, and children were walking and playing over it; natives, barefooted, were sweeping and turning it.

Pink bananas, quince, oranges, pineapples, plums, papayas, cantaloupes, and watermelons were being displayed in bamboo stalls. The fruit was fresh from the haciendas and had a wonderful flavor.

These people were nicer looking, appeared cleaner, and seemed happier than those of the border towns and regular route towns.

Some of the toughest driving of all has been today. The Colombian government is rebuilding a road over a 12,000-foot pass. It took four hours to go twenty-five miles.

The nicest fellow from San Jose, California, who is a construction engineer with the Utah Construction Company of the USA, but down in South America on this project, came up to the car, while waiting for the road gang to level off a strip of road.

He said, "Well, well, well, look who's here. From Texas, eh?" walking around and eyeing the car number and inspecting the car in general. "Ho, ho, ho, nobody but fool Texans would come down here in a Cadillac! Say, ain't you just about twenty years too soon?" and then, "Well, where you heading?"—Rio—"You mean Rio de Janeiro, Brazil??? Oh, now folks, don't kid yourselves, that just ain't being done in this kind of a car! Are you trying to tear the car up? Why don't you folks just stick around a few days, there's a good little village about a mile back. I'm hankering to talk to and be with some Americans for a change. There's a fairly good road on into Buenaventura, it's a good town, too, where you can get a boat home. Oh, but you can't get through Ecuador into Peru. There just ain't no good road through them parts. I know—I've been there. Well, so long folks, you can't say I didn't warn you. Here's my address, drop me a card when you get stuck in some God-forsaken mudhole down the way, I'll pull you out."

Just then a native came up and talked with him in Spanish for a few minutes and then went away. When it was mentioned that a good knowledge of Spanish would make the driving through the country easier, he replied, "Sure, it's easier, I learned Spanish in a hurry when there was no one to talk with in English, and a given job had to be done in a certain length of time. You will, too, when you get in a tough spot, the words will just come to you."

Waiting more than an hour while a big bulldozer smoothed out a road from a blasted mountain, and to keep from getting impatient over the delays, the time was spent sketching trees and flowers, natives and animals and birds.

The trees and the thick underbrush in all the green colors captured the heart this day—never could there be more beautiful or greater variety of plants in one given place. Looking up overhead, a twisted, half-unearthed tree bent over the road was holding clusters of white and pink centered orchids which, thirty feet up, nature had nestled securely in the arms of the tree limbs. These orchids had unusually long stems and very dark green foliage and were a rare and unusual specie, a native conveyed by blowing a kiss toward them and seemed like was saying *raro planta*.

The roads were horribly dusty, dry, rough, and rocky; while progressing slowly along, rocks as big as water buckets were right in the middle of the road. Trucks and pickups could possibly go over them; after all they were the only vehicles that come this way and should be able to go over them. It was simply a question of taking things as they come—otherwise one would go out of their mind attempting to do this driving.

These trucks on these roads have lots of punctures; they scotch the wheels with these big rocks and then just leave the rocks in the road, which accounted for many rocks and slow driving. One can't swing off from these rocks 9,000 feet up, with the road barely wide enough for one car, so getting out and moving them is the only thing left to do. Putting in a claim to the Colombian government for clearing the road of all large rocks might be something to add to the record.

A landslide was missed by seconds today—rocks as large as a washtub struck the front bumper. Getting the car in reverse pretty quick and backing into a tree on the edge of a canyon saved the situation from further disaster. Thank goodness, there was this tree, and a road building crew not far away who cleared the boulders away.

About ten miles further on, several cowmen came along, riding horses and yelling at a herd of steers. There was barely room for the car on the 7,000-foot ledge of road. The car just had to stop and wait there and let those animals and men go by, one at a time.

It was almost dark before arriving in Sevilla, where the night was spent in the craziest kind of a hotel. Everything, including kitchens and dining rooms, was upstairs—except the baths and toilets. These were lined up on either side of the first floor, with clotheslines all strung in between. The people upstairs would wash their hands and brush their teeth, and then dump the bowl or glass of water over the rail on to the tile of the first floor, splashing on clothes and flowerpots and adding to the messiness.

All during the night could be heard marching, talking, singing, laughing, hollering, and hammering. Much confusion was sensed. In the morning, when the hotel doors were unbolted, the entire plaza was fixed up with tables and stalls from which was hanging fresh meat in bloody array or hacked in great hunks on tables.

It was a great display if one likes to look at tons of fresh meat. Hides of animals were piled high at one corner of the square; some were left stretched on poles from tanning.

The whole populace of the countryside was pouring into the square with buckets, sacks, and huge wagons with two oversized wheels, and smaller pushcarts, to take away the meat. A brisk business was in progress. This was meat market day for the country folk. The millions of flies were also doing a brisk business that day.

The people in this section of the country are very ingenious and seem to make the most of what they have. Every bit of ground is cultivated to the topmost top of the mountains, in a small patchwork effect. There are fields of yellow grain, aquamarine fields of flax, fields of a lupine kind of clover, and fields of yellow mustard, which grows in abundance. The fields are just a few acres at the most, and are bordered by hedge flowers, so one can imagine what a riot of color is to be found on all these mountainsides at this season of the year.

The natives live in small bamboo huts; the bamboo is put together similar to our log cabins, but daubed with a mixture of wet mud and manure, dried and then whitewashed. Some of the older homes are very attractive with flowers climbing over them.

There were many such huts in the process of building, with a hole dug out nearby where naked children were tromping and blending this mud and manure mix. For larger homes or business houses, horses or donkeys were deep in the mire, being driven round and round to get the goo to the right consistency.

The roofs of these houses are of grass and it's the craziest thing to see a blackened-up place where smoke is coming right out of the grass top roof.

There were sheep tied to trees on the mountainside to keep them from falling. The mountain pastures for cattle were tromped in a terrace effect to keep the cattle from going over. Sometimes cattle do fall, and they are left to die wherever that happens; the gruesomeness of it was seen many times.

There is an abundance of turkeys, chickens, and pigs surrounding every hut; the people and animals seem to live together.

The whole Cauca Valley looks like a paradise where every hut boasts a bougainvillea tree in gorgeous bloom, climbing its walls and roofs. There are poinsettia trees fifteen feet tall, the blooms four times the size of those in the USA; there were red and yellow flowered trumpet-like vine or trees with massed blooms, prolifically dominating wherever they grew, and castor bean trees full of rich, red beans showing through mammoth zig zag leaves and with trunks the size of hackberries at home—these were the most amazing trees of all.

Eucalyptus trees were to be found in all sizes, the very old being cut down for timber. The fragrance from these trees was refreshing. There were many groves of mesquite and pepper trees, so much alike; the best way one could tell them apart was that one had long red beans hanging down, while the other had huge clusters of red berries.

There just can't be enough said about the geranium trees, loaded with rich red blooms; then the dwarf plants nearby, which served as border plants, were startling in color.

The rose trees, six inches in diameter, with great thorns thick over the trunk, were similar to the Dorothy Perkins in color and shape, and were in massed clusters. Once today there was seen a climbing white rose covering a wall, then running frantically on in a mad rush of looping across the road into another tree, leaving a garland effect, all of which was collected together in perfect arrangement, showing the centers of the roses to be yellow.

Daisies, forget-me-nots, rosemary, sweet William, and a yellow sage, grew wild all along the highway and in pastures. An odd, deep red, thorny-pronged cacti plant and yucca were to be seen right along with these other tropical plants.

The cable on the emergency brake was sheared off this afternoon when a young child, rolling a hoop with a stick, darted right out on the highway in front of the car. Making a quick swerve to the left, a large rock caught the cable. Arriving in Cali about twenty minutes after the GM plant had closed the parts department was a disappointing experience. This was Saturday afternoon and the manager had gone on a fishing trip for the weekend, and it looked to be a delay of at least three days.

The time element was important. In three days Ecuador and the rainy season had to be dealt with—three days of rain and the chances of getting through would be slimmer.

An Italian family, living in the hotel, who spoke English, were extremely nice and hospitable. They wanted to talk to Americans. In their apartment, they served delicious fresh roasted coffee and dainty sandwiches and cakes.

In the course of the conversation it was brought out that a brake cable was needed for the car. The man contacted his brother, a mechanic at the GM plant, who took the cable he was using for his radio and, with the help of the brother, they had the car ready for travel by noon the next day. They wouldn't take any pay for service or cable and when one finds such generosity, it's best to accept the kindness graciously.

Cali is one of the richest agricultural sections of the country, as is shown by its prosperous, thriving business section, its modern homes, manufacturing plants, coffee plantations and parks. The vast distances of cultivated lands between the city and the snowclad mountains was quite impressive, as could be seen from the hotel windows.

Funny thing, the hotel had added 33 American dollars to the hotel bill when checking out. The corner had been chipped off the bathroom mirror. When telling the clerk about the broken mirror, we offered to pay $3.00, but refused to pay the $33.00 they were asking, finally threatening to call the American Consulate if they insisted that amount had to be paid.

After repeated calls for the manager, he finally showed up. He went up to the room and when he saw that the door of the cabinet was stuck, he apologized for the clerk giving so much trouble and sent us on our way, graciously refusing to charge anything. The hour's delay was worth it.

Driving through a sandy, dirty, dusty, low road to keep from doubling back through Palmira, was to be seen a sample of Sunday afternoon doings in that part of the world. There were hundreds of negroes, in flashy Sunday garb, on the streets, in the churches, sitting in large groups guffawing, playing baseball. Children were playing what looked to be soccer. There was horseshoe throwing, and a new game to us—a boxed-off strip of leveled dirt with large balls to be pushed to the other end, similar to our bowling, but without pins.

Finding time or place to write is a great problem; the lighting systems of the small villages are so weak it is necessary to keep candles on hand all the time to see by when writing or going to the bathroom or toilet. The candles in this part of the world put out such a faint glow it's difficult to know whether it's because of poor tallow, poor tallow cord in the way they are made, or poor and older eyes using them.

So much of the time is taken up keeping the car oiled and greased, getting visas and automobile papers, and following these silly customs regulations, that exhaustion overcomes duty at the end of the day.

Washing clothes at least every other day because of the dirt and grime from the car and the road is another great problem. It's absolutely necessary to do this or find the car full of soiled clothes. Two flats today, near Tunis, caused untold worry, and soggy, dirty clothes, and made it necessary to stay in this place for the night.

A half-finished hotel was all that could be found—it had awful beds, poor toilets, no bath—they never heard of a bath. The manager of the hotel kept watch over the car during the night; otherwise, dozens of ragamuffins would have broken handles, stolen hubcaps, and literally torn the car to pieces.

He sat on the steps, with a large wool poncho covering him, while these children and some dirtily clad older boys and men milled about the car all night, keeping up a jabbering lingo which disturbed the night's sleep.

There were two Indian women squatting near the car all night, with cans and what looked to be a pile of blankets. At 4 o'clock the next morning they had rigged up a little stand and were serving truckers hot, black coffee and rolls warmed up over a charcoal brazier. It looked good, but fixing our own coffee, Sterno style, seemed to be the best bet. Heat out of a can amazed these natives.

Preparing our own food the night before, as the kitchen looked completely bare, was an amazing thing to these people; they peered wide-eyed from every doorway. Their method of cooking is very much like barbecuing in the USA.

Set out in the center of the kitchen so all can work around it, they have a long trough-like square box of brick or stone, with a metal rack about a foot from the top. On this rack they put charcoal or wood and when there are coals of a red glow, they put pots and pans right on the coals and start the cooking.

Handing the leftover foods to the hotel owner's children to put in the garbage, they were later found to be eating the last little scrap of food. After seeing this, all the good bread and canned food, fruits and bottled drinks left in the basket were turned over to them and they ate and drank hungrily.

It takes good stomachs to stand the filth, the outmoded comfort stations of just triangular holes in the ground—maybe the best word would be "guts."

The mother of these children was seen making a skirt for one of the older girls, on what looked to be a 50-year-old, but good working Singer sewing machine, and the skirt had a nice modern style and a wide tucked belt that should be remembered. Clothes seem to be of more importance than food down here, as this young girl beamingly pranced to and fro when trying the skirt on.

Another trying day with two more flats. The tire with the broken rim that was almost thrown away in Bogota has brought the car and occupants more than a hundred miles since. Every mile made on these tires is "velvet"—they have been all over Canada, the west coast, and Europe. Some might think it foolish not to have bought new tires before leaving home, but with all the grief up to now, it doesn't look that way, yet.

Swinging around a treacherous cliff, there was La Union, which looked like a good town on top of a high plateau—the Guide Book says it is noted for its panama hats.

There was no hotel fit for a dog to stay in, but it was a question of staying or facing another bad mountain pass next on the agenda, and not daring to risk those tires on that road so late in the evening, it was necessary to park there for the night.

Dozens of roguish-looking urchins clambered over the car, then followed us into the patio of the hotel and hung around all night watching every move made; even matches and soap were not safe from their quick slippery fingers. The manager of the hotel was paid to watch the car during the night, but a tire was slashed and the red taillights were missing.

It seems a custom in the country hotels of Colombia to economize by using very short sheets on the beds. They bring the sheet up to where the pillow comes, then there is a naked, old straw mattress under the pillow. If one does not sleep on pillows, there is the remaking of the beds most every night. Sometimes the feet are against the mattress, but rather than risk having feet against the mattress, the coverlets are used to cover that part of the bed. The natives must think the Americans are "nutty" when they find the beds fixed like this after leaving in the mornings.

This night at La Union Hotel, after trying to cope with these goofs and the hard driving of the day, found us too tired to change the sheets. Instead, a coat had been put at the top of the bed to sleep on. Having left the hotel early the next morning, going about ten miles out of town, we suddenly realized a good coat had been left on the bed. Turning back to the hotel, the coat could not be found on the bed.

The hotel keeper kept saying, "No, no coat," but continuing to look all the while, saying, "We get *Aduana* if coat not found," going from room to room until finally the coat was found back behind the kitchen tucked away in a small room.

That turn back cost two flat tires and proved pretty expensive. A slashed tire gave out completely, there was a chance of saving the second and a nail was found sticking in a third tire just before it had gone down. The situation was rather glum. There had been three spares, now there were none left, and fourteen miles to Pasto!

Driving a while, then stopping to pump up the tire with the nail, then going again, kept up all the way into the city. But the worry of the tires was completely forgotten for the time on reaching the summit of the pass and looking down to view the jewel of a city, with the high plateau of varied patches of golden wheat and other grain, fields bordered by hedgerows growing completely up to the top of the extinct volcano Galaras in the background, forming a picture of unforgettable beauty. There just can't be any place in the world more inspiringly beautiful than this.

Wonder of wonders, the city of Pasto could boast a comfortable hotel with the best food to be found so far on the entire trip, and so reasonable in price. A nice young American who lives in the hotel and has a new factory making flour sacks introduced himself and has been a constant companion, acting as interpreter and guide. He wanted all the Express checks available as there are a lot of American supplies he needs to get from the States. So, each were thankful for the other.

He is also to be thanked for negotiating for new tires for the car—four tires and tubes were bought much cheaper than they could have been bought at home and, as has been said, what mileage has been accumulated on the old tires is velvet up to now.

The highway construction men say the Colombian all-rubber tires are far better than US tires for these rocky roads, and they use them altogether for replacement. Though the last inch of service has been extracted out of the old tires, three of the better ones were kept for spares and were to save the day in the future, but that's a story to relate later on!

It was with deep reluctance when the third morning found the car and occupants wheeling south again. A little world in itself, Shangri La, shut away from worries, it had been like heaven in Pasto. The good hotel with the friendly service, the delicious foods, beautiful surroundings, was what had been needed to soften up weary bones and give courage to continue on. The four new tires gave a feeling of relief and removed all worries from that score for some time to come.

Driving on the outskirts of the city, the police (*aduana*) were there to send us back into the city to get permission from the chief of police to leave the city. It was necessary to get recommendations from the hotel saying the bills had been paid, no traffic violations, no time in jail—with these things cleared up, permission was granted to leave.

Two hours were wasted on that turnback, but the friendly visit we had had in this city and with its people brought about a nonchalant feeling as to not minding whether we ever got away or not; however, that delay, coupled with trouble with Colombian border officials, made it impossible to arrive in Quito that night as planned.

4

Ecuador: July 7, 1953

A few hours later and south of Ipiales, the customs officials dumped bags and clothing out of the car and on to the ground, while a bunch of rough-looking natives crowded around. Remembering losing hose the last time things were dumped out of the car, it was with great determination to avoid a repeat of that situation, so a belligerent attitude was turned on them to no good end.

The official, a snaggle-toothed upstart named Oscar Warno, sent another with us into the town of Ipiales to see the head of the police department. Not understanding what they were saying exasperated us and we broke away from the officers, inquired and found an English speaking fellow who explained that they wanted to see the car papers, which we had already shown them twice, but they had never seen a carnet and could not understand how to fill out papers as there was no AAA Club to help.

They tried to keep the passports to check and said they would send them on to Quito, Ecuador, all because the visas had been stamped in Cucuta. But they were told, in no uncertain terms, that an American citizen would be a fool to give up passport for any reason whatsoever, and then stepped to the phone to call the American Embassy in Bogota.

The bluff worked. They filled out the car papers, and then they let us go. From the ignorance displayed, we must have been the first American car to go through there with a carnet.

Talk about snaggle teeth, it seems like a third of all the young people of Colombia from one end of the country to the other have four teeth missing in front—many girls included, but 18-year-old boys especially—and so many of them are cross-eyed, too. One explanation was that they do a great deal of fist fighting and usually the fist lands on those two front teeth—the cross-eyes must stem from lack of care at birth.

Darkness was overtaking the light on entering the small town of San Gabriel. If it was possible to find a room, this would be the logical place to stay for the night. Circling the square twice without seeing a place, the first thought was to rush on in the night and not waste any more time.

So many of the hotels in these smaller villages have business houses in front, with just a door entrance to a long hallway leading to a large patio in back, with rooms surrounding this patio. The best and the humblest of these hotels have these patios filled with rare, tropical and exotic plants, making up for their drab and undistinguishable entrance.

In a debatable frame of mind as to camping on the square that night or risking a dreaded difficult pass looming ahead, we had stopped for a moment's discussion when a young man, wearing a blanket Indian fashion (poncho) and a black sombrero on his head and moccasins on his feet, came from a large group of people dressed similarly, walked over to the car and asked, in good English, if he could help us.

He said, pointing to an opening, "The hotel is old, but the owner, a fine man, will do everything he can to make you comfortable." This hotel proved to be all he said and more—clean, restful, and gorgeous orchids and other flowers blooming in profusion. There were running vines climbing over columns and stair rails. We were thankful for this young man and thankful for finding this comfortable place.

This young man was a midshipman at Annapolis and had returned home for a holiday for the first time in two years. He had won this training in the US through competitive examination, and hopes some day to be an officer in the Ecuadorean Navy.

He introduced his father (who was a city official), his English teacher in the college there, and his sister. He insisted the car be taken to the city garage for the night, as there was danger of having it broken into. Acting as interpreter, he took care of the smallest details.

He said when he was at home, he dressed just like all the home folks and they felt freer with him. The father, son, and the teacher were guests for breakfast the next morning. Breakfast consisted of papaya, thick black coffee with the addition of brown sugar and hot milk, two poached eggs each, and rolls, cooked on an antiquated grill, as mentioned before.

All the people in town, covered in heavy wool ponchos, came down to see us off that morning, as we filled up our car with gasoline and prepared to leave early.

All of that day the driving was done without a very good map, as the Esso Company does not furnish a map of Ecuador. The roads were mostly ancient cobblestones, with slow, but sure progress.

Each dangerous hairpin turn gave a new, majestic view of the wild, beautiful region. The 11,000-foot pass was unguarded all the way, and the turns were so sharp the horn got hoarse from so much use.

Finally making it down into the valley, a valley dense with jungle undergrowth where was to be seen plenty of animal life, two armadillos got in front of the car and proceeded leisurely across the road, forcing the car to slow down. An enormous iguana crossed the road at one time, not very far from where some native Indians were clearing out a wooded section. When trying to tell them about the enormous-looking lizard, they looked goggle-eyed at us and the car.

A few miles farther on, when trying to make up time at a pretty fast clip, suddenly before us was this sheer drop down into a swollen stream—no warning of any kind to show the danger.

Fortunately, good brakes stopped the car—a foot from the broken road. Another car full of people went over and were killed at that spot that same day. Workmen, unperturbed, were cutting timber and scraping undergrowth for a new circle highway to the left, and we got through very soon.

Chota, a typical African village, where the thatched-roofed houses were all built up on stilts, was the next interest. The school children were lined up as the teacher stood ringing the bell at the end of recess. They all waved in the merriest fashion as we drove slowly along and honked and waved in return.

The women, naked from the waist up except for strands of beads around their necks and with scarves over their shoulders, were grouped on the opposite side of the road from the schoolhouse, in a very picturesque setting. Some were nursing babies, others weaving colorful baskets and bright woolen materials. Some were humming or singing, others were laughing, and all seemed happy and contented. Everything in the whole village was neat and clean.

Near Otavalo, where the natives are nationally known for weaving fine woolen materials, it was amazing to see dozens of women walking toward the town, all dressed up in gaudy clothes, with string after string of beads around their necks—some looked to be choking.

We stopped one girl and asked her to come over to the car and, while doing this, trying to carry on a conversation with her. To avoid self-consciousness or embarrassment, only words were used as came easily to mind, such as, *buenos dios, hermosa rosario* (pointing to head), *bonito* Ecuador (waving overhead), *camino peligro, no* (pointing straight ahead) *buenos camino*.

An old, old soul, practically in tatters, was noticed sitting by a fruit stand begging, when looking over and buying some fruit. Giving her a couple of sucres she, too, though a beggar, was almost choking with strands of beads around her neck.

Entering the center of the village, it was readily understood why so many of the natives were on the highway coming toward the town. Sight of sights! The most colorful Indian market was in progress and all the women there were choking with beads.

Everything imaginable was on sale—colorful materials, clothes of all descriptions for men and women, rack after rack of hard shoes, animal skins, pottery, baskets, needles and pins, fruits and vegetables of every description.

A first introduction to the cherimoya was experienced that day when the attitude of "trying anything once" was uppermost in our thoughts, and these bead-choked natives were flocking around a two-wheeled cart and eating the fruit with such gusto.

Another fruit, a variety of orange, brought in by natives and tied up in long bunches, full of gelatin or tapioca-like seeds, was good to look at and deliciously good to eat.

Milton Eisenhower and his party are in Quito. A Baptist World Conference group is also in session here; so finding a good, reasonable hotel now has been most difficult.

We like this city, the people of Ecuador and the way they do business—they are fine, honest, thrifty and a lot like Americans in their way of life.

Quito is one of the most picturesque cities to be seen anywhere. It is built in a valley plateau, surrounded by the colorful, overpowering, majestic Andes with the volcano Pichincha to one side. It lends itself to many true and fancied stories about their national hero, Marshal Sucre.

The first drive was up to Cerro Panecillo, a large hill overlooking the city, where a wonderful view of the low-pitched, red tile roofs and the cathedral towers of the city could be seen at their best, and the distant mountains seemed to hem this in in a protecting sort of way.

Quito, called "City of Eternal Spring," would be more suitably called the "City of Four Seasons," as was enjoyed the delightfully spring-like mornings, the hot, stocky (shed all wraps) summer afternoons, the brisk snappy autumn evenings, and the cold sit-by-the-fire nights.

San Francisco, the oldest church, with its gold encrustments, is still in good repair and has a most colorful history. Other churches, such as La Compania and La Merced, with their heavy gold ornamentations, were inspiring.

It was a day to remember when walking around the narrow old streets paved with cobblestones and peering into shops and cubby holes while hunting for good maps to help on the journey south.

The choicest food was enjoyed in old famous restaurants; delicious coffee, freshly parched, was ritually served morning, noon and night. This coffee has the best flavor of any in the world.

In the shops they display many good buys of handmade and hand-woven woolens; the native costume dolls are complete down to the last eyebrow; ponchos in somber black to vivid reds are to be found in every shop and most reasonable; and the hand-tooled leather belts and bags are really works of art. Seeing these things makes one wish they were a buyer for a million dollar concern, as there is not one you would want to turn down—they are that perfect.

The Indian Market is worth a whole day's browsing to bargain on foods of all kind, flowers, baskets, and crockery. There were many American shops with nationally known American brands of products in abundance, and people were flocking in to buy. These things were high-priced, but represented "home."

An American from St. Louis, now living in Quito, came to the hotel this morning to invite us to the 4th of July picnic for all Americans visiting in the city. It would have been great fun, but a date had already been made with a garage man to grease, wash, and change the oil in the car, having learned from past experience in Bogota to never leave the care alone in a garage when having work done on it.

The South Americans can't understand a woman looking after a car and staying with it while having work done, but if one does the driving one needs to know the condition of the car. It was Saturday and the last chance to get it serviced for many days as plans had been made to start south on Sunday morning.

The American gave some good advice about the

roads, but it was too late before realizing it was good, and we didn't have sense enough to take it.

He had been over this road only the week before, through Latacunga right to Quemado, Vincie and Babohoya. The garage man, who should have known road conditions, marked what he thought was a good route on this new and good map of Ecuador. Later we found out that the American knew more about our problems and our needs.

The drive south out of Quito was one of the most beautiful to be found anywhere; the road was ancient cobblestone and slow going, but it gave us an opportunity to study the volcanos—Cotopaxin on the one hand, and on the other Chimborazo, rising over 20,000 feet and perpetually topped with snow. It was a perfect time to see numerous other snowcapped peaks of the Andean chain, as the distance was crystal clear.

The night was spent at Ambato (garden city)—the summer home spot for Quito people. Tomato trees were growing there, ten feet tall with trunks four inches in diameter, the limbs hanging down in umbrella effect from the weight of the ripe, luscious fruit.

Delphiniums were as large as those seen in the cool northern regions of Canada, and there were large rose trees again to be found, full of choice blooms. The pruned and trimmed appearance of these summer gardens left the feeling that only the choicest buds were allowed to bloom forth.

Peaches, apricots, pears, plums, and grapes also grew in abundance in this locality and were so reasonable in price it was a temptation to gorge on them and then pay the penalty of dysentery.

About ten miles out of Ambato next morning, when approaching a turbulent mountain stream on the rise, the bridge going across the stream was found to be about halfway washed from the bank.

While debating on trying to attempt crossing it or not, a large truck came bearing down very fast toward the bridge and barely made it across as more soil fell away into the water. Turning back, the only alternative left was to take the high and dangerous pass through Isidro.

Going through a place called Four Corners any number of people had cautioned to watch carefully to get the right road, but on arriving in Cojabama, we found we had gone forty miles on the wrong road. We had a hunch to not turn back and that hunch was proved right, as can be seen later on. Turning back, wasting half a day! Turning back on to the narrowest, most dangerous, muddiest, dirt pass one could be on!

A light rain was making visibility difficult and the rarefied air was affecting the carburetor so the windshield wipers were not working very well. The foot feed being clogged with mud made it necessary to press very hard on the accelerator. That pass was dangerous with a car in excellent condition—this situation was maddening with drunken Indians following in a truck, honking, hollering, and whistling to let them by. The first thought was that they just wanted to pass, but there was no place to let them pass. This honking and whistling kept up so long, the situation became desperate. It was impossible to go faster on account of the mud and narrow sharp turns.

Finally, looking ahead, we found a small mudhole turnout and, after locking the car doors and hiding the extra money under the seat, we decided to let them pass. They did go by, but stopped in such a position that it was impossible for our car to move an inch.

These six drunk Indians came back to the car and started jabbering for sucres, sucres, and put their faces right against the glass, and leering, or grinning, tested the door handles to find them locked.

Shaking heads, showing them empty purses, gesturing with hands to mouths indicating that we were hungry, putting hands to head in sleepy sick fashion, and saying *inferno nauseade* and constantly and continually motioning them to go ahead finally brought results. They did go ahead after what seemed an hour of parleying around and many whispered conferences between them.

After going over two more dangerous, narrow ledge passes, then winding around a deep, dark, rock canyon, with water gurgling from many crevices into foaming, frothy waterfalls, pouring down this dark, shiny, wet rock into a river at canyon bed which led into the little town of Gurando, we circled the plaza a couple of times looking for a hotel.

From every direction young men, boys, and small children flocked over and around the car, testing door handles, windshield wipers, lights, and generally peering in. It was impossible to find a garage to lock the car up in. With all the jabbering, it was difficult to get it over to them that someone was wanted to watch the car during the night, and out of that group of what looked to be hoodlums, it was impossible to select one to watch the car.

Saying, "*Se habla aqui Ingles?*"—"*Si, si, momentito*," was a quick reply from a good-looking chap, about eighteen years old, as he walked away.

Locking the car and going on into this old hotel, we started exploring every corner from the dining room and bar to the kitchen, where many flies, some chickens, and a pig were running around on the mud floor.

Famished from the day's driving, decided to look in the pots on the stove and see what they had cooking. Found a potato soup, chicken meat with rice, what looked to be a bread pudding, and hard fly-specked rolls on a plate on the table. The potato soup, being covered up, looked to be the best bet.

Pointing to the soup, then going into the dining room, we sat and waited while they warmed it up. This soup proved to be an exceptionally tasty dish of fresh, small, new potatoes, boiled in milk, with butter added, and was worth waiting for.

In came the young man who had said, "Yes, yes, one moment, please." He said, "This man *habla Ingles, el misinero*," and with that introduction, an American shook hands with us and for two hours sat and talked about the problems of Ecuador; about the great thirst for knowledge of these young men who were hovering around by the dozens, and who were listening to the talk but understanding very little of it. He spoke of the slow progress he and his wife were making in a country steeped in superstition, fear and ignorance.

The missionary continued, "The more knowledge they acquire of the world and its affairs, the less they will conform to unreasoning fear or marked beliefs they've grown up with since childhood; and, with the knowledge they acquire, they proceed to develop into useful human beings, anxious to help others see the light and get the same knowledge they have."

Another subject he touched upon that was surprising was his views on communism. He said, "I can talk about this now that my mission here will be over in the spring."

He explained their missions have always been to go into a new field, teach cleanliness, help the sick and afflicted, and teach that Jesus Christ is the son of God, and convert and train the natives to take over the work, as natives can do so much more good than outsiders, if they are sincerely converted.

He went on to say, in dynamic fashion, that too much emphasis could not be put upon education, medical care, the teaching of cleanliness; and that a workable friendship with these natives helped them to develop into a fine country of people, away from communistic tendencies brought about by past suppression of these very important things.

He spoke of the longing and desire of these young men to learn English and eventually come to the United States. This was a high spot in their lives, seeing Americans driving around in an American car, from one of the best-publicized states—TEXAS! They kept saying "Tex-as," with much emphasis on the first syllable.

The missionary said the young man who had brought him there would watch the car all night if we would pay him fifty sucres. Funny thing, a policeman stood guard with the youth. Wonder who was watching whom?

This hotel had a patio filled with magnificent flowers, which made up for its old and dilapidated ugliness. It also must have been at one time a shining example of tile work, a Victorian type, as tile in browns and yellow colors was high on the walls.

An antiquated tile walk, of same blend, centered and bordered the flower beds—this tile made a splendid background for calla lilies, with stems higher than our heads, the large, waxy-white flowers with yellow centers glistening in their freshness.

Fuchsias in deepest, velvety purple hung down in clusters, and a pansy tree!—a tree four feet tall, full of the most beautiful blue and yellow blossoms; the lower petals were yellow, with dark tracings, more like little faces than anything else could describe them.

There was also a deep red velvet double-bloom hibiscus, the elongated yellow stamens pointing out in a sprightly fashion—much, much too gorgeous for the ragged, common leaves they boasted.

Late morning, while sitting by a table placed on the tile floor separating the flowerbeds, the hotel served coffee and rolls. As the sun brought about a reflected light through the glass overhead, the question was asked, was it the climatical location, the warmth inside the building, or the excellent care that had produced such loveliness—or all mixed together?

A gentle old lady, who, like the hotel, had seen better days, probably in her eighties, tottering around, tried to talk about the flowers, but her Spanish was such a mixture of other languages, the two put together was beyond understanding. Understanding words is not always necessary if one can convey, by simple admiration, the beauty seen in a thing, which was certainly conveyed to her that morning.

This day was a lulu, one that out out-lulu-ed a lulu! Rain during the night had softened the red clay road that was in the process of being widened all the way into Babohoyo. If you've never driven on a wet, red clay road, 10,000 feet up, don't! There isn't anything on earth as treacherous or as sickening to the person driving, especially if the driver is on the outer rim of road and can look down and see where, with one mistake, they could easily drop hundreds of feet below.

Highway trucks had made deep ruts on the lower road. The car got stuck many times on account of the ruts being deeper than the wheel base; by backing, then going forward, it was possible to extricate the car most of the time. But one time it was so terrible a highway truck pulled the car some distance, with the use of a cable belonging to an old native lady, who was standing by for just such a chance. Ten sucres seemed a fair price to pay her for the use of the cable.

Then a Model A Ford jitney bus, with big wheels in circumference and narrow rubber tires, came along and, in trying to get out of their way, the car bogged down considerably. These Ford jitney buses are the most surprising cars to be found in this country. They take the roads mighty good. They are about the only cars to be seen outside of the cities. Many Americans think they have to buy a new car every year, but when these remarkably well-kept and good running cars, twenty-five years old, or more, are seen on these horrible roads still going strong, it's not only amazing, but it could be a lesson.

The old lady was asked for the use of her cable again, but she wanted fifty sucres this time, so we decided against it. She was just taking advantage of the situation, being the mother of the road truck-man. They were together deliberately making this opportunity count for themselves.

There is a possibility their help would not have been refused so definitely had not one of the natives, barefooted and muddy, standing by, grinned and motioned he would help. He jacked up the back of the car and put big rocks in the rut; then, he jacked the front up and put more big rocks in the rut; and he added more rocks until he had the road ruts filled twenty feet ahead.

When he took the jack down, and the motor was put in motion, the car pulled out of the mud without the least difficulty and started up and made the steep embankment. This native looked thrilled when he was given ten sucres, and he was the hero of the hour as others patted him on the back. The old lady had a look of disgust on her face as she and many of the other jabbering natives standing by, hissed at the worker lifting rocks into the rut—they must have thought putting rocks in ruts would not do the job.

Every inch of continued climbing over this pass was nightmarish; sliding, slipping in the sticky mire, all the while trying to keep on ridges of the road, even having to ride the ridge over the narrow ledge because the ruts were too deep. Imagine sliding around on a wet, red clay ledge, barely wide enough for a car, the good earth straight down hundreds of feet, a swift, deep, running river the only alternative!

That's what had to be done for the longest hour ever lived. There just couldn't be a turning back, and every step ahead was frightful. The alternate road through Quevedo would have been dry and dusty, so the American had said in Quito, and it was much safer for a low-slung car, was the belated, chiding thought as the dangerous driving continued. If one ever got through, there was a desperate declaration and promise to listen to intelligent people who had actually been over these roads, and to follow their advice from there on out.

Should one quit and give up going any further south than it took to get a boat home, was always the talk as one more difficult situation was overcome? However, the natives kept saying these were unpredictable rains, the rainy season was usually over a month before, never in the history of South America had the rainy season lasted so long, they knew this was the last rain and the roads would dry up quickly.

When finally, going into the lowlands, the brakes could be felt getting weak and the foot was shoving the floor board, there was one thing to be thankful for, that this smooth, low road had been reached before the brakes gave out.

An old, dilapidated jitney bus was coming toward the car and a young man in a ship navy uniform was standing on the step. He jumped off the bus step and stood with arms extended in front of the car. Quick use of the handbrake was all that saved him from being run over.

He was an advertising messenger from the ship company at Babohoya, they having already heard, by phone, of the couple trying to get through in a car and this was their method of trying to get the car to go on their ship to Guyaquil. He wanted to take over and drive, but he had never heard of or driven Hydramatic and, with no foot brakes, it would have been dangerous for car as well as occupants to ride with his driving.

The mechanic in Babohoya found the brake rod bent from rocks and clogged mud, and the fluid had leaked out of cups—no parts could be had there and no method could be found to straighten the rod. It would have been necessary to wait several days for parts to be brought in, and this dirty little seaport, roughneck sort of town, had no hotel accommodations.

The Delta Road to Guyaquil was good but, with just a handbrake, it was not safe to risk. The best solution to the problem was, if possible, to try to get the car on a boat and go down the river Babohoya into the city of Guyaquil, where there were many car agencies that could get parts and repair the car. Since the boat was sailing in half an hour, it was decided to try to get the car on the boat. But getting the car on the barge, going down a steep dirt incline, was a hazardous undertaking with poor brakes. The primitive method of using twelve-inch boards from bank to boat to drive up on would have been a dangerous drive to risk with good brakes; with nothing but handbrakes, it presented a perilous situation. Could someone have been found familiar with a Hydramatic drive, the car and baggage certainly would have been turned over to them.

The interpreter said he would have the crewmen hold the car back as it was guided down the steep hill, but the weight of the car was too much for the few men holding it, so they had to let go and, with handbrake on a very little, the car went down the hill at a terrific speed. With the fast application of the handbrake, the car was stopped on the barge, and car and driver were saved from going into deep water.

The shock of nearly plunging into twenty feet of water, after looking about extracted another promise, a promise to stay on terra firma from there on out.

A taillight was unscrewed and taken by a young boy who kept leaning over the car jabbering, while all the time, with his right hand hidden from view, he kept working on the light. He looked to be begging and, without being rude we had, by signs of hands and saying *"vamoose"* repeatedly, tried to get him to leave the car alone. He did finally, like a blue streak, leave with the taillight in his possession.

Later, awakening, there was a big, burly, ragged, half-dressed man trying to take off the windshield wipers. Quickly honking the horn and flashing on the lights, he left in a hurry, going into the big boat.

Arriving in Guyaquil, they used the same crude boards, extending from barge to riverbank, to drive the car on. Explaining the problem of no brakes to a motorcycle policeman at the docks, he cleared the way of traffic to the hotel and on to the garage for repairs.

The hotel manager was a Hungarian. He spoke seven languages and was very kind, first acting as interpreter and showing the way to the Cadillac agency, but the Cadillac manager would not allow anyone to stay and watch the mechanics as they worked on the cars.

So, the hotel man insisted on going to another garage, owned by the secretary-treasurer of the newly organized AAA Club. This garageman was so understanding and fixed the car as good as anyone could have done and, no doubt, charged much less than the Cadillac man would have charged. It was a relief to find that by simply straightening the rod the brakes were not badly damaged.

This garage owner gave out several pointers that have been useful over and over. He said cars would drive better, as well as be in much better shape, if washed more often after going through the gumbo mud of South America. The great amount of mud washed from underneath the car had to be scraped into the street to keep from clogging the drains of the auto shop.

They put five gallons of high-octane gas, from the airfield, into the tank with the regular gas, changed the motor oil, put in a new filter, and changed the transmission oil. It was advised to not wait 25,000 miles to change the transmission oil, as the Cadillac manual suggests, because of the muddy, dusty roads, and the continuous driving. The car ran beautifully when leaving the garage, and seeing the city was for the moment the main objective.

Guyaquil is a bustling, prosperous city—like many of the seaport towns of the world, it has sawmills, breweries, and all kinds of American car agencies. The Municipal Police, one of the finest public buildings in South America, is the pride of these people, and the statue of October 9 is an unusually impressive work of art, high enough for all to see, and flanked by a magnificently decorated square.

A promenade, with beautiful flowering shrubs, ran along the waterfront. Benches and chairs were filled with the natives, seemingly with nothing more to do than sit, laugh, and eat tamales, and more tamales.

There were ten teachers from Pennsylvania State Teachers College, on tour and sightseeing here today. They were typical teachers, effervescing a desire to practice their Spanish.

There's an interesting looking fellow from the USA, who goes around here in white, crisp suits all the time. Many shrimp and fishing boats out in the bay are his problem. He says there's good fishing and better shrimping all along these waters.

Another American has put in an ice cream bar just around the corner from the hotel, and is sure going to town with it. It's by far the nearest cream-like stateside ice cream to be found so far; most of the stuff tasted is just a sherbet or ice, but this has sure-'nuf canned milk in it. Ice cream sure helps to cool one in this sticky heat.

There are possibilities for many businesses to be established down here and make money hand over fist. Another would be ready-mix concrete, with this continuous slow building forever going on. Adventurous young people, with know-how and American tools, could make a killing in ten years in the building business, so it seems.

This old tub, a stinking, disreputable hunk of wood, which one might call a boat, was foundered with a hundred people aboard near the Isla Puna. The tide had gone out about seven feet and unless it got started soon, it would be stranded in a mud marsh with jillions of dead sea gulls to add to the stench. It had already been here four hours.

After promising, a few days back to stay on terra firma, another stupid blunder has been made. How completely fooled can one get? Only fluttering idiots could have made such a bungle!!! At the docks in Guyaquil, when making arrangements for transporting the car, this old tub was alongside a big, white boat, so clean and nice. It was supposed, without an interpreter to help, that this boat was tied to the big boat and would go alongside it all the way to Puerto Bolivar, like the barge did from Babohoya to Guyaquil. But after the car was placed on the boat, it pulled away, and too late it was realized what a poor decision had been made. Let's not call it a boat—it's beyond description, and the natives on it are definitely lower class.

One's stomach has a feeling of being on the outside looking in and land will be cherished if land is ever touched again. An Indian woman passenger is desperately seasick—she has a baby about six months old, all strapped up in tape, and another little girl about seven or eight years old.

The mother lies flat on the deck and looks dead. She's been given aspirin, ice packs put to her head, smelling salts to her nose, but she just lies there. The baby cries and cries—it should be hungry. They just changed its clothes—watching them uncoil the many yards of tape from around its arms and body, which took a long time, gave one the feeling of its emerging from a straitjacket. Watching them coil the strips of cloth over the baby again reminded one of a stuffed, stiff scarecrow.

They fed the baby some juice from the boiled shrimp. It smacks its lips and acts like it's still hungry by crying for more as the woman crooks her hand and fingers in the juice, retaining about a tablespoon at a time. She then puts her fingers in the baby's mouth. The slogan, "Fingers were made before silver," could be aptly applied to this primitive method of feeding.

Most of the people on board are typically native mixtures—they keep up a continuous hubbub of conversation and giggling until there is some movement made with relations to the car—fixing the coffee Sterno fashion and such—then they get quiet to watch everything done.

It's hard to know just what they must have thought. There was a feeling they would knife and rob one without batting an eye—on the other hand they could have thought of us as very selfish by keeping away from them and staying with the car, watching vigilantly until our eyeballs felt like fried eggs look, but we dared not leave the car—even on so small a ship the car wouldn't have had a piece left that could have been pried off if left alone. It is said these parts are taken to resell, or for souvenirs, or just for the heck of it. One fellow was caught under the car trying to remove some bolts.

A typical Southern-type looking negro, who is the general flunkey, had the job of boiling shrimp all morning. He looked to be the only one to be trusted on the entire boat. He would bring batches of shrimp and try, in his Spanish lingo, to show respect and friendliness. He tried several times to explain that the repairs would be finished in a short time.

The owner of the old tub is worried and can be seen down in the engine room, sans clothes, and working desperately to get the old boat going again. This is an experience one could never forget.

A pair of shoes, a butcher knife, and a can of soup have been stolen while one or the other would go to the back of the boat for a short time. It's funny about the foods being stolen, but it could be serious if something important to the car was taken, and one would have to wait for weeks until a replacement could be sent in. It could be a terrible calamity even to be without windshield wipers in a blinding rainstorm. That's the one thing they most often try to pry off. They are so easily taken off, but with an extra bit of fine wire wrapped around them, they've been saved up to now.

The lifeboat has gone ashore to a waterfront, high piling, crude-looking village, and brought back a lot of bananas and other food stuff for the passengers—the bananas are small and pinkish in appearance, and very delicious in flavor.

They are continually working on the ship repairs—they had the motors going for a few minutes, but it went zing, and they've taken the thing all down again.

It's getting stifling hot. The old darky just came by the car and he tries so hard to tell us the delay will be several hours more before the repairs are finished and they can get started. The Coast Guard finally arrived and took off all the other passengers except the sick Indian mother and her two children—she tried desperately to make it, but was too sick, or wasn't fast enough in gathering up her belongings.

The logical thing to do was to stay with the car, for the safety of the car and the future safety of ourselves. There was a relaxed and relieved feeling after the passengers left—dozens of eyes were not continuously staring from upper deck, cabins, and portholes. The cunning look of trying to put something over on us was also a relief to be away from, and most of the human, sweaty body stench was gone.

At last the old tub got going—it got going into a channel of cross currents and hefty winds, plying through a terribly rough sea all the way into Porto Bolivar. If there was ever going to be seasickness, that would have been the time. With the pitching and creaking of the boat, the chances of not going to the bottom looked very slim at times.

And to add to the horror of it all, there were literally thousands of dead sea gulls on the water, washing in and out, around and over everything, which had a stinking, rotten odor.

Arriving in port at one o'clock at night, or early morning, was the next horror. The tide was still out and the only way of getting off the ship and onto a twenty-by-twenty floating dock, about four feet lower than the ship, was to back off on two twelve-inch boards, and the ship was tossing and bouncing about from six to eight feet from this dock, which would give a rebounding quiver as each wave came in.

It was a most paralyzing situation. Everything from bribing to begging was used to get the ship's owner to wait until daylight to take the car off; however, it would have taken the nerve of a brass monkey to back off of that place could they have seen the scary situation by the light of day.

To delay the process of getting off the boat, a deliberate delay was resorted to for a time. Pretending not to understand, every pretext that could be thought of was used in trying to gain time for the time to come up.

Then, too, there was a signed receipt, taken care of in Guyaquil, for putting the car on the boat and taking it off, but the dock workmen in this port of Porto Bolivar wanted two hundred extra sucres, which certainly would have to be paid; insisting that they explain over and over, using the conversation book, helped delay while waiting for the tide to come up. But when they started to throw bananas—the ship's cargo for the return trip—on the car, it was then realized that the car had to be taken off quick.

A tall, blue-eyed blond from Scandinavia stepped up while the arguing was going on about paying the dockhands two hundred extra sucres to take the car off the boat. The fellow sure caused a lot of extra trouble. He pried into the situation more than he should have and, when he found out what the argument was about, he kept trying to get the workmen to raise the price to four hundred sucres when he had been told, confidentially, that it was just a case of trying to hold out until the tide came up.

He was certainly a troublemaker and didn't realize a Spanish conversation book was being checked as he tried to agitate these dockhands, and that most everything he was saying to the workmen was understood.

When he was told the car and occupants were planning on going south through the jungles, he said, "Ecuador and Peru are in a state of war over their boundaries and it will be impossible to get through with your lives." He said, "I have tried, I have gone to the government leaders, and they refused me a safe passage through the jungle."

He was told they would let an American couple go in a car where they wouldn't let a belligerent young man on a motorcycle, who might be a spy or a labor agitator. Arrogantly, he said, "What do you Americans think you are anyway, that you think you can do anything you want to do?" He added, "I'm willing to bet you don't get through."

He kept saying to the ship owner, "This old couple don't realize what they are getting into." He was trying to persuade the ship owner to take us on down to a small port in Peru, a port like Babohoyo, without any kind of dock facilities—much worse than the present situation. It was located about thirty miles about Huaquillas and, had he succeeded in persuading that that proposition be accepted, a magnificent jungle area and some wonderful experiences would have been missed.

What he wanted was a free ride to Guyaquil and he told the captain of the ship that if he could get the old American couple, that didn't know any better, to pay the captain fifteen hundred sucres to take them to this other port, he wanted the captain to give him, in exchange, a free ride to Guyaquil. Seeing through the ruse he was trying to pull, it was with great determination that the car was taken off that boat.

He talked on and on, one wild story after another, about not going through the jungle. His tales of Peru, Chile, and Argentina were blood-curdling enough to make anyone want to turn back. He said he had been in all of those countries and such a state of unrest existed that revolutions could break out at any moment in Argentina and Bolivia, especially; and, with political developments such as they were, only fools would go there in a car.

Others might have believed his stories, but it was getting to be common routine to hear these fantastic tales of not being able to get through in a car. There was no turning back; there was always the one thought of finding out for ourselves what was ahead.

The longshoremen had a hard time getting the car in position to take it off the boat—they had to pour buckets of water on the deck and sort of shove and then rock it back and forth. Just one little mistake and the car and driver would be lost, was uppermost in thought as the backing of the car commenced on the two two-by-twelve planks, with the water thirty feet deep below, then on to the slick, greasy, floating dock without rail or any kind of side protection, twice backing up and down to get in position to go up a steep ramp to the permanent docks being built above.

At the top of the ramp they had to put sacks of flour, salt, and sugar to help give clearance, as the car axle had struck the ridge when first trying to go up the ramp.

Suddenly the car went dead—no amount of buzzing would start it. Right there, in the car, on the half-finished docks, was the only place to stay until daylight. There was barely room for the car with the bananas, sugar, salt, flour, and case after case of Coca-Cola and other bottled drinks.

Men, continually passing in the night, tried to turn the car handle knobs; some drunks would stand for what seemed a half hour, pressing their faces against the glass, licking the glass with their tongues, or just leering at the inside of the car.

Without sleep, hoping and quietly trusting this situation would be overcome some way, daylight arrived and showed better than imagination of the night what a horrible place this was. A toilet nearby explained why so many men were passing in the night, as they were always either coming from or going to it; this condition was probably caused by the wine which these men drank continuously.

Some fellows, mostly native Indians, offered to help push the car off the dock, when they saw it couldn't be started, but the Scandinavian and his partner just stood by and looked on disappointedly. Groups of dirtily clad men, women, and children followed as the car was guided off the dock, over the bridge, and past the railroad tracks to a nearby garage.

No battery charger could be found nearer than Machala, seven miles away, so the next effort to get the car going was to tie a cable to another car and have it pulled off. The Cadillac manual said, "Neutral first, 20 speed, turn on ignition into low"—and it worked! Then through low, wet, but passable road to the enterprising little town of Machala.

A mechanic in Machala said the battery was okay, just a poor connection. An English-speaking Ecuadorean came up and asked if he could help out. He's been in and lived in Dallas. One realizes how small the world is when he named a familiar street and number where he had lived, and a nostalgic feeling was temporarily indulged in over just talking with someone who had been home.

This man, an architect, who was supervising the building of a bank in Machala, said any wish would be his command as people in Dallas had been so wonderful to him. He's to be thanked for many things. He helped get a room in an old overcrowded hotel—such a hotel! The bath facilities were laughable—a bucket of water poured in a trough, but the main thing was to get rid of the putrid smells carried away from the boat. Mosquito nets over the beds were a blessing as flies, mosquitoes and chinch bugs were seen, felt, and heard.

The sick Indian woman, seen on the boat, lived here in Machala. Her husband, a piece goods merchant, had a showy little place. She couldn't speak a word of English, and her Spanish was not understandable, but she tried to show her friendliness by showing all the materials they had—some of the gaudy patterned material would almost stand alone in its garish gaudiness.

Eating in a Chinese restaurant with pigs, chickens, and general filth from animals and fowls over the floor, was an experience not soon forgotten. The food of rice, chicken, snails, and little wormy-looking shrimp mixed together, was good, if one is hungry enough and has the courage to sit down to eat under such circumstances.

Through the architect's efforts to help, plans were made with the road engineers to go through the jungle border and he, knowing the army officials personally, phoned Colonel Pineiras, who commanded this outpost, for permission to go through the closed roads. Troops were stationed all along the border and had to be informed if permission is granted to people to go through.

Colonel Pineiras came in person to see and give permission to go through. He shook hands and said, "I just had to jeep over here to see this American couple I've heard about who wanted to drive a car through this God-awful swamp country."

He said he was educated in the US and had spent three of the best years of his life there. Americans had been wonderful to him while there, and he made it a point of being nice in return to all US citizens whom he contacted in Ecuador.

Jeeps were going through the muddy lanes, but he suggested that the car be put on the flat railroad car for the first thirty miles through the jungle. Much more could be seen that way, it was safer, and this narrow-gauge road, with the cutest sort of miniature train, would be fun to ride on.

Saying goodbye to the architect was like losing a "fairy godfather"—he had helped to do so much, so quickly, so easily; and just the day before the Scandinavian said it could not be done.

As this Sunday morning trip started through the jungle, it was with enraptured minds we beheld the shimmering beauty of the millions of morning glories, white and blue and as large as saucers, lining the roadway for many miles in their dewy freshness.

Orchids in many varieties were clinging to whatever limb or trunk of tree was handy; the baby clusters of yellow ones flecked with Meissen brown were literally having a fair all by themselves, reaching out to be gathered up, and one trying to outdo the other.

Then there were deep yellow flowering trees, which lifted their blossoms heavenward—the sky-blue background against the yellow gave out an aesthetic feeling.

Big-leafed ivy and delicate ferns, intermingling with elephant ear plants, could be seen, and a thousand more plants whose names are unfamiliar, but which God and nature placed there, were admired and exclaimed over.

Wonderful singing red birds, green birds, black birds, in pairs, their wings folded together like lovers holding hands, could be seen by the hundreds. There were nesting places of aigrettes, cranes, ducks, and pelicans; the pink ibis, which seemed to be easily alarmed, would wing themselves through the low-hanging trees, their legs going in a horizontal pattern. Parrots, gaudy of plumage, were most timid; the owls, easily heard, were hard to see, they were so much like tree trunks; and the macaws were fluttering everywhere in their gaiety. It was more interesting than you see in pictures.

Going through Santa Rosa and other small villages there were to be seen many handsome, interesting, clean people—all wearing nice clothes as they boarded the train for church; the children were intent on reading the funnies of the papers as do the children in the US.

Arriving at Aerenillas about twelve o'clock, Captain Francisco Mejia Silva, who had driven from Machala through this part of the jungle in a jeep, was at the train to bid us welcome to this military post. His invitation to the officers' barracks for a delicious Sunday lunch was thoroughly enjoyed, as was talking in English with many young men who were stationed there—it was like "old home week" in school. For the officers who spoke, or were learning to speak English, this was a good day to practice words.

The main course of the dinner was chicken with rice, flavored with cumin seed and a mixture of vegetables, after egg on toast, sprinkled with a goat milk cheese, was served as an entrée. A dessert called *quinvalito*, which is Ecuador's national dessert, was a rare treat. These are individual cakes baked in a banana leaf; the tang of the banana leaf lends something extra special to the flavor of this sort of yellow pound cake.

It seemed to give the men so much pleasure to be allowed to drive this new and large American car with Hydramatic, over the town and countryside, as they had never driven anything before except a jeep or Model A Ford.

The cleanliness around this camp and entire village was surprising, while the filth and the squalor of the town left that morning was sickening. There a bottled apple cider drink—good, too—had been the only drink to safely quench one's thirst; while at this camp fresh water, drunk to the heart's content, was enjoyed for the first time in many days.

A church processional was in progress that Sunday, made up of all the townspeople following a statue of the virgin being carried high up on a truck with a group of marchers playing a loud band. Then came men, women, and children marching up and down one street after another. The music would die down for a while, then start all over again. This kept up most of the day.

The officers talked about their ambition to come to the US and what could be done to help them achieve their goal. They wanted names of good schools. They said they wanted to travel and see all the marvels of North America they had read and heard so much about. When asked why they did not explore the marvels of the South American countries, equal in beauty to the US, they said the red tape necessary to go through the suspicions of one country for the other made it not worth the undertaking; while in America, they had heard, no one was under suspicion.

It was a pleasure to be elected honorary mother of the group. They showered upon us every attention, thoughtfully getting out their photo albums to go through, showing pictures of fathers and mothers, brothers and sisters, and relating interesting things connected with their families. They also got out maps and pointed to the different towns they came from, explaining what these villages were noted for.

Some of the fellows insisted on giving up treasured souvenirs to us; and the cook, after finding the great interest in the cake dessert, insisted on giving the recipe for the cake.

A young officer, Nick Zambrano, who has relatives in Mexico, and who spoke good English, was one to always remember and help if he should come to the US. Another fellow, called Bill Shakespeare, was so anxious to please, and had good knowledge of his namesake.

Other things to remember: these young men took pride in showing the unknown soldier's tomb located on a restful knoll very near their quarters, saying they did not want war, neither did they want to have their land taken away from them, as Peru was always threatening to try to do.

It was four o'clock when we bid farewell to this wonderful group. They loaded the car with luscious fruit and extra cakes to eat later in the day. The captain insisted on putting a pick and shovel in to take along in case there was trouble.

We started the sixty-mile jaunt to Huaquillas on what was once a one-lane jungle road, but was now so overgrown with bramble and wild foliage it was just a cow trail—the trees and foliage were so close they would scrape the car and hold it back as we inched along.

It was easy to get lost and we got lost twice due

to the road being so indistinct; this road was ordinarily used only for military purposes and was kept this way for protection.

Getting stuck in the sand was the most difficult problem to overcome, but memory served us well and we jacked the car up, digging out the high ridge, then piled rocks in the ruts as a native near Babohoyo had shown us. In other places the pick and shovel were indispensable in digging out ridges and filling in the holes. It took many minutes to make a mile, but the scenery was so startlingly beautiful, there were no regrets.

Night overtook us and we dared not go on but had to sleep in the car. Mosquitoes were big and strong-voiced. It was hot and close inside the car, but we could not risk leaving the window down or go outside in the darkness, as there was danger of snakes (several large ones had been seen), wild cats, monkeys, and lizards (iguanas) five feet long—an unusually large iguana had crossed the path earlier in the afternoon. In the night, a wild cat was heard scratching on the car, but must have slunk away when the lights were turned on, as there was no more trouble from him.

As the morning sun was casting its first glow over the jungle, a patrol jeep from the camp came searching, and seemed relieved to find the car safe and the occupants finishing coffee, Sterno-fashion, and ready to go on.

Though arriving very early in Huaquillas, the whole population was up and out to see the Americans coming through in the big car. The town was immaculately clean with flags flying in the breeze. The police chief, a Swiss, had ready a delicious breakfast, consisting of papayas, ham and eggs, and a pungent black coffee.

The officials prepared the papers necessary for leaving their country; then they brought out attractive Ecuadorean hand-painted bags for gifts, and cards of "Auf Wiedersehen" were passed around.

All this gracious attention was being showered upon us through the kindly influence of Colonel Pineiras, who will always be remembered as the kindest and most thoughtful commander.

5

Peru: July/August, 1953

Being anxious to get on Peruvian soil, as the general understanding was that the roads were much better there, we soon regretted the rush made trying to get out of the friendly country of Ecuador.

The Peruvian officials were most suspicious because of strangers with a car being allowed to go through the jungle of Ecuador, as this was a most unusual precedent.

They examined the car and every piece of luggage thoroughly for guns, demanding that the travelers take all of the baggage out and then put it back in the car. This was a far cry from the wonderful treatment of the Ecuadoreans a few hours before.

The first office, near a large statue, was passed as it was closed up. They checked everything very friendly-like at the second place but, when leaving, they said something about a statue, which was not understood; and supposing everything was okay, we went fifteen miles ahead before an official, blocking the road with a chained post, pointed a gun at the car, saying, "Turn back."

Arriving at the border again, it was decided the best thing to do might be to circle around the big statue, just in case they had wanted us to do that—some of their regulations looked to be that foolish!

After that it was necessary to sign up six more times before arriving at Tumbes. A general stationed at Zarumilla, where this assiduous searching went on as already mentioned, insisted on going to all the places for signing up. He would stand by the car, as proud as a peacock, motion us into the place to get the papers registered, then salute his men, get in the car and, with a benign smirk on his countenance, wave a hand to continue on.

Arriving in Tumbes, the general waved the car and occupants to the police station, where they examined the car very carefully and would pick up bits of leaves, weeds, and dirt, and look them over almost with microscopic intentness. When they found the good Ecuadorean map, which had been bought in Quito, they very confidently confiscated it. It was highly prized, as few maps of Ecuador were available.

The next morning when it couldn't be found to be put away in the bag of used maps and pamphlets of each country, it was decided to return to the police station to get it back. Wrangling with them for an hour brought no results.

Asking for the courtly general of the day before, the second fellow in command at the station left in a run to a building a block away, then he rushed back, out of breath, saying, "No mapa." It was decided if this stay in Peru was to be enjoyed, the best thing to do was to forget the map.

A nice Tourista Hotel, owned by the government, was a restful abode for the night and made up for the experience of the night before in the jungle. These hotels, so the Tourist Guide says, are located at all important points in Peru. They are clean and comfortable, with good food, such as broiled steaks as low as thirty cents in American money. These hotels will be looked for all through Peru.

The road out of Tumbes started out good, all weather, but not paved as the maps and people had said. Following the Pacific there was a cool, brisk breeze to add to the comfort and pleasure of driving on these better roads.

Then coming into a lot of sand dunes, away from the ocean, all the enjoyment was soon gone, as it turned terribly dusty; the fine dust penetrated every inch of the car, adding to the stifling heat. In this maddening heat, the car would pick such a time to go dead!

Having to wait a long time for the Esso garage man, several cars came by, all stopping to offer help and staying to chat. A Scotchman, in his burly, slurring voice, kept those gathered around in gales of laughter, with his jokes and wisecracks, all the while tinkering with the car. He, at last, was the one able to find the car out of gas, although the gauge registered full!

A New Yorker, one of the fellows who stopped to help, told about the many boats in the harbor near Mancora and said he was part owner of this, the largest tuna fishing fleet in the world, which was gathering in and canning tons of the delectable product.

After many confusing crossroads and magnificent views of the sea, we arrived in Talara in the later afternoon. There was an outmoded hotel, for such a modern city in every other respect; but nevertheless, a good bath was first thought in an effort to get a layer of sand off of sweaty bodies.

The city of Talara boasts the oldest oil field in South America. A very friendly young Swiss, acting as a welcoming committee of one, took over and showed all the most important buildings and business concerns over the city.

They have unusually well-equipped schools with American teachers selected from the US. The American Club was very lovely with every necessary form of entertainment from swimming pool to movies. The commissary had American foods at reasonable prices, cold drinks, late American newspapers and magazines—which were keenly appreciated as they had been missed for weeks.

All of this comfort, inexpensive domestic help, good salaries, choice homes, good schools, good everything, is bound to entice the better oil petroleum worker from the US to that country.

The president of the oil company and his wife were gracious and charming when visited in their beautifully appointed home, which had a magnificent view of the mountains and the surrounding city colony of lovely homes.

The next morning the oil gauge on the car started registering danger. At the Esso station they found there was plenty of oil, and could not find anything else wrong, but traveling on through the morning the gauge continued to register "danger" and, with every mile traveled, there was a vision of a burnt out motor, which caused stops many times to check and double check before proceeding on.

A garage at Sullan found the entire electrical system out of order, due to the terrific shake up of the car in the storm when coming down the Channel of Jambell, or to the rocking and shoving back and forth of the car on the boat when the dock men were trying to get the car in position to take off at Puerto Bolivar.

The battery had given trouble, as already mentioned, soon after getting off the ship. That's what had caused the gasoline gauge to not register, and explained the running out of gasoline. It was a great relief to have that problem solved, and there was a thankfulness that, if this had to happen, it was on a good road and not in the jungle area of Ecuador.

Having used up so much of the day checking and fixing the car, darkness closed in upon arriving at the small village of Olmos, and there couldn't be found a hotel fit for a dog to sleep in. Getting permission from the police to camp on the square, in the car, was the only thing left to do—for the next twenty miles to a good hotel, the road was under construction and much too dangerous to attempt at night. So often these roads are without warning lights of drop-offs where work is being done.

Inquisitive children, carrying baskets of bread and cookies, came by for a "look see" and, for a few pennies, offered a week's supply of the fresh baked and fragrant bread. Opening a can of tuna, with fresh tomatoes and avocados bought by the roadside, a wholesome meal was enjoyed. After this, by sleeping on the car seats, the best of the situation was made for the night.

There was a good lunch at the government Tourista Hotel in Piura the next day, but could not stay there for the night as it was much too early to take out, and they did not have hot water in the bathrooms. So often a nice room with a beautiful file bath is obtainable, but no hot water is to be found in the faucets and, with all the sand and grime saturating one on these roads, a hot water bath is very important at the day's end.

The supposed good roads worsened traveling south. Dysentery, coupled with the bad roads, caused a most uncomfortable feeling—the same food had been eaten and the same water had been drunk by both of us, but only one was the sufferer. The best thing seemed to be to continue on to a larger town with better hotels where comfort and rest could be had.

At long last a good paved road, beginning at Lambayeque, made it possible to arrive in Trujillo in the very early afternoon. This was the first city of Peru of great importance from an historical standpoint. The pre-Inca ruins of Chan Chan are nearby, and the museum, Larco Herrera, has the most outstanding archeological exhibit to be found anywhere in South America.

A good hotel, a better night's rest—with the aid of some medicine manufactured in Switzerland, which looks like charcoal, and boiled canned milk—helped to make a quick recovery from this most dreaded of all diseases found in these South American countries.

The houseboy at the hotel was amazed when asked for boiled drinking water to fill the jug. He turned on the hydrant and said, "*Mucha bueno*"—but one dared not risk that *mucha bueno* after such a siege, and insisted on having it boiled to the houseboy's look of disgust.

The following day there were good paved roads into Huaco, but travel was slowed to observe the weird and fantastic sand formations in every direction on either side of the road.

On the right, extending from the road to the ocean beach, this sand could be seen in the most grotesque shapes; sometimes mounds looked like prehistoric dinosaurs with long, crinkled, tapering tails. Again, there would be seen a cone-shaped formation, so finely pointed it would be easy to believe there was just one grain of sand on the tip top.

Then there would be a mountain of sand suddenly cut straight down as if sliced with a knife. There were large doodle bug-looking holes covering mile upon mile of nothing but sand, sand, white sand! One could believe that a colossal giant had rushed through this sand and whacked out, with powerful knives or scythes, some of these crazy gigantic shapes. Then in other places there were reclining forms and castle-like caves and tunnels, as though molded by monstrous, fabulous hands.

All these fantastic, crazy formations are said to be brought about by the wind, but on stepping out of the car, there was only the gentlest of breezes blowing. One would think it would take a terrific gale to produce such phenomena—maybe this is nature's way of going berserk over having to cope with so much sand.

To the left were the dramatic green, yellow, orange, and red Andean mountains—many covered with snow. The white sands of the desert, blown and filling the crevices of the mountains, blended so with the snow, it was difficult at times to tell where the snow began and the sand ended. Cold desert and colder mountains was a crazy combination to persons who had been through the hot desert sands of New Mexico, Arizona and California.

At the Huaco Hotel they served such badly prepared food for the evening meal that a miserable night was spent getting rid of it. Next morning, going into the kitchen to try to get eggs boiled, found the cook was frying eggs in deep, hot lard.

Reaching for a fresh skillet and turning the heat low, a teaspoon of butter was placed in the skillet, then slices of cold boiled ham were fried for a few minutes. Taking the ham out of the pan, four eggs were added for scrambling, or shipwrecking, as one would call it, and the whites were cooked a bit before stirring up the yellows.

After scraping the eggs out, the bread was

browned in the same pan. The bread in that part of the country was a sour dough concoction, similar to English muffins, and very tasty.

The chef, all the while, looked on goggle-eyed—I suppose he had never seen such simple doings before. A fourth of a cup of cold, thick coffee syrup, common in those parts, was added to hot water and produced an aromatic fragrance similar to New Orleans coffee, and a good breakfast was enjoyed.

From Huaco into Lima was one of the most unexpected, dangerous highways to be found so far. A very high sand mountain was overhanging the sea with the road winding in and out over this narrow highway.

On the right going toward Lima, there is nothing but sand and rock hundreds of feet straight down to the sea. On the left in many places, the mountain side of the road was a rock wall which helped keep the sand from sliding on the highway; however, there was encountered two sand slides covering the wall and portions of the road.

But oh, brother, the right side of the road and the right side of the driving wheel was the danger spot, as the driver could not see just how little or how much it was safe to get off the pavement in an emergency when other vehicles were blaring their horns to get by.

If the car wheels got off the pavement, there was danger of sand and car sliding right into the sea, hundreds of feet below—and it was necessary to get off that road many times to let the wildly driven buses, trucks and some cars go by.

A girl said she actually went over in a car landslide on that road. She and a companion landed on the rocks in a high spot and survived. Going to the AAA Club in Lima to ask for mail, she (the secretary of the club) told of her narrow escape.

Without knowing of the above happening at the time, the great danger was sensed as the car was maneuvering slowly along. It was a great relief when the double lane Franklin Roosevelt Highway was reached. This highway extends from Ancon, a good fishing and ten-story hotel resort town, on into Lima.

Now that better roads were ahead, it was with a sigh of relief that one found one's self retrospectively checking many of the tight places lived through—dangerous spots where lives could easily have been lost—just out of a great determination to try to get through at all cost. Some terrible chances had been taken—some foolish things had been done!

If a person had known the actual condition of these roads, no one but a blithering idiot would have gone over them like they were. And, yet, now that they've been gone over, one feels they wouldn't have missed what has been seen for anything.

There was much to be thankful for, was the grateful feeling on arriving in Lima with no more than dysentery wrong with the humans, and no more than a leaky gas tank wrong with the car.

Lima, the beautiful City of the Kings! The most fabulous gem on the Pacific shores. This city, with the smaller cities encircling it, can be classed with the best everywhere. Cherillas, a fashionable resort suburb, with high promenades, has a casino and boating and bather. Miraflores, adjacent to the city, has a very modern shopping center, and is noteworthy for its garden homes overlooking the Pacific. Callao, the shipping center, is teeming with many ships in the harbor.

Adjoining is the city of La Punta, the seat of the Naval School—it is also a good bathing resort.

We arrived in Lima on Friday, too late in the week to get the car work done, such as repair on the gas tank, change of oil, etc. Deep holes and large rocks in the middle of the street in Chancay, where much repair and paving plans were in progress, caused a bad gas leak in the tank. We had it plugged with airplane glue to be able to continue on to Lima.

It was real funny, always arriving in the larger cities on the wrong days. These business houses which close on Saturday delay one's schedule and keep one from seeing the sights in one's own car. Many places do not open up at all on Saturday when they are having a holiday, and every week there seemed to be a church celebration of some kind. The Catholic church celebrations cause the stores to close and they have more of these celebrations in South America than any place in the world, it seems, and they always end in much consuming of wine as is shown by natives marching in staggering formation through the streets.

It was a joyous experience to register at the swank Country Club Hotel in the suburban part of the city, where it befits weary travelers to rest and relax for a change, and where there was ample space for parking the car.

An American doctor at the hotel said most all Americans coming here get this dysentery from eating shrimp; yet eating shrimp, fruits, lettuce and all other fresh vegetables, which most English-speaking people warn against, has been the food we most craved and, at the risk of being sick, we have literally gorged the beautiful fruits and vegetables, and not one trace of the disease has been felt since eating them—which proves that not everyone coming down here gets this dreaded dysentery.

There was a gray mist overhanging the city—not once had the sun been shining for a week. They say this gloominess continues for several months. The weather, however, was of very little concern as the luxurious hotel and its good food, with a much-needed rest, was being enjoyed to the fullest, and was the most important interest at the moment. One day on the menu were charcoal-broiled filet mignons, with all the trimmings, for only 75 cents. Were they yummy! You bet!

The Peruvian money is called sol. It is necessary to learn a different name for the money, and how to make the exchange in each country—sometimes it's very confusing.

Venezuela-its Bolivar (Bo-liev-er): 3.3 to 1 US dollar
Colombia-its Peso (Pa-so): 2.5 to 1 US dollar
Ecuador-its Sucre (Su-cre): 16.4 to 1 US dollar
Peru-its Sol (Plural: Soles): 15.5 to 1 US dollar

In the modern and newer part of the city, the castor bean trees were growing along fence rows, and as background for flowering plants. The poinsettias were blooming in lavish splendor and are larger than dishpans. The bougainvillea, in many colors, is everywhere—clinging and climbing over high brick and adobe walls and on magnificent California-style homes.

The coleus plants, dainty at home, grow here into large, various-colored leafed bushes, and are a riot of color on a wide avenue for miles back of the hotel. Palm trees line most of the boulevards. Geranium bushes and trees bloom in profusion. Everywhere there is a great variety of coloring and more beautiful and exotic flowers than one can name.

There are many lovely drives following the oceanfront. There's ugliness and destruction, too, the destruction wrought by the earthquake in 1940. The tumbled-down homes, once beautiful, are stark reminders of the havoc wrought by part of the land cracking away from its past position and sliding several feet down into the sea.

There were fishing craft by the hundreds off the bay near the "old city"—the old part of Lima, so completely charming in Spanish architecture, with the narrow streets and the wooden filigree balconies. While out at Callao, where ships dock from all the other countries of the world, there was to be seen one of the larger Grace Line boats in port.

It goes north through the Panama Canal, then sails on to New York—sure gives one a homesick feeling to see these ships getting ready for departure to the USA. For two cents and a little persuasion, one could be induced to go home on this big liner, but the other half insists on continuing on. There have been so many chances taken and so much spent on coming down here, that it would seem a shame to give up when officials say the roads are much better all through Peru.

These South American people, and especially the Limanians, are like no other folk on the face of the earth. They act as if they have a lifetime to do the least thing. It's easy to make plans for each day, but the day always ends up with the plans making the travelers.

Having arrived in Lima on Friday, as already mentioned, there was a weariness from several days of hard driving. But the car had to be looked after first, regardless of weariness. It is very important that it be kept in good running order, because the pleasure of the whole trip depends upon it.

Had heard of a repair shop that would be open on Saturday, so rushed downtown to find it. This Buick garage didn't want to understand, or couldn't understand, what was wanted—this being a Saturday they, perhaps, had rather have missed a repair job than get involved on something that would have kept them three minutes after twelve o'clock.

Decided that the sensible thing to do was to phone General Motors and ask them to recommend a good shop. They are the company, in all of South America, who deserve more praise and thanks than anyone for helping out of a bad situation, although they recommended the shop to which the car was taken, and this shop later caused so much trouble.

General Motors sent a young man down to interpret and help out—a Scotch-Irish, good looking blond from Chile. This young man was unusually nice—such a likable chap. He was the one to thank for seeing so many out-of-the-way places of interest, and the unusual types of celebrating, in full swing over the city.

The national holiday of Peru was to begin on Tuesday, but everyone takes off a couple of days before to get themselves primed for the festivities. It takes two days to unlax and sober up after the week of celebrating ends.

The entire week had gone by with the car in the garage. The General Motors man had said it would be perfectly okay to leave the car there for the week, while resting up from driving; however, there was an uneasy feeling over leaving the car with this shifty-eyed garage man. When we went to get the car the tank still leaked, the carburetor had been substituted, the Hydramatic had been tampered with, the horn was definitely a different low squeaky sound; so the General Motors man took over and made the necessary repairs saying they were checking that particular garage off their list.

It might have been just as well without the car, if the garage had been a good one. The wild activities of the holiday, streets blocked off for miles, having to wait hours for the parades to pass, was continually experienced for three days—the same thing over and over.

Taxis weren't so high, if the price was asked before getting into one of them; but oh, brother, if one fails to ask the price, they sure stick it to you, especially if the USA is written all over your face. The best bet was the streetcars for three cents each, if it could be explained very simply where you wanted to go and when to get off.

This Peruvian holiday was some goings-on. They were celebrating their Gran Feria. There were thousands of young men marching on foot, then men in tanks with guns, and men riding on horses—in all their military array. Indians, in all their colorful regalia, were stoically marching with all the pomp and pageantry of olden days.

There was a great display of airplanes zooming down in noisy formations from overhead. There were all sorts of colorful costumes among the people, and there were only quick glimpses of the parade, unless from second story windows or forcing one's way through the large drunken, whooping-it-up throngs of Indians and mobs of men, women, and children, who had brought lunches along and were lining the sidewalks and streets for the day.

One of the most interesting things found to do, after the Peruvian holidays were over, was to go with the young man from General Motors to a famous and exclusive eating place ten miles out of the city—a place called "Granja Azul" and a place much off the beaten path.

It is the farm home of a Swiss merchant who has capitalized on his knowledge of foods, especially chicken. He serves the most wonderful chicken, charcoal broiled, ever tasted. This is all visible to the guests, while in the process of cooking; dozens of golden brown chickens can be seen on skewers, oozing out a fragrant aroma. It makes one ravenous just to sit and watch the barbecuing.

The waiter puts a bib around each person's neck, to protect one's clothes, as the chicken is eaten by hand. They place hand painted pottery ashtrays around for use—these ashtrays have people painted on in typical Peruvian garb, with llamas, alpaca and vicuna animals in motion designs over them—they make good souvenirs.

This Swiss has hanging in the various rooms and the bar many clever paintings and lots of quick sketches eulogizing the "Chicken"—and an especially tricky one was of the chickens roasting the manager.

There were exhibition counters arranged and lighted, which showed a most effective coloring of many antique Indian relics. He had old wooden antique plows, such as the Indians in the isolated areas still use today; there were Inca treasures of gold, dating back hundreds of years and placed in most artistic cubbyholes. It was worth the price of the dinner, just to see these lovely old tings.

There were plenty of homegrown garden vegetables, in large earthen crocks, to fill up on. The manager said these vegetables were perfectly safe to eat, as he grew them in his own garden on the farm, and there was no raw sewage dumped on these plants, as is the custom in most of the truck gardens around Lima.

It was most gratifying to watch the chef mix all of these chlorophyllous gems from the garden, into a tossed salad, with fresh olive oil, and an assortment of ripe olives, radishes and avocados to enhance the eye appeal.

There were potatoes similar in flavor to the Irish potatoes, that were little and yellow and fried a deep brown. There are more than 57 varieties of potatoes grown here; some of the markets show them in many colors such as pink, yellow, green, and brown, and their shapes and forms are most interesting—from long roots to star-shaped.

Broiled chicken livers and hearts, served on bamboo sticks, anticuchos fashion, were the entrée, and were brought around and served continuously to the guests, wherever they might be, at bar or nosing about looking over the relics.

It was amazing to see such a successful business so far off the highway, and the question was asked the owner of how he got started. He said he sent out his first invitations, in beer bottles, to a selected group of friends and prominent, cultured people with automobiles. (He did not want for clientele the people who ordinarily passed on the highway.)

He has no signs up showing directions to his place, but there was a well used back road, which wound in and out among old adobe huts, but finally led to his palatial pink stucco home with magnificently kept grounds dotted with comfortable chairs, and swimming pool and game yards.

They serve all the chicken you can eat for $2.50—some eat three to five chickens—if a person eats eight chickens at one setting, they are given the meal free. Imagine how he makes it up on the price of the chicken, with the unusual drinks he serves, as they are cleverly concocted in many unusual containers and are terrifically high priced.

These drinks have seductive names such as Virgin Viciosa, El Roncador, Slims Poison, Bachelor's Desire, Wedding Night, La Novia Cristola, La ChiCha Milagrosa, Gentle Murderer, Largo Tiempo, and La Gallina Vinda.

His guest book included many famous American names—Rockefeller, Louis Bromfield, M. Bratts, John Moyn, and the names of lots of movie stars. It was one of the happiest evenings this Mañana Land has had to offer so far.

Lima is bewitching—there is so much of the unusual to do and see. It costs much more to live in the city than all the magazine articles have said. There aren't many apartments to be found, the only one that looked good at all was a tiny, one-bedroom affair, and it would have been necessary to sign up for three months at least.

Many who come down here use Lima as a center of activity to take in all of the historical interests of

Peru. Staying in a pensione out near Miraflores was a happy solution for many Americans who come here; it's in a most attractive part of the city and was recommended by the Embassy.

A lot of American Embassy girls were staying there—they gather around in the evening over coffee, and talk and play games—it's great fun. A new game, Spite and Malice, was taking up most of the attention of the guests—the girls even bet good stakes on it.

There were many other interesting people staying there: a Belgian couple in the Belgian Embassy here; some Hollanders with two boys, who had arrived from Chile and were looking for a home to lease; and an English girl whose father lives here and is president of the English railroad, known all over as the highest railroad in the world.

This girl and her beau, who also works for the railroad, helped with reservations and perfect plans for the tourists to go up on the train over this high pass. The officials and some doctors say it's very dangerous for anyone with high blood pressure, or extremely low blood pressure, or anyone with a heart condition, to make this trip; however, the conclusion has been reached that one can't afford to believe everything heard down in these parts.

Our hats are off to two American girls traveling around the world, who were staying at the pensione. They were most nonchalant about telling how they stop and get jobs for a few months in one country, and then go on to the next. They were going to Chile soon, then on to Argentina, and from Buenos Aires they sail for Europe or points in Africa.

The cost to get to Europe from Brazil or Argentina is as cheap as going from Dallas to New York, so they say. To look at these girls you would think they are just the typical American secretaries, without a venturesome trait in their makeup—they are nice, very nice, and attractive, too.

While waiting for the car to be repaired, the streetcars with the three-cent fare, and the trains, have been the favorite mode of transportation for the past week. These trains have made it possible to go to some of the most interesting spots of the whole Andean mountain chain.

The highest spot on the Central Railroad, with the highest tracks in the world, was reached at Ticlio in the Tunnel de Galera, 15,805 feet altitude—this is reached 100 miles before arriving at Huancayo, with 10,000 feet altitude. The trip was most exciting and well worth the two days given to it.

Early on Friday morning there was a grand rush to the station to get choice reserved seats on the "buffet" coach. They served breakfast of coffee and rolls, and later on they served a half chicken, stewed with rice and cornmeal, and vegetables in a soup plate for lunch.

The first stop and city of importance on the way up was Chosico, about 3,000 feet above sea level—a resort town where most of the Limianians go during the gray, murky weather. The Chamber of Commerce advertises it as "The city where the sun shines every day of the year."

Its flower bedecked parks on either side of the station were a welcome sight, and swarms of colorfully dressed Indians, selling their pottery, fruit, honey, and flowers, lent much interest in their intentness to sell their wares.

After a ten-minute stop, it was amazing to watch the train continually climbing higher and higher by a zigzag method of backing up to a higher level, then climbing to higher rails, to back up again, climbing again the higher grades.

The scenery was spellbinding. The train went through several tunnels and, when emerging into the beautiful new views ahead, it was realized what great foresight this English Railroad Company's engineers had had sixty years ago when this road was built by imported Chinese coolies.

This road was built primarily to take care of the minerals of the country, of which there are abundant supplies left after a hundred years of production. Copper, silver, gold, lead, zinc, vanadium, bismuth—there's much unexploited reserve yet to be taken out of the Andean mountains.

Many times, when emerging from tunnels or rounding the rims of mountains, one could look down to view the perpetually green valleys of vegetation and flowers and fruits, with the heavy ice and snows above, surrounding—the contrasting situation was beyond all expectation. There was so much to see it was difficult to take it all in.

On one side there were glaciers and snowcapped mountains, coal-black rock, white sand, and then a terrific sand slide would confront one; on the other side of the tracks there would be lush vegetation of many kinds, including lupin trees in full bloom—like the Texas bluebonnets, but on big bushes—six feet tall.

Old granddad cacti was growing in massed patches among dark rocks and boulders, and many other familiar desert cacti plants could be seen.

It has been explained that this unusual warm and cold condition is due to the semi-tropical latitude of this part of Peru, which keeps it warm, and the Humboldt current, which keeps it cool.

One canyon, El Infiernillo, or "Little Hell," was so deep and had such a complicated network of roads, that trucks driving on the lowest highway looked like small toys from above.

There were many Indians on the train going up, and the most unusual thing was, as the train climbed higher and higher over the passes, the Indians would get sick and have to have oxygen, which was carried on the train for such emergencies.

There were several Americans, a few English, many Irish, and a couple of Jewish people who seemed to not be affected by the altitude. It was unexplainable, as well as amazing, that the natives would fall over on their faces and look lifeless, while all the foreigners could take the high altitude.

As they backed the train into Jauya for a ten-minute wait, there could be seen lots of Inca ruins on tops of mountains surrounding the city. Many interesting people, well dressed, got off there, including several immaculately groomed Peruvian officers. One gal with the party of officers was oh! so striking. In beautiful, well cut clothes, she had an air or poise that one could not help but especially remember. She was definitely a mixed breed—dark skin, luminous eyes, limpid swagger, and boy, was she clever with these men!

Arriving at Huoncayo (pronounced One-ky-ya) about four o'clock, we rushed with great haste to the Tourista Hotel to get a room, and then went out to see the sights and watch the Indians parade up and down.

The Indians were already gathering in the square by the hundreds for their national holiday fair which started on the morrow. They would select a place for their stalls and with their trinkets, weaving, and food, would squat there for the night for fear someone would get their places.

It was amazing to see the women, they look like they had at least twenty skirts on, beautiful blendings of many colors. Tall crown panama hats, with ribbon trim, were the choice of so many of these women for headdress, and were worn with dignity and pride.

Every woman, regardless of age, seemed to be pregnant, or to have already a baby and it strapped to her back, all wrapped up in gorgeous colored blankets. With all the skirts they were wearing, and a baby in the womb or the baby in a blanket, they were bound to be carrying a tremendous load, and some of them did fall out, or squat down in the most surprising spots, sometimes right in the middle of the sidewalk. They would shove the blanket to the side, take the baby in arm, pull out a breast and start the baby to feeding.

Many of the women were wearing aprons with pockets, just like American women do. These aprons practically covered their skirts and kept them fresh for the next day's festivities.

It was noticed how they would reach in their apron pockets, or sometimes dig way down in their skirts, to get out ground up cacao leaves and a small white ball, which they would then put in their mouths and chew. They say these Indians have to chew these cocaine leaves to be able to live for a great length of time in these high altitudes.

There were Indian bands practicing all night for the parade next day; Indians were staggering around half drunk, their capacity seemed unlimited as they continuously cavorted about here and there on every side; then they would get into line and start marching while saying a succession of words that sound liked right, left, right, left, then would go into low catcalls that ended up in weird crescendos—like nothing ever heard before. They paraded up and down again and again and would start blowing on their reed pipes and flutes in an eerie chant. The noise would die down for 30 minutes or more, just long enough to doze off to sleep, then the catcalls and reed music would start all over again. What a night!

They had wonderful food in the hotel—fresh asparagus soup, trout, thick luscious steaks. The trout was caught right up in the mountain streams. There was a mixed vegetable dish of corn, cauliflower, beans, squash, almond and cashew nuts.

This was just one day ahead of the festival, which lasts all week. It's their Fourth of July, and I think it was seen much better at this time than with such crowds as were expected next day; and there were lots of laughs just watching them making the preparations and training the fellows. One funny sort of a guy would fall out of line when marching and slip quickly through the crowd to the next corner and join up, so unconcerned, which got lots of laughs out of the natives.

This has been an unusual experience to see 20,000 inhabitants living at an elevation of 10,690 feet—a city of uncommon interests with a temperate climate, architectural beauty and a Sunday Market of international fame, attended faithfully by Indians of surrounding districts.

It was a relief to arrive back in Lima—the high altitude was rather difficult to take and had provoked a dizziness after several days of it—maybe the Indians do have to chew the cocaine leaves to survive, was the conclusion reached.

At the Braniff offices at the airport, it was wonderful to find and read a *Dallas Morning News*. (These papers are flown in to the pilots each day and tourists are allowed to read them, but they can't be taken away.)

A fine looking young man came in and said, "What part of the States are you from?" When told Dallas, he said, "Well, I'm from Sherman and have lots of friends in Dallas."

He then asked that we go out to his car and meet his wife and little daughter, who were homesick to see someone from Texas. They insisted we go to their home for lunch, and the perfectly delicious American ham, pineapple salad, asparagus, and luscious lemon pie, reminded one of the good old USA.

They were very wonderful people—he is with the U.S.A.F. Mission to Peru—a mission to promote good will and train the Peruvian young men to fly. It was amazing to find that most every South American country has leased land to the US to establish these missions, and a flying unit of selected officers from the USA are stationed down there to teach the men better methods of flying and repairing and rebuilding planes.

There are many other missions down there—map, mineral, game and fish, educational—all functioning to promote better relations with Americans, and to help in the development of the resources of these countries.

This young man finished in law at the University of Texas and knew our son, Earl, who was a flyer and was lost off the *Enterprise* in the Marshal Gilbert Island group during the first aggressive action after Pearl Harbor. He remembered Earl and his old car at the University, and he knew Bill Robinson, a friend of Earl's, who was lost in the Philippines during the war.

He was in the Pacific during the war—Philippines, Guam, and he remembers that first aggressive action of the *Enterprise*—Bull Halsey, and a lot of other fellows.

His wife said she craved some good Mexican food more than anything. It was decided, if some good canned chili could be found, to fix some for her that evening.

They decided to go explore the Indian Market, the most fantastic place to be found in the country. These markets have everything in the world for sale—it's real fun just to walk around and practice Spanish by inquiring prices of merchandise.

The natives are very colorful in dress and arrange their wares so artistically—they alertly and industriously try to sell what they have. They seem to lose all of their slowness, displayed when walking along or just sitting, when they are in these markets selling. It's a study in psychology just to see the difference in action. Could be there is a difference in the species from the slow, often stupid, drunken type seen on the streets and roads.

It was tempting to load up on green peppers, avocados, beautiful tomatoes, onions, garlic and cheese.

The Carters had some canned tortillas (good, too) from the USA. After the tortillas were fried, sautéed onions and green peppers, grated cheese, melted all together with milk, was put on the torts, which is usually called tostados; then more onions, peppers, and grated cheese, mixed all together with garlic and cumin seed, was rolled up in the tortillas; the chili mixed with a can of tomato paste was poured over the rolled tortillas and cooked for about 20 minutes, and out come the enchiladas.

In the meantime, individual tomatoes had been peeled and cut three-fourths through several times, then pressed down to give the appearance of an open flower. Into the center of this was mashed up avocado, seasoned with garlic, tobasco, salt, pepper, and fresh tomatoes mashed. This on a lettuce leaf and topped with an olive, made a most attractive guacamole salad, and the meal came out very well, and looked good, too.

It would have been perfect if better chili could have been found, or there had been time to make chili, as the kind found in cans was mixed with beans and, of course, the beans predominated. It was like old home week to get in a kitchen again and help prepare a meal.

Mrs. Carter has two regular servants and a yardman. She pays all of them less than one girl is paid a week in the USA. Her home was beautifully kept, the butler (and chauffeur) was most courteous at the door, and served dinner and supper superbly.

One night, with the Carters and a group of friends, we all went down to Pildarin Restaurant, a very famous eating spot, for anticuchos and other Peruvian foods. Anticuchos are prepared on bamboo skewers and made up of beef hearts, chicken livers, shrimp, and diced fish, broiled lightly over charcoal fires, and served to be eaten right off the skewers.

One of the most unusual appetizers was raw fish, called *"cebiche de carvina"*—freshly pickled in lemon juice, and served with a tomato sauce.

Then followed *"arroz con mariscos,"* which is rice with a conglomeration of fresh sea delicacies, such as snails, shrimp, mussels, and fish with hot red and green peppers and onions, all mixed together into a colorful dish. After the first mussel, then snail, it was easy going. If one is venturesome enough to just try these foods these other countries eat, they will find out what good flavor and fine foods they've been missing.

Sitting in the dining room of the Jockey Club. The horse racing will start in about an hour. The Carters lent us their club membership card, which made it possible to be here.

This is a beautiful track and the club is magnificent with hundreds of feet of glass enclosure, making it comfortable for those inside, as it is pretty cold out in the open.

All of the tables in the front section have already been reserved, but having arrived early has made it possible to get a choice seat in back, almost behind the finish line.

A typical, five-course Peruvian Sunday dinner has been served—avocado and lobster cocktail—a marvelous combination; long spears of fresh asparagus with a pat of mayonnaise to dip asparagus in, was the entrée; roast beef with curry sauce was the main dish; peas and carrots (carrots have a sweeter flavor here); corn, cauliflower, squash, with almonds and cashew nuts, all mixed together, was a colorful combination of vegetables and would be easy to serve at home.

For dessert they had a custard cooked like pie with rows of fruit on top, very artistic in looks and delicious in flavor. They serve the blackest coffee that has to have *"ague caliente"* to make it at all drinkable.

With as beautiful horseflesh as can be seen anywhere, the horse racing in Lima is something! Earl bet only 10 soles on each race, until he got the swing of the thing. They disqualified the winner in the third race, so he got his money back. In the fifth race he won 100 soles. One bet was made on Putty Tat (Pussy Cat) some name! And he lost by a point.

It was a swell time for the money—the entrance fee was just about 30 cents in American money. It was more than worth it just to see the crowds of beautifully dressed, sparkling bejeweled women—the elite of Lima.

After the races, going downtown to see *Moulin Rouge*, it was necessary to stand in line as all seats were reserved. This was the first American picture show seen since leaving home.

Then on to the Crillon Hotel for dinner in the sumptuous dining room, where everyone gathers in the evening for relaxed, talkative time and ritualistic served foods. You don't have dinner in the evening until from 9 o'clock to 12 o'clock. From 5 till 9, most of the natives and guests can be found over teas and cocktails, so it's a long, long evening of talking, drinking and eating.

This dinner was superb—couple of charcoal broiled lamb chops with all the trimmings, then a fruit dessert called *cherimoya* with cold orange juice covering it, one of the favorites of South America, and deliciously good. A good, English speaking waiter suggested it. Whenever there can be found an English speaking waiter to help out, they are more than worth a generous tip in giving service and selection of choice foods. This fruit had been bought when traveling in the car—bought at open markets and at fruit stands, and found to be very good, but prepared in this way it was heavenly.

A couple of California movie men who are here filming an old 18th century galleon that's still in good shape, and was marooned on dry land nearly a hundred years ago, sat next to us and chatted about food, people, and scenery down here. They said for us to be sure and try this *cherimoya* dessert with orange juice.

This *cherimoya*, or custard apple as some call it, is a most unusual fruit. If it could be grown in Texas Valley, it would bring a mint of money to producers. It's a hard fruit to even describe. It is green outside with appearance similar to an artichoke, but formed in lots of crazy and different shapes—no two alike. When peeled it has a white milky look, with large black seeds scattered about. The flavor is a cross between a pineapple, avocado, papaya, and very fresh coconut. Well, there's just nothing like it ever tasted before. If this fruit wasn't so perishable, it would be sensational to send some home—that is, if the South American officials would allow one to do so.

Prices on food and hotel rooms are not half as reasonable here as had been expected. *Holiday Magazine* should be written a letter, telling them the story they printed regarding the cheap prices is not true anymore. Large groups of Americans, with their free spending, increases the prices wherever they go down here—that's one of the reasons it's so nice to travel by car and see the out of the way places where the humblest of people in a car are treated with extra special kindness and attention.

This city would take the starch out of you, the salespeople are such idiotic people and not being able to speak the language fluently, causes them to charge double prices on everything, and one has to stand and wrangle with them for a half hour. The best thing to do is to offer just half the asking price; however, gold and silver prices are very reasonable. The little gold and silver trinkets of monkeys, Inca idols, snakes, and llamas, characteristic of this country, are carved out of pure gold nuggets and are very heavy compared with those at home.

There are many places of interest—the cathedrals have large numbers of priceless paintings, solid gold altars, carvings, much baroque and rococo style work can be found in most of these older buildings. The old government buildings, with their dark wood carved balconies, still remain as reminders of the pomp and glory of this "City of the Kings."

The Plaza de Armas is one of the most historic spots in all of South America. From a balcony where the municipal building now stands, San Martin proclaimed Peru's independence from Spain. In the Inca period, the Indian chief lived there and built a temple where the now ancient cathedral stands.

There were shoppers from all over the world, every nationality under the sun could be seen shopping along the Jiron Union, the most popular street of the city, buying gold trinkets, gold jewelry, silver tea services and other of the most modern of silver household objects; in the most beautiful shapes and delicate carvings were copper objects; then there were vicuna and llama blankets, rugs, shoes and jackets by the thousands, which are the most oversold of objects they have for sale.

The next thing of importance was a visit to the National Museum of Archeology to see the Paracas pre-Inca exhibits. Paracas is about 200 miles south of Lima and that's where these exhibits were excavated; these are the most unusual and best preserved exhibits known today, having been buried in dry sand, a wonderful preservative, from about the 6th century before the Christian era, until the present day.

This exhibit shows the high textile development of ancient Peru and the cultural race of people existing in those days, by their well-developed features and originality of designs and fine quality of materials worn by them.

These Paracas people are buried in a sitting position, with layer after layer of hand woven linen covering the bodies; then for an outer covering of the fardels, there is a cape of the most marvelous hand woven, soft, muted colors, with geometric, mythological or natural designs, which signify many and carried experiences of their existence.

Days could have been spent studying and making drawings of these designs, and there's never been an exhibit that made a more profound impression than this one.

They say there are thousands of these mounds near and around Paracas, yet unexcavated; so for many years there will be much interest centered in these excavation activities as they continue digging, and there is no limit to what they may find in this fabulous country.

Leaving Lima early Wednesday, we digressed on the way south, about 30 miles out of the city, to see the ruins of Pachacamae, which was built long before the Inca civilization. Excavations of more recent years show a gigantic grouping of overlapping terraces, narrow streets, temples, altars, tombs, homes with plastered walls and painted decorations, a lodging place for visitors, grain and other supply warehouses, secret enclosures, reservoirs for the water supply, irrigation ditches, and many other things to indicate they had a cultural civilization and a flourishing city a thousand or more years ago. It is amazing to see the uncivilized condition of parts of this country now, and yet know that hundreds of years ago they were so versed in learnings, crafts, and creeds.

The newly paved highways were being enjoyed to the fullest—they were indeed a great improvement over northern Peru, or any other place in South America. The view of the mountains to the left, in greens, mauve, and copper, with great splashes of snow on top, was awe-inspiring; to the right, following the sea, the blue, green-blue water was magnificent.

There were, at times, piles of sand three feet deep on the pavement to slow the car down, but workmen were all along this highway, literally sweeping this sand off with brooms, so there was not much of a delay, and excellent time was made through Canete.

When crossing a good bridge, we sat and watched a swift stream of churning water coming from the snow-clad Andean mountains. Going through the fertile valleys below Canete, it was almost unbelievable to see cotton trees 12 feet tall, with huge leaves and thick cotton hanging from bursting bolls. They do not have to replant this long staple cotton each year, as is done in the States, but trim it back and new growth develops each year for three years, without seeming to weaken the quality or quantity of strands. These most productive of plants will have these snow white, long streamers of cotton, then there will be large yellow bloom and boll, ranging from small ones to the bursting point—it's really fabulous—one could take proper equipment into that virgin soil, lease the land, and with the cheap labor, come out of there with millions—in ten years!

The pink bananas, watermelons, cantaloupes, and other fruits—such as oranges, papayas, charinoyas, had a most unusually delicious flavor, which shows the possibilities of this country if they irrigated over larger sections of the land. Vegetables were such intense colors, as though dipped in strong dye.

Then the next driving was back to sand and more sand to Chincha Alta and away from views of the Pacific to wild stretches of desert and sand; then inland to Ica, where they had an earthquake recently and some old buildings were destroyed.

Then continuing south through mountains of sand to Palpo and on to Nazca, a modern, well laid out little city where they have lovely garden homes surrounded by orange groves, and many other tropical fruits. The oranges had an unusually tart, sweet flavor, and it was a temptation to buy a whole carload, as up to this time there couldn't be found oranges as flavorful as those found at home.

There, inquiries were made about the road inland up to Cuzco. They said it was very good at this time of the year, but there were possibilities of not finding gasoline plentiful. At the fork of the road we hesitated and debated for ten minutes, trying to make up our minds, and waiting and hoping a car would come along that might be going that way. But no one came along and finally it was decided to follow the better marked road.

There was a very lonely stretch of road that seemed to take hours. Not one car came along to keep us company into Chavina. The only thing to break the monotony of the hot desert sand was the unusual formations of white rock and black coal streaked mountains—fantastically striking with zigzag layers of rock, then coal exposed to the elements in the same zigzag fashion. It seemed like nature was trying to create a symphony all in black and white.

Again we started following the Pacific over treacherous, winding cliffs, drifting sand, and no habitation whatsoever, into Puerto Chala, where there was found a beautiful hotel overlooking the sea.

All along there the sea was blue and green as the Mediterranean. A little spot of heaven had fallen down, and it was a temptation to stay there and fish for a week, as others were doing, but weather conditions were right to go on the next morning. We were afraid to linger and hoped to make it into Arequipa, in spite of the reported bad roads over mountainous passes, hairpin curves, and heavy piles of sand on the road.

We continued on toward Camana and encountered the most treacherous and dangerous road for a low slung car to travel on. Drifting sands had obliterated the road in so many places, and the sand was so treacherously deep the car would slide right and left as on ice, and it was necessary to keep going fairly fast or one would bog down.

All of this was happening on a one-way road, with turnouts every now and then to stop in when cars were approaching, which was overhanging the sea, water from 30 to 1,000 feet directly below. High waves were pounding the rocks and against these sand mountains. It sure puts butterflies in one's stomach and weakens the strongest nerves to the shaking point.

A most spectacular pass, with limitless views of the surrounding country, led into Arequipa, just a few minutes after the gate had been closed for lunch at the Pontiac agency. The brakes were beginning to shove the floorboard, so the only thing to do was wait right there until they opened at two o'clock.

They took the wheels off the car, cleaned out and put in new cups and fluid, then suggested that they make a protection pan to put on the bottom of the oil pan and over the Hydramatic, to lessen the danger of damage by large rocks in the road. When told it would cost only seven American dollars, it seemed the thing to do.

This G.M. manager of the Pontiac agency advised us not to try to drive up to Cuzco, as they had some serious bridge washouts just the week before. He was most courteous and rushed out to get train tickets for Cuzco. It will cost about $20 for two to make the 500-mile trip and that includes one night's Pullman. This trip is over several passes, one is up over a 15,000-foot pass. The trains here are amazing, and are the practical mode of traveling when getting off the main highways—the main highways are bad enough and there are many workmen on these roads all the time, trying to keep them open.

Arequipa, an Indian name meaning a place of rest, is absolutely just that. The hotel is all one could ask for, the nice people who run the place are most solicitous the way they cater to people by putting hot water bottles in the beds each night—makes one wish they could stay here forever.

Food is the choicest, with service unexcelled—wonderful steaks for 60 cents, are as good as you could find for $5 at home.

The beautiful landscaped gardens, surrounding the hotel, are full of many varieties of blooming flowers and make this a perfect setting with these impressive snowcapped mountains just back of the hotel. What a picture, with the volcanoes Misti, Chachani, and Picchupicchu—all nearly 20,000 feet or more—hovering above this attractive green valley!

Six tiring, but wonderful days have been spent on the trip up to Cuzco and surrounding country. A Pullman out of here Monday night for Cuzco brought us over several 14,500-foot passes during the night, by way of Juliaca (Hul-yaca) next morning.

At Juliaca a wonderful experience was enjoyed while waiting for the train. A very attractive woman, dressed in a gray suit and a vari-colored scarf tied around her throat, came up and wanted to know if she could practice some English words. She said she was learning English from records, which she played over and over on her old talking machine. She lived on a ranch at Allantaitambo, which is near Cuzco, and spent her leisure time trying to learn English, as she hoped to some day send her two sons to the US to be educated.

So the two hours between trains was spent slowly reading and explaining words in the Guide Book to her. She commented, "You pronouncie de words more slo-ly. I (patting her chest) more understande you, de records queek, no understand altime." Looks like this slow Southern drawl came in handy again.

From Juliaca on into Cuzco the seats were in what they call a buffet car of the train, and the wide windows made it possible to enjoy the scenery to the fullest. Most of the time the training was traveling in a valley (plateau) 12,000 feet high; snowcapped, copper-hued peaks were to the right, paralleling the whole trip.

There were pastures of vicuna, llama, and alpaca sheep; goats; cows; donkeys (and a few horses) all along the way. These were tended by Indian women or children—the women dressed in hat and flashy garb, even in the fields, with a blanket tied around their shoulders and a baby's head popping out.

These women always carry spinning pins and spin diligently as they walk along, or just stand and look, or sit on the ground. Their hats were many and varied—tall derbies, panamas, pie-shaped and parasol shaped with tassels—depending upon the place they live and the tribe to which they belong. Some were absolutely fetching in these hats.

Small adobe houses, dilapidated adobe fences and outhouses with a few trees around these buildings, dotted the landscape as far as the eye could see.

At each railroad stop the Indians were squatted by the road and in front of each, they had their handmade wares arranged artistically and for sale. There were vicuna and alpaca rugs in blending light and dark colors; pottery of every description from little figures in very original positions to large earthen pitchers and bowls—one pottery piece, a ferocious looking bull *(toro)*, is the "prize" most tourists try to get direct from the Indians. There were metal hand carved llamas, in solid silver and copper, depending on which color one liked best. They knitted woolen caps and bags, scarves, ties, and shawls in the gaudiest of colors, so terribly showy they looked good; vicuna bed blankets in the softest of wool, though there is a law against taking them out of the country; beautiful and hand woven scarves of plaid material, in soft wool that would delight the eyes; dolls and animals knitted in all colors and sizes for the little folk.

They were serving meat cooked on long sticks, anticusto fashion (many people were going through the train eating this delectable smelling meat)—they were also eating a honey looking candy out of small round boxes.

There were halves of raw lamb, pork, and beef on sale, and people on the train were buying it up like mad. They would just wrap it in a blanket, cloth, or paper, and away they would go, sometimes with the blood oozing out over the ground, or on the train floor. The smelly stench of the car was sickening by the time the train reached Cuzco.

It was after dark when we arrived in Cuzco and found a good hotel with a wood fire burning in the large living room. There was a young Peruvian on the train who graduated at Southern California and wanted to practice his English; he was very helpful and our constant companion for the next two days.

He owns a canning factory at Trojilla and is making great strides in his business—his tests on many of the perishable foods, such as tomatoes, greens, fruit juices, and some fish, have been used throughout Peru—and what he is striving for now is a tin can factory, as his greatest difficulty is getting tin cans imported from the USA.

An Indian student at the University, who spoke good English, acted as our guide. He showed us the most important ruins in and near the city. Early in the morning we went up to see Sacsahuaman, once a gigantic Inca fortress, on top of a mountain, commanding a magnificent view of Cuzco City and the surrounding valley.

The stones of this fortress are tremendous in size, and how they were ever placed there by human hands, is beyond the imagination of experts. Some of these stones are ten feet tall and weigh hundreds of tons, with smaller stones fitting so close and so perfectly that one cannot slip a razor blade between them. All of these stones are "battered" out with each corner rounded. Centuries and the earthquakes have not pulled them apart, though no mortar was used. They are magnificently placed in their odd shapes and forms, with corners, squares, and indentations all fitted together in perfect form.

At the Temple of the Sun there was to be seen portions of the old pre-Inca wall being restored; the niches and hinges chiseled out of rock to hold doors was the work of masters; all the pre-Inca foundations, on which so many of the Inca buildings were later built, are just fantastic in form and workmanship. How this was accomplished without steel tools in those days is a debatable question.

There are lots of churches in and around

Cuzco—the largest one on the square has many wonderful paintings similar to Murillo's work. These paintings are copies and the work of Indian artists in the 16th century.

We just happened to be in this church when the bishop was showing two priests the gold and silver ornaments of the vestry—we've never seen such gorgeous gold things outside of St. Peters in Rome. There were rubies, emeralds, and diamonds, and many pearls on this large candelabra sort of vessel of gold. At the base was an indentation with delicately carved images of the Virgin Mary in gold and other figures gathered around.

A large solid gold thorn crown, with pearls at the end of each thorn, was the pride of the church and the city, as it has remained on the Christus head throughout a terrible earthquake.

There were heavy gold goblets, beautifully etched in historical designs; there were large gold platters for sacrament; pitchers studded with precious stones for wine; and in the main part of the church, the altar was hand wrought of gold and silver. The pulpit showed many laborious hours with wood chisels.

It was told by the guide that at one time a solid gold chain was linked to each post around the square in front of the cathedral, but it disappeared when the Spanish took over.

In the center of this square is the statue of an American Indian man, with feather sticking in headband, a loincloth around his waist, his feet in moccasins. It looks out of place where these native Indians are heavily dressed with a big poncho sort of blanket covering them almost to the ground. It's easy to see the resentment the Indians must feel about this statue, with it dressed so differently from them, or one might say, with hardly any dress at all.

It is said this is the work of an American sculptor, who was commissioned to do an Indian for the City of Cuzco. He probably thought all Indians looked alike. There's been a great deal of controversy over it for many years, but the statue remains standing there to this day.

Another impressive church was one of mirrors; every inch of the building seemed to be covered with mirrors and draped with lace bunched up with blue and red artificial flowers. It was gaudy, but brought about a reverent and subduing effect. Crowds of Indians were sitting, kneeling, and prostrating themselves on the floor while a service was in progress.

Up on a hillside overlooking the city there was a small, intimate church, which had exquisite lace on the altar rail, dating back several generations, but still in fine condition. A nun, dressed in white, was getting ready to take her final vows and was praying at the altar; so intent was her supplication, it's doubtful if she was conscious of anyone being there.

There were beautiful old paintings just standing on the floor and scattered about. One painting of an Inca runner or *chasqui*, as they were called, was of great interest. Every day, so the story goes, these runners brought letters, important papers, fish, and other sea delicacies from the coast several hundred miles away to the Inca kings.

Walking down these old streets, going into the shops and looking through the souvenirs, one could tell by the well-spoken voices and the well-dressed appearance of most of the natives that this was a cultured city—a city with a great future. Many schools and two universities have been established here for generations.

Late in the afternoon the Indian Markets were visited, and the poorer sections of the city around the markets; somehow the markets tell a better story of the people than can be found anywhere else. They had much to sell, melons, squash or pumpkins, many green vegetables foreign to American eyes. There were wicker stalls and all kinds of basketwork, pottery in muted tones, Inca idols, flowers of the surrounding country, including delicate orchids potted and in wire baskets.

Then to one side were a dozen or more Jewish merchants with stalls of everything conceivable to be found in a five and ten store at home. The Indians were crowded around these items, examining them in amazement and curiosity. Much buying, trading, bartering was going on. The Indians would buy a thing just because they liked a thing and not for its usefulness, or knowledge of what it was. They would hold up what they had bought for others to see, then giggle and laugh about it.

Often there was to be seen a white flag on a pole sticking out from different adobe houses; sometimes there was a bouquet of flowers tied to the pole. Upon asking the guide what it meant, he said, "These people have *chicha* and other drinks for sale today; they've just got it fermented to the right consistency."

If it is possible, would the guide take us into a place to see and try it? He said, "Would you like to drink it made the Inca way?" What is the difference? He answered, "After you have tasted it both ways, I'll tell you the difference."

Going into a dark, poorly lighted room where all the chairs around the tables were full and several men and women were squatting down, or with legs outstretched, leaning back against the wall of the room with large mugs in their hands, we found a happy jabbering was going on.

Americans must have been a novelty to them as they quit talking, got quiet, and watched closely as the keeper dipped into a wooden keg to fill our glasses. This gave the feeling of being conspicuously prominent, and the thought was voices—"If the home folks could see us now!"

These drinks were very good in taste and reminded one of a childhood drink an uncle concocted of corn in the home many years ago, without Mother knowing it. However, just a single sip of each was all we ventured drinking, then handing the remains in the glass to some of the Indians, a broad smile spread over their countenances, and the jolly, happy talking noise started again.

On the way back to the hotel, the guide said the first drink we tasted was prepared the Inca way—their method of grinding is to have the corn chewed by women, then they spit the chewed corn into a barrel. They cover this mix with water and wait a few days for fermentation. Such a sickening feeling it gave when he told us this, but there's a possibility he was just pulling a joke on us, as he had a wonderful sense of humor, which he displayed several times that day—but dinner could not be enjoyed for thinking about it.

Thursday morning it was necessary to get up for

breakfast by 5:30, with about 25 other tourists, and take this bus with train wheels, called an *autocarril,* over the mountain pass. By backing up and then going forward four or five times, the bus kept gaining altitude.

Finally arriving on top, a magnificent panorama of the city of Cuzco and the surrounding mountains was being oohed and aahed over. Climbing over mountain after mountain, the beauty of the distances unrolled before the passengers—then the ride was terminated on the downgrade to the small village of Machupicchu.

Cuzco is 11,440 feet, while Machupicchu is only 8,000 feet, but there was the feeling of being much higher at the ancient citadel because of the tall mountains surrounding it, many snow covered, several perpetually so.

Alighting from the *autocarril* at the end of the railroad line, it was necessary to go in a station wagon, winding around many hairpin turns up a steep pass, to the ruins.

It would take years to actually describe the place. That is one place that has to be seen to believe. It's a place beyond the comprehension of the layman—even experts ponder over the magnitude of this and other similar fortresses of the pre-Inca and Inca periods.

There is so much of perfectly fitted granite rock to see, so many intricate turning streets built around the contour of rocks that nature has already placed there. There are unusual winding stairways leading to many levels of buildings with peculiar styles of construction to delight an architect's eye.

Then with curious intentness, it was possible to look down into a deep, dark pit. This deep, tunneled stairway leading into the bowels of the mountain is forbidden to visitors, and it is said that no one has been able to survive, so far, in attempting to explore it in these ruins.

There was one rock in the entrance hall to the king's home, which was the most surprising of all. So much had been read about the stones in these ruins having unusual angles and turns, some had been pointed out as the most significant of all.

There is much supposition as to how they had been hewn out and fitted so perfectly without metal tools, and this one in the king's entrance room deserves more recognition than has been given it.

It had been cut or chiseled out to form a corner of room in an oblong, rounded top, effect; and at the same time on the left side there was protruding out a part of the same stone, chiseled out to form a hook shape, about five inches in diameter, with a hole about two inches across, cut through this hook part of the stone, which looked as though it was used to hang things on.

Five hundred years ago they had apartments as we do now, hundreds of units with separate entrances, bedrooms, living rooms, and kitchens. There were community toilets and baths. There was a slide hewn out of rock for children, a cemetery, a crazy cut stone altar which was supposed to tell the time of the month and the year. Legend says priest astronomers "tied the sun" at the time of the equinox.

There was a large council room with three windows, very wide and symmetrical, which overlooked the valley on one side, and out of each window the opposite valley could be seen.

There were places hewn out of rocks for persons being punished to have their hands forced into these locks, and they were forced to gaze directly into the sun.

They terraced the land to stop erosion and did a much better job than is done today; also, these terraces were used to grow their corn, potatoes (wild potatoes and strawberries still grow there) and other vegetables.

They had a complete water system hewn out of rock—some say the only reason this citadel was ever abandoned was because the water springs gave out—probably the effect of an earthquake. Some say the place is 500 to 700 years old, but it's hard to believe this work could have been done in thousands of years, with only the crude tools in existence of that day.

When the guide started piloting the climb up to view the ruins, it was surprising to see a lot of new tents, cots, tables and chairs placed about on a ledge near the hotel; and while getting drinks in the dining room, there was to be found lots of American canned foods of the well-known brands. These looked so out of place in an atmosphere of antiquity.

The guide said that just a few weeks before a group of Hollywood movie people had been making pictures of these ruins, with hundreds of the Indian natives in the scenes. They say this film will be released in the United States soon, and will probably be called "The Legend of the Inca." It should be most interesting and well worth seeing, if for no other reason than the background of the ruins.

It's possible to climb and explore a week and not see all of the interesting works in granite—we left reluctantly in mid-afternoon; younger tourists spend the night to explore and climb over narrow steep trails the mountain Huaina Picchu fronting the ruins to where burial tombs are hewn out of solid rock into the mountainside; but that is not the thing for older people to attempt.

Down the bus went on these hairpin turns to train level. There was a good chance to enjoy looking at the flowers and to examine them more closely on the cliff and surrounding riverbanks, while waiting for the bus company to bring the second load of passengers.

Fragile pink begonia was growing all over the mountainside; clinging to tree limbs and niches were rarest orchids; pampas grass seemed to serve as soil protector at bottom of ridges; piso-may, a red blooming tree, was tall and background-ish with its magnificence; a purple tree called humehuine that looked similar in shape to our catalpa tree blooms, but without leaves, gave out a rare fragrance—can you visualize a huge all-purple tree?

There were peach and wild plum trees, all in bloom; there was another tree, not known by name, that had great clusters of blooms in the shape of an umbrella, sometimes white, sometimes pink—they were so delicate, so airy, they lent a softening effect to the mountainside.

There were many kinds of ferns with big leaves; tropical plants like those at home and for which fabulous prices have to be paid were growing wild on these banks of the headwaters of the Amazon River.

Arriving back in Cuzco after dusk, down-tracking from one road to another on the descent into the city and enjoying the view of the mellow lights of the bustling city below while progressing down—there was the feeling that the day had been spent in another world.

Ever so many people had talked about how cold and horrible Puno was and, had the tickets not already been bought to return by Puno, we would have failed going there and would have missed a wonderful experience.

It seems like everyone we contact just puts themselves out to be nice. A young teacher from Cleveland, Ohio, who speaks Spanish like a native, was on this train going to Puno. He said, "I've found that you just can't trust the judgment of others abut places; I'm determined to go to Puno to see if it is as bad as they say." After shaking hands on that, we said, "Those are our sentiments, too!"

A light snow was falling on our arrival in Puno. The blustering flakes were digging down in the wraps and all over the luggage. It was very cold, colder and higher than one would like; and along with the high altitude it was necessary to walk; and as the snow was crunchy and slick, it was necessarily slow progress to the hotel a block away, as there was no taxi to be found at the station.

A card from the hotel manager in Arequipa to the hotel manager in Puno brought about wonderful results. He had the boy build a fire in the dining room immediately and brought freshly made coffee. Later, after serving the choicest of steaks, he got hot water bottles for the beds and prepared hot water for baths in big kettles in the kitchen.

Next morning early, the hotel manager suggested things to do for the day. With this teacher and an 83-year-old Floridian, we took a car ride about the Lake Titicaca, which is 12,500 feet, the highest navigable lake in the world.

The first stop was to watch the natives making what they called balsa boats, when in reality they are made of dried bulrushes, or tatara grass, of which the lake has acres. These rushes, strong and durable, are formed in round layer after layer, then tied together with a grass twine.

These layers are then tied on top of each other, bulging out and protruding in the middle or center, then they are brought to a point at each end and all tied together. They do look like a crude makeshift of a boat, but are very strong and durable and last for years, with these bales laced securely on top of each other.

One large boat, with a clumsy looking sail made of rush laced in fan shape, had eight or ten natives going slowly, but going, across the lake. The slow going was due to the mild, calm weather after the night's snow flurry.

Some of the smaller boats were carrying what they call a *"mallo net"*—this net is made of the grass similar to a cane chair bottom, and is v-shaped with a long pole in the center for support, and with a braided grass rope extending about 10 feet from the pole to the boat, as it glides along.

On the backside and top of the net is built a sort of flange of net to hold the bago fish, as this net skims along in the water and forces the fish to glide in. They lift the net up when it is full and dump the fish into the boat, then start all over again until they get a capacity load for the boat.

This bago fish is about eight inches long and

kind of flat. When fried or broiled, they are perfectly delicious. They were served the evening before as an entrée, and the waiter was popeyed when asked to serve them for breakfast, as coffee, rolls, and a small pat of butter and jam is all they usually serve—it's a big problem to try to get anything else.

This is Saturday, August 15, a day celebrating Indian Independence Day, and there's to be much activity in the form of dancing and folklore displayed.

The squares and marketplaces of these small towns near the lake are full of Indians wearing a riot of colors—reds, yellows, with aquas predominating—every Indian is in his best clothes for the occasion.

There were many hand woven materials for sale, some delicate and soft, others of the coarsest and roughest of feel. The market squares were full of everything imaginable for sale; in one spot there were young vicunas brought in from the range to be sold or to be looked at close up—they are gentle little things and remind one of baby deer in their grace of face and limb.

Great quantities of food were on sale; fringed shawls with embroidered patterns were selling like hotcakes, as were heavy shoes and coarse black and white socks and stockings; blankets and a ducking material were exchanging hands.

Dye tenders were doing a landslide business, with delicate looking apothecary scales weighing out colors for the people, and it was easy to recognize the colors the Indians had used in their garments.

There were all kinds of fruit and vegetables tied up in big duck sheets. The Indians squat and clean and sell right from the ground—if no luck, they pick up and move on to another location, leaving filth right on the street, wetting before everyone, with back turned. Odors of excrement and the smell of beer and liquor combined left such a stench it's impossible to understand how the Indians stood it; but it's been said the Indians never bathe and wear the same clothes until they rot off.

One could never forget the celebrations going on in each town passed. These celebrations were not being put on for visitors, like in so many of the well-advertised tourist spots. There were only two other cars seen, in one of which was a buyer of an animal for slaughter, and we were the only visitors.

Some of the oldest churches of Peru are in these villages. The hand carving in red stone, done by the Indians, formed a pattern of their legends, and was in a wonderful state of preservation.

In Juli the most fantastic affair was in full swing. In front of the cathedral were three drummers in weird mask faces, beating drums in a tom-tom chant. Surrounding the drummers were ten men dressed in the most dilapidated organdy and silk skirts, which looked like they had been packed away in water-soaked trunks for years. Their pants legs showed from beneath these skirts. They had on ordinary men's vests, trimmed with gold and silver braid shields nearly the shape of butterfly wings. Over their faces they wore masks of the silliest looking kinds—one-eyed, bleary-eyed, cross-eyed, wide-eyed, blind, scary-eyed, etc.

All the while they were dancing around and around and blowing on Indian reed pipes, the uncanny and eerie notes never in tune, but somehow blending.

Another row of men, circling this other group,

was wearing ordinary suits, but with stockings up to their knees and pants legs put in, giving the appearance of knickers. They had their faces covered with the funniest masks of all—one was a typical, long-lipped African with mirror teeth; another face was like a fox or pig, then a turned-up nose affair, skull and crossbones; a two-handed monster; a monkey; and a bird with a long beak.

It was comical how two of these fellows would back their butts together, shimmy, and then dance away to the weird, wild notes of the music; then back-to-back again, shimmying. This kept up for an indefinite length of time with the natives standing by, clapping hands, making a Ho-o-o Ho-o-o sound, swaying and stepping a one-step sort of movement to the reed pipe notes.

At Pomato the most colorful affair of all was going on—a lot of barefooted Indian women in so many skirts that they stood right straight out and looked to be weighted down, they were so numerous and so full; red, kelly green, aqua, purple, pink, every color of the rainbow, with a contrasting shawl, was in that group and being worn by them; while the men with whom they were dancing wore ordinary black suits, but colorful fringed shawl around their shoulders.

There were abut 20 couples in this blocked off square, and the way they danced in and out, stooping down, then raring back, was a reminder of some of the rougher square dancing done in the States.

In the center of this group were the funniest and queerest dressed fellows playing flutes. They had black masks covering their heads of what looked to be stocking material, with holes for eyes, and those eyes slanting crazily in an oriental fashion, and a funny hooked effect protruding out in front for a nose, with two feelers, with a blob of color on each end, similar to a bug of some kind, extending from above the eyes.

These fellows were wearing long cotton socks, blouse and knickers, all in coarse white gunny sacking. Over this was a frock-tailed coat sort of thing made out of same material, with all kinds of weird colored (black predominating) embroidery over this coat.

It looked like they were imitating grasshoppers, or some similar insects, and the way they hippity-hopped about, with the flutes making off-key cheeps, chirps and shrills, was further verification of their representing the antics of some insects—could have been the locust.

All this would have made a good movie; the chanting of the natives in unison, with the reeds vibrating to the pat, pat of their feet as their marching off of the grounds was intensified to the beat of the drums when their dance was finished. It certainly was an awe-inspiring sight, until a group of the women started fighting.

When one stooped to retrieve her shawl, the heavy, clumsy skirts fell completely over her head, and she took an awful walloping right there in the street, landing headfirst on the ground, with the lower part of body exposed to the elements and for all eyes to see. Needless to say, she wasn't wearing drawers—they've never heard of such a garment for coverage, except the three-cornered kind for babies only. From the looks of the Indian babies and children, the three-cornered version were few and far between, and if seen, was just a colored piece of cloth. They were all so heady with their corn *chichi*, or beer, and another crazy drink made of sugar cane and called *aguardiente*, that as they got from under the spell of the reed pipes and drums, and when trying to help the girl recover herself and find her face, they practically all went berserk in dizzy grabs at each other.

Going on to Yunguyo, there was a real Indian dinner prepared by Indian women, some in derby hats with red trimming, others in tall white panama hats. They reminded one of the Ladies Aid Society at home, or a Dallas Fair church group selling plate lunches.

Mr. Bailey and Mr. Fraser were just lapping up the good food, but the effects of being in rarified air for so many days, and the stench around, was enough to weaken anyone's appetite. The Indians were upset because we did not eat all the soup of rice and eggs; they zealously wanted to earn their money; so they offered some raw kidneys from a big hunk of uncooked meat nearby!

In a stone's throw of Copacabana, we let the young teacher out to go on to Bolivia and La Paz; it sure was a temptation to go on there, but decided not to risk it, even by car, as so many had said the car might be confiscated, as a division of land was in progress, and much unrest and hatred was in evidence, and a revolution was likely to break out at any moment.

Exhausted, but with exciting things to remember and lucky to have seen something out of the ordinary for visitors to see, we returned to Puno very late, had a quick steak dinner (best ever), got the luggage and beat it for the train.

The train man at Cuzco told us that a sleeper would not be available until the train reached Juliaca, forty minutes away; but upon getting on the train and entering the day coach, the conductor looked at the tickets and then motioned and insisted that we take berths 11 and 12 on a sleeper that was available and already connected to the day coach.

Saying to the conductor, *"No, Hul-ya-ca"*—but the old fool just wouldn't listen and kept saying *"once, doce"* and shoved us in, it was reasonable to believe that a mistake had been made by the trainman in Cuzco and, tired as we were, we felt it a pregnant idea to go on to bed.

About an hour later, there was a loud knocking. On opening the door, two men saw us undressed and went away. About 10 minutes later, there was more loud knocking, and two army men in uniform burst right into the berth, and the conductor and the men had an awful fight there in the aisles of the car!

The conductor, after much parleying, finally asked us to get up—with the train already going! Getting clothes back on with the train lurching forward at a fast rate of speed was a problem, but these men were forcing themselves right on into the berths.

Next door was a nice man who asked, in broken English, for us to come sit in his berth until we reached Juliaca. He made many apologies for the bad way these officers had acted. He wanted to take us to dinner when we arrived in Arequipa. Giving us his card showed that he was Judge of the District Court in Puno and was on his way to Arequipa to try some cases.

Arriving back in Arequipa on Sunday morning, it sure was good to get back in a lower altitude. A bad case of sniffles had developed in the higher altitude, which was suspected to be hay fever, but a few hours in the lower altitude had us feeling much better, and the whole thing cleared away.

Sunday afternoon we drove out near Arequipa to see the airport, where some planes arrived daily from Lima. One plane was full of a tour group, with destination Cuzco. They see so little of the people and country. By car is the best way, if one has time on their hands.

Later, it was fun to drive over the city and see all the lovely buildings and homes, mostly white with streaks of volcanic layers. This stone is quarried from the lava beds surrounding the city, is used for all their buildings, and produces a glistening effect with this backdrop of snowcapped mountains.

Early Monday morning, when a Norwegian with whom we had been talking said he was leaving in a few hours for Maquegua and could help us through one stretch of bad road, we decided to tag along.

He was driving a big-tired jeep truck. He works for the American Copper & Zinc Company, who are building a large new plant near Llobaya. It was a relief to go this short distance with him, as this part of the country is supposed to be very dangerous from several standpoints.

There had been some wild tales about this road south; they said there was no road visible, due to the wind velocity blowing the sand in ridges in washboard effect—just a few hours after making the roadbed, the imprints were blown away and it was easy to get lost and go in circles. It was also said that roving caravans of dangerous and desperate men had been seen in this section, who would mislead, waylay, rob and kill those who were brave enough to venture through there.

That was not a pretty picture to think about while driving along. After bidding *Adios* to the Norwegian, there developed in the mind a feeling of insecurity and a lostness in a stretch of beautiful, towering mountains of sand, with deep dry riverbeds, and a few straggly trees which encourages the traveler to believe that some form of life did exist in those desolate stretches.

It is understandable why the wild tales got out regarding that section of the country. We did go, by dead reckoning, through some horrible stretches, where there was nothing but sand. We did see a car of four wild-looking goofs coming toward us—they slowed down, then stopped. After quick thinking, we kept going on and in a short time they turned around and were following. We figured the sensible thing to do was to try to outrun them—this was easy to do in a fast car with them in an old jalopy—but when rounding a curve into a canyon road, in our haste it was with great difficulty that we kept from going overboard into the depths below.

Every hundred miles or so there would be rivulets winding to the sea. There would be some green trees and a little underbrush, but mostly yellow, pink, and copper-colored mountain ranges and sand roads were all that would be seen before us.

Rounding hills, or in the valleys, the car following could be seen and the determination was to keep far ahead was much safer than running any risk of stopping. After such an experience, we can understand why most people want to fly through this section.

It was with thanks that we finally came on to a more visible road, which wound around over a wonderful mountain pass, and the beautiful valley of Tacna could be seen in the distance. Strange to say the old jalopy with the four men disappeared completely upon arrival at the good road.

In Tacna there was this lovely new Tourista Hotel with good food and hot baths, and our nerves were restored from the wild chase. There was also a swimming pool and the terraces were covered with bougainvillea and other climbing vines. Many exotic kinds of flowers were growing in this flower garden—a real oasis in the desert.

It took most of the day to get the oil and grease work done on the car, and it was late afternoon when we started for Arica, Chile, which was just a 45-mile drive over bumpy, poorly paved roads.

The Intrepid Donnells Cross a High Mountain Pass.

Roadside Shrines of Red Flags
Dedicated to Gauchito Gil
in Argentina.

A Friendly Helping Hand.

Day of the Dead Festival (Peru).

Masked Day of the Dead Celebrant.

Coming Down a Mountain Pass.

Reed Boats of Lake Titicaca in Peru or Bolivia.

Women Wearing Bowler Hats in Bolivian Market.

Bolivian Woman in Colorful Shawl and Pollera (Skirt).

Llamas in the Andes.

Ecuadorian Child with Fishing Pole.

Dance Parade in Streets of Cusco.

Street Musician Playing Mandolin.

Reed Boats of Lake Titicaca.

Ecuadorian Festival.

Andean Quena Flute.

Fishing From an Improvised Platform.

Peruvian Alpacas.

Peruvian Quechua Indian Woman in Traditional Dress Knitting While Tending Sheep.

Reed Balsa Boat on Lake Titicaca.

Folk Dancing in Buenos Aires, Argentina.

Villarrica Volcano in Chile.

Children Going for a Swim.

Quechua Woman with Her Stubborn Llama.

Brazilian Woman Carrying Basket of Fruit.

Men Drinking Mate with a Bombilla, a Straw Made of Silver to Filter Mate.

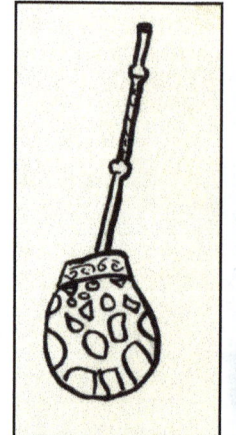

A Bombilla Straw.

6

Chile: August/September, 1953

Two hours were used up going through customs and to get into Chile. They were the slowest officials imaginable. One learns it is best to just be patient, not get upset, let them take their time—there isn't anything that can be done about it anyway.

It was a relief to be in Arica, a typical seacoast town, after going over what was supposed to be the worst part of the trip south. Things are much cheaper—the hotel room and food for two people is only four American dollars—not bad! This is the place to stay for a long while if one wants to save dollars.

This antiquated hotel, Pacifico, was built more than 40 years ago for a South American conference of some kind. It is still very lovely in some respects, as it commands a view of the blue Pacific from the bedroom windows.

The plumbing in the bathroom is gold bronze—very continental in aspect—with a rear end soaker thrown in. The bathtub on legs is nearly three feet deep, with a shower spray above on gold prongs that looks like a light fixture.

It's excitingly interesting to watch and hear the millions of seagulls nesting on the mountain within a stone's throw of the hotel, a mountain housing a beacon light on top to safely pilot ships into the harbor.

There's no other country like this Chile in South America. There's so much of it, it would take a lifetime to tell all about it. Chile is ten times nicer than Peru. Many people speak English here, which helps a lot in getting about. These people are so clean in the cities and surrounding countryside; they look, act, and wear clothes like Americans. The food tastes much better—not so over-seasoned one can't tell what it is, like the food in some of the hotels in Peru.

Peruvian roads are the most overrated in the world. The pre-Inca and Inca ruins of Peru are the attractions for tourists to that country and make it what it is. One would be a fool to go in a car and take the chances on these treacherous sands and isolated, lonesome roads again that one has to take to get through Peru.

Peru has been ruined by tourists, mainly school teachers, who think they know Spanish. They start spouting their college Spanish and not one native can understand a word they say. It's been laughable more than one time, their trying to get things over to the guides. It does seem like Americans can understand the natives' broken English better than they can understand the Americans' poorly pronounced Spanish—you've got to get the correct sound into a word, and then only can they understand you.

It's hard for college teachers to get that tongue-twisting sound to words as the natives do; then, too, the different Spanish speaking countries have a difference in the sound of words. The young teacher from Ohio said he had learned more in six weeks living with the Indians than in his four years of studying Spanish in school.

Of course, getting the grammar down pat helps. The best system learned so far is to point to a word on the map or book, let the native say it first, get the sound correct, then the motion of their hands will show if it's right or left or straight ahead, when getting directions for travel. If the native can't read, then a stab is made at the right pronunciation, saying the words over several different ways until it rings a bell in their minds.

There is a very nice drive around the mountains, by the oceanfront. Here they have some clean sand beaches for play and swimming in the summer, which is November, December, January, and February. There are a lot of nice beach hotels, a casino, inside swimming pools, and a novelty store.

It's been very cool here all day and coat suits are comfortable, with toppers handy in the car for the evening. The climate is just right—really wonderful.

It could have been a beautiful spot, but they have spoiled the north end of the bay with docks and ugly shipping paraphernalia.

In the park adjoining the hotel are some bougainvillea trees, surmounted by wire netting to hold the limbs to the top of the pergola roof—the trunks are at least a foot in diameter. Underneath is a cool, shaded parkway with inviting walkways and comfortable seats. These bougainvillea are in full bloom just now—can you imagine an acre of massed color? Several types of palm trees are growing down the avenues of streets, which show it's very tropical, if cool.

Many people, including three skiing couples, came in by bus from Tacna, 45 miles away, this afternoon—they will fly out of here early in the morning for Santiago.

The Panagra air rates into Santiago are much higher than the Chilean rates, due partly to the dollar exchange in Chile; anyway, that's why so many people make a stop-off here—at least these people coming through keep the town alive. Buying an air ticket here, on to Santiago, they save about a hundred American dollars.

Lots more people speak English in Chile, and

on the whole there's a better class of people. All the people are predominantly white.

Leaving at daybreak for Iquique didn't help much, as a pea soup fog plagued us for hours. There were to be seen many extinct salt or nitrate mines. The land for miles was all rolled up in chunks, and the crazy, plowed-up effect was sprinkled with white, like frost.

Near frequent intersections of nearly obliterated roads it was easily possible to get lost or wander around in circles—several times when we failed to watch carefully, the old half-made roadbeds were going in every which way and there were few signs to go by, so dead reckoning, or guessing, was resorted to most of the time.

To ease the fear of getting lost, we kept saying, surely we had enough sense to go to the right, or coast line, which was always to the west—if there was any doubt about a road.

It was difficult to stand the loneliness after the first hundred-mile stretch of road, where there were no cars to be seen, only one or two trucks, and very few people.

There was a good stretch of road into Iquique—a typical seaport and fishing center town, with a good-looking hotel. But, as it was only one o'clock, it seemed foolish to sit there and wait all afternoon, when there was a much dreaded isolated desert highway to go over.

The Esso station attendant said Antofagasta could easily be made by nightfall—but cross roads, bad roads, dangerous roads, and customs kept us from accomplishing that.

There was so little of attraction in these small towns, and it seemed the quicker we could get these bad roads behind us, the better off things would be.

There were two extra cans of gas in the car, Hydramatic oil, one change of motor oil and, with all that, it looked safe enough.

The roads in that northern section of Chile were hot and dry—very bad indeed, but the low desert roads were less risky than the high winding sand-slidy ones of Peru, right next to the sea.

Knowing that American Esso maps had been accurate in their way up to now, they surely wouldn't be less accurate in Chile, though so many had warned us to stay out of this horrible ghost country.

Many years ago, there were village after village flourishing in this section, but not a living thing was to be seen now. All that was left was just thousands of half-torn-down, dusty old rock houses and cross after cross, weird graveyards, sometimes with hundreds of open, gruesome, concrete crypts, where bodies had been placed and taken away. All of which reminded one that this was once the land of the living.

The roads looked so untraveled and, in the maze of crossroads, a definite right turn should have been made at the ghost town of Pintados, when the better road looked straight ahead.

Traveling mile upon mile, much of the time following a rocky creek bed with huge rocks to slow us down, there was the feeling of being completely lost. One car did pass, but decided it was dangerous to stop and get directions, after looking at the drunken-wild-looking fellows inside the old beat-up car—they probably were fearful of us, as they rushed on past.

For miles, while creeping along, there was indecision in the thoughts of turning back, but it was terribly hard to make up our minds to go back over that awful strip of road, as the rocks had already broken the handbrake.

Calculating there was barely enough gas to make it back to people who could give directions, but scanning the horizon with hopes of just anything showing up, there could be seen some trees in the distance and what looked to be houses. Usually, a group of trees spelled a small village or some form of habitation, and the safest bet was to get to that spot. Following the hunch, upon arriving closer, we saw a dilapidated old rock house, fenced-in yard, and two children playing in the yard.

A burly looking Englishman came out to the car and said, "What in Heaven's name are you two crazy people doing in this car in this Godawful country?" We told him we were trying to make it to Antofagasta and couldn't tell one road from another, and it looked like we were lost. He said, "You are jolly well right. You are lost!"

Then we told him he looked lost and asked what he was doing in that Godforsaken country. He said, "It's a long story and you haven't time to listen. What you need is to get going and get somewhere before darkness overtakes you. I don't want to be responsible for your driving in this ghost-ridden land at night. It's my job to keep these roads open and I've been lost at night on them and I know what it's like."

After giving the proper directions, he said that we would need to go through customs first, about five or six blocks down the road, where two other men were stationed. That was all the inhabitants left in the torn-down village.

It took a long time for the officers to get the papers prepared, having to print the words out slowly. All the time this slow procedure was going on, there was a restless, uneasy feeling that this night would have to be spent out in this open, stricken country, unless inspection could be finished soon.

Continuing to say *rapidio*, it seemed the best thing to do was to snatch the papers out of their hands and rush to the car, get in and start. If they didn't whistle us down, we figured everything was okay and we could keep going, progressing as fast as was safe for the car. When patience was completely threadbare, trying to rush them seemed to cause them to delay that much longer.

The darkening shadows of evening were coming quickly, when a sign was seen to the right—"Tocopilla" and below it "79 miles." Circling down and around a downgrade canyon pass all the way, we reached this coastal city with all the night lights blinking at us, as we rounded the last hill and looked down on this quaint town.

Trying to find a hotel, great excitement seemed to spread over the streets when the people saw a Texas license on the car and hundreds of them gathered around. The hotel was definitely on the old-fashioned side—but after the hard driving over such desolate country, it was with thankfulness to find this port.

Early morning found us searching all garages, trying in vain to find a cable for the handbrake. The only thing left to do was take a chance and go on south.

The coastal road on south was the most

dangerous, but nearer to our destination, and by now it was unusual to have a handbrake. This is one of the outstanding drives of the entire trip so far. With every turn of the road, a breathtaking view of the blue Pacific, and to the left were wild, craggy formations of rocks and overhanging mountains in rich reds, intermingled with pinks and aqua—there's nothing anywhere in the whole world more majestically beautiful than that drive—not even Amalfa Drive in Italy.

Antofagasta was a bustling city with a new, modern hotel, half-finished, right by the dilapidated looking old hotel with a boarded-up face. But with a good room, excellent food, it was wonderful to relax again, talk with and just see many interesting people living and eating there. People from all over the world were there and in some way connected with their mining industries.

The Automobile Club has a beautiful clubhouse and restaurant out on the beach, where they do lots of entertaining. Many Americans are also established in this section of Chile, as the Chuquicamata copper mines, one of the world's largest, is not too far away, and the activity of this mine is fabulous.

Every car agency in town was contacted, but no cable could be found for the car—it was dangerous to go on, but there just wasn't anything else to do but go on, hoping and praying to make it on to the next large city safely.

The coastal road was chosen again, through Papaso; there had been enough of the dry desert, desolate sand roads to last a lifetime. Here was another outstanding section of wild beauty, hairpin turns, death traps, and narrow roads, all the way into Toltal—but every breathtaking moment was worth the danger and the risk.

Then again, the inner circle of copperous green mountains, wild deserts, torn-down villages, large cemeteries, nosed behind us mile upon mile; dusty washboard roads through Chanard, Pueblo Hondido, Inca de Ore, and on and on south to Copiapo.

This Copiapo is an unusual town. At one time it was called the "Gold Coast" of South America. More than a hundred years ago they found gold and silver here, and it became a boom city. The mines were discovered by a fellow named Goday, who promised to pave the streets in silver, as he said, "Them thar mountains are full of the blanket-blank stuff."

There are many reminiscences of the "good old days," such as the old hansom cabs (*coche*)—dilapidated, but fun to ride in. Operas from New York played here. The first railroad of South America was built by Norris Brothers of Philadelphia in 1850, and the same tracks pass along the side of the Carrera Hotel. This first train, on the original tracks, is preserved in a schoolyard nearby—just like pictures out of Currier & Ives.

The School of Mines was unusually interesting, where they have every conceivable metal mined in Chile, including uranium for atomic bombs.

The Club Libones is the place to eat, where a wonderful combination of fish, shrimp, snails, and chicken combined with rice is served in typical Chilean fashion.

Very interesting people live here and a young Chilean has been exceptionally nice and kind. He lives at the hotel and speaks English like an American; in fact, he learned English first in a mission school, and that's why his pronunciation is so good. For safekeeping, he asked that we put the car in his garage for the night.

His company is an iron ore and magnesium tungsten company that has discovered a fabulous new vein of iron ore near here. A letter from Lloyds of London giving an analysis of the stuff says it averages 78 percent iron, the next to greatest percentage finding in the world—the other being in Sweden.

A young Ecuadorian, married to a New York-Long Island girl (a nurse), is the chief owner of the company—some day he will be worth millions.

They got out the first shipment of ore last week—by Grace Line to New York; they got it out on schedule in the face of many handicaps: the old, half-torn-up trucks have to climb steep hills and mountains, and it's the greatest difficulty to keep them going under such strenuous conditions. They have four trucks out of commission now and are waiting for parts from Santiago.

A German, their chief mechanic in their garage, is repairing the handbrake on our car. This is the second time a rock has broken the handbrake; we are very lucky (the luck of the Irish) to find such good help, after going for so long and over such dangerous roads without a handbrake.

There are several high, narrow mountain passes to cross near Vallenar, which is about a hundred miles south; then there is a dangerous pass, with terrific hairpin curves, right by the ocean, and near La Serena, that has been warned against, but must be gone over. It's an uneasy feeling when thinking of going over such places without the handbrake, though we've traveled all the way from near Arica without brakes, nearly a thousand miles.

Chilean people are wonderful, there just can't be enough said for their kindness. They think like Americans, they act and dress like Americans. They may live in an old shack-like adobe home without baths and without modern kitchens, but there is always a lovely flower filled patio of rare and beautiful blooms. They, of the better class, come out well dressed in the latest American-looking styles, though they aren't allowed to import anything from the United States without paying heavy duty.

This is a man's world here. We went with Mr. and Mrs. Buenaventura, owner of the mines, to a basketball game last night. Copiapo played Antofagasta (darn good game) for championship—and Antofagasta won! Ninety-nine percent of the attendance was men.

There's a tradition that each couple that gets married in Chile must get a family book to start a record of the family and children. The first two pages are for records of his and her family; the third page is devoted to his illegitimate children, of which he may have many—up to ten; then his marriage children are listed on the fourth page.

Unmarried mothers are most common and respected. Their children can take her name or the father's name—it's very common to take the mother's name.

At the border of Chile, it was required that we given our mothers' first names, then maiden and surnames. It was not understandable at the time, but having learned of these national requirements and conditions, it is readily seen now.

The Buenaventuras have two boys in New York with his mother. They were born in Quito, Ecuador, but he has established a home in New York in order to help form a company for these mines. He's up and coming and works hard, is very friendly to us, and wants to help in every way possible. They are waiting for parts for their trucks and want to keep their men busy—was one of the reasons they so generously offered to fix the handbrakes.

He has just bought a two-engine plane to fly to Santiago to bring in car parts—that's his greatest headache, getting parts and men who will try to keep the cars running to the mines, loading stuff and getting it to the docks—there's untold millions to be gotten out of these mountains around here, if they can only get equipment to get it out with.

These Chilean natives take their time to get this iron ore out—maybe that's the way God intended that they should be—Americans are rushing around in such a hurry all the time, trying to extract the last ounce of metal from the earth.

The Chilean government is trying so hard to get its people to use what they already have, as importing a lot of material from other countries would only weaken their already weakened economy. This is the cheapest place on earth to live—it would be great fun to just sit here for a while.

One more day had to be spent in Copiapo than schedule called for, due to heavy rains reported in the south. Since we are having such a wonderful rest, why bother! Really, this is the place to stay in all of Chile, and save money—today, they are giving 190 pesos for the dollar.

At the best hotel here, they charge 400 pesos per day, that includes breakfast and two heavy meals for just a little more than two dollars per day. Today's lunch gives one a good sample of just what they serve—first course: lettuce salad, radishes peeled back in flower form, slivers of roast pickled pork cut in long strips; second course: soup with short-ribs, rice, potatoes, carrots, and other green vegetables mixed with seasoning; third course: wonderful large black beans cooked to perfection and taste like our navy beans, but the skins are shiny-purplish black. There's to be seen in the juices a little tomato, garlic, and green something like parsley sprinkled over the top of them—oh, they are out of this world! For the fourth course: broiled steak—almost a pound—with natural gravy and parsley potatoes, and a dessert of apple rings with maple syrup, and then thick, black coffee, to which they add hot water. Most everyone has a half-gallon jug of wine on their individual tables, which they drink all during the meal.

The same thing, equally as good, will be served tonight. Soup is a must for both lunch and dinner, and is to be found simmering in the kitchens at all times.

These men working on the car only make a hundred dollars each month, and that's tops; but they look well fed, well clothed, and seem contented. These people are more intelligent than most—so many are refugees from Europe.

One old fellow is a Russian, but lived in Germany for years, and is an excellent mechanic. A Polish helper, who speaks good English, had just arrived from Shanghai, China. He told us he was asked to leave China—when trying to find out why, he just shrugged his shoulders. He wants desperately to get to the USA. That's the story everywhere.

There is great opportunity here if American capital can be brought into these cities and these mines developed. Just since this mine has been opened up, in four months, this town is literally on a boom again.

As has been said before, government regulations keep the people from importing things. This mine owner could use 20 American International trucks if they were only allowed to ship them in. Something surely will be done to relieve the situation. The more iron ore they could deliver to America, the more prosperity the city would feel.

The geologist who had given such terrible reports on the roads in Chile had said the road from Vallenar, which is about 75 miles out of Copiapo, was a death trap, and that he would not advise anyone to take it. There were a couple of trucks going south over this road the following morning, and if they could go over this road, so could we.

Nerving ourselves up for a horrible road, it was surprising when it turned out to be a good gravel road for a change; some dreadful hairpin curves, yes, but there had been plenty of hairpin turns as bad in Peru, in Columbia, and in Venezuela; and just a few days before at Paposo there had been many such turns and without handbrakes.

Arrived in La Serena about four o'clock in the afternoon without a single mishap. Found a very modern city and a good hotel room. The story goes that the immediate past president of Chile was born and reared in La Serena.

When he went into office, he wanted to do something outstanding for his hometown, so he cleared out all the old adobe buildings and built new, rose-colored apartments and a hotel; put on pavements on all streets; built an esplanade with streets on either side; planted trees lining the streets, with beautiful copies of famous statues on pedestals placed on the outer edges of the park for miles.

They say the apartments are half vacant; there were also new and beautiful school buildings, churches, and homes. They have a new president now in Chile, and that's ended the improvement in La Serena.

It was a great relief to arrive at La Serena, as people of good authority had said there would be pavement from then on into Santiago and Argentina.

Carburetor trouble was giving some worry, due to sand and low grade gasoline. In Santiago a friend had given the name of an American mechanic connected with an American petroleum company. Stationed at La Serena, he supervised the work on hundreds of cars. The sensible thing was to look him up and see if he could adjust the carburetor and check the spark plugs of the car.

Found he lived in an apartment next door to the hotel, and he came over with another American from New York State, who is a representative of a national USA concern and who has traveled all these roads of Chile, having gone as far south as Puerto Montt in the summertime, when the roads are usually good.

They were most interested in our experiences in the other countries and how we were planning the trip on south. He said, "No one but a fool Texan would pull the stunt you are pulling and take a trip like this in a car and, of all things, a Cadillac." He said we must not dare leave La Serena, going south, until he talked with the Engineer of Road—they had had a four day and night storm in Chile that had washed out 32 bridges and undermined the highway to the extent that it was dangerous. So there went the good roads people had said were ahead, and we had been looking forward to driving over.

Several trucks had come through this road, and when talking to two men who had made it from Santiago, they said it could be done if one would take their time.

Wednesday morning found a flat, and a hubcap stolen. We were afraid to contact the New Yorker for fear he would say the road engineer would advise us we couldn't go on. Taking the bull by the horns seemed the best procedure, if we had to sleep in the car.

Excellent time was made the first hundred miles, then detours and washouts were encountered. One time it was necessary to back up over a treacherous mountain pass to let six big trucks through, which was nerve-racking, but if trucks could make it, so could a good car.

In many places they had built temporary fill-ins. These once beautiful roads were built upon sand, without solid foundations—the sand had washed right out from under the pavement and approaches to the bridges.

At Hintelauquen, a large bridge had a gap in it the length of the car, where the water had washed out the embankment. There was water flowing over a good fourth mile wide, and it looked deep and scary.

One wouldn't dare venture into that, so the only thing left to do was to turn back, but the road men took a big cable, which was attached to a bulldozer, and tied it to the car and just started pulling it across the water.

The car was so light the swift water seemed to keep it floating along—there was a feeling of seasickness or fright. It took more than an hour to get across that stream, and it was with a sigh of relief when the car was on dry land. There were several cars waiting to be pulled across in opposite direction to where the car had come from. The luggage got wet in the back seat, but the bags were opened upon arrival at the hotel, and everything dried out, so all was okay.

At Las Vilas, a quaint fishing center, a stop for lunch was enjoyed, and there had a chance to see the fishermen bringing in the most wonderful fish fresh from the sea.

There had a first taste of sea urchin. As they would take them out of the porcupine quill-looking balls, they looked and smelled so good; but, my, one can never forget that taste! After watching men gulp them down with gusto, it was a temptation to keep trying them, but it would take half a lifetime for a woman to learn to like them. Could be their supposed potency is what appeals to the men.

Night was closing in when crossing over a dangerous red clay pass, a detour near La Ligus—a once beautiful highway had literally been eaten up with too much rain, and the only chance to get through was to take this old unused road. These big gaps in the road were unnerving, and sudden washed out areas, not blocked off with lanterns or warning signs, were too dangerous to risk. So the reasonable thing to do was to take out at La Calera.

Hotel accommodations were supposed to be poor there, but anything was better than risking going over an embankment, or sleeping in the car. The Rex Hotel, a very old one, proved to be better than said—it had clean beds and good food, and the night's lodging only cost two dollars, including food and bed for both.

In the early morning, taking the long road around by way of Vina del Mar, a summer resort city, it was found to be one of the most beautiful spots on the South American trip so far. It had been built up so fantastically in the Guide Book, it was hard to believe such a place existed; but there was no disappointment in all of it, including the Hotel Mirimar where a second breakfast was enjoyed, having had only coffee and rolls earlier.

The morning was spent just driving around looking at scenery; Valparaiso adjoins so closely it's hard to tell where one city ends and the other begins; just driving and driving north to see the lovely summer homes and apartment hotels along the coastline was a thrill never to be forgotten, as the buildings were magnificent. Then back into the city again and a drive to the top of the hill on which is built a lovely tower and many castle-like homes, which have a commanding view of the ocean.

The entire morning was spent looking around, fearing something would be missed. Big ships were in the harbor, but none with the American flag.

Valparaiso is a terrific place—reminds one of San Francisco—up and down one mountain after another, with steep grade roads, dead end streets, flagpole views of surrounding country, until everything had been seen of the place; then and then only did the car nose its way on the road out to Santiago.

Climbing up on a mountain pass, a dense fog was a plague to keep one from getting the panoramic view at that point. It was the pea soup kind, which lasted for half an hour. It was wonderful to come into the sunshine—the big trucks and cars rushing along seemed not to mind the fog, but would scare the wits out of one rushing past.

The sunshine broke over a fairyland world with everything in bloom—peach, plum, cherry, what looks like red bud, yellow mimosa, cherimoya. The yellow jasmine clinging and falling over hedges and fences was beautiful; geraniums, some tall and others dwarf, were lovely in all their coloring; the grasslands were so green and freshly clipped looking. This was, indeed, a beautiful country and made up in part for the trials of bad roads of the past few days.

After Casa Blanco, there were two more high drives. The view of snow-clad mountains for a backdrop, with a hazy, flowering middle distance, coupled with a foreground of calla lilies, day lilies, daisies, iris, forsythia, asters, bridal wreath, bordering roads and pasture lands, and all seeming to grow wild, was enough to make one feel they were in an enchanted land.

When descending into Santiago Valley, it was thought there had never been anything lovelier in Switzerland or the Bavarian Alps. These snowcapped mountains literally surround this valley—through some atmospheric phenomena they seem so close, one had the feeling they could reach out and touch the snow.

The miracle of spring is upon Santiago, and it is beautiful to behold. It's easy to love this Chile better than any other South American country. These people look, think, and act like Americans. There are just the two classes in Chile—but so many of the lower class speak English.

The city was entered by way of the airport. A large bus with passengers, their bags on top, was just in front. The thought was broached, if we could keep up with that bus, it would go directly to the hotel. It was going at a pretty fast clip, and it was necessary to do some weaving in and out all the way down the heavily congested O'Higgins Boulevard; but sure enough, the bus finally turned left and made it right to the Hotel Carrera.

The hotel is gorgeous, lots of Americans are here, mostly air-minded ones who've been in the air only and know so little of the land. They've missed so much—and think of all the money they have spent, more one way than is necessary to spend for the whole trip in a car.

Immediately after registering and before taking the bags out of the car, the first thought was to get over to the Embassy, very near the hotel, to see if there was mail from home. One letter from Miss Gasparo and a note from Mr. Frazier, the young man who went to Puno and around Lake Titicaca.

He went on to La Paz, Bolivia, and had a wonderful time, no danger whatsoever, and he made some wonderful purchases there, as the money value is lowest in the history of that country. It never pays to listen to other people about these countries, but just go on and see for one's self.

You just can't imagine how badly one feels unless you've experienced it, when there are no letters from home. A telephone call home is the best thing to relieve one's mind of worry, and it only took five minutes to get a call through—a call through one of the highest telephone lines in the world. It was like a miracle to hear so clearly a voice so far away, just put cold chills over one. The low cost of only $7.50 was surprising.

Friday the Automobile Club of Chile, which functions better than any so far in South America, talked about the roads to Argentina and they said, due to the heavy rains and snow, the roads would not be open into Argentina for six weeks.

They had a terrific snow slide last week on the Argentina side, and killed a lot of people—which was in the International News. Well there go all the good roads, the plans, the hopes of getting to Brazil for a long time to come.

Mrs. Rodriguez runs the AAA Club in Santiago, and she has been unusually nice. When she found the great distance the car and occupants had traveled, she called the Cadillac agent here about it.

The manager of the agency left his card in the hotel box—it never occurred to us to look—then they phoned repeatedly to bring the car to the plant.

The car had been cleaned out and washed, and they were very pleased to see it looking so good, and could not believe it had been so far over such horrible roads as they knew them to be, and they said they wanted to have a picture made of it.

On Saturday the manager's son, Alberto Reyes, took it upon himself to show us the city, driving all over Santiago, including up Cerro San Cristóbal, a mountain centering the city, on which they have a large statue of the Virgin, hands outstretched, flowing robes—on the topmost point, and which dominates the countryside. It's a wonderful place to get a panoramic view of the old and new city and the surrounding mountains.

The La Monedo Palace, dating to the 18th century, was interesting in colonial architecture. The Cerro Santa Lucia, a cone of rock 230 feet high in the center of the city, is beautifully landscaped, and it was pleasant to walk around and view the bustling city streets.

Later, the drive out to the Polo Club for tea was inspiring, as the mountains were so crystal clear in the background, with flowering fruit trees and flowers of every description in the foreground, which enhanced the beauty of the place.

The Polo Club building is Old English in inspiration, beautifully built and placed in a perfect setting, with wide picture windows, for a view of the Andean snowcapped mountains. A delightful tea hour was enjoyed, with Alberto Reyes talking English.

Mr. Reyes, as well as Mrs. Rodriguez of the Automobile Club, have said they have before never heard of a Cadillac venturing on so long a jaunt down in South America. The car runs like new, though it has a few scratches outside to show the hardships it has been through. The trip south is anticipated with pleasure now that the Cadillac people here have put the car in such good condition.

They have checked the Hydramatic, tightened the bands, readjusted and cleaned the carburetor, checked handbrakes, and changed the oil—and refused to take any pay for any of this work. Mr. Andrade, who was once a famous racer and now head of that department, was most kind in going over the car, insisting the mechanics would be happy to have us watch as they worked.

Sunday evening while looking for something to do, a young fellow who wanted to talk English explained all about the shows of Santiago. He said they were crowded on Sunday and all seats were reserved. But why not go to Violen Gitano and have a cup of tea and hear the singing. He could not explain just what it was, but we decided to take a chance and see for ourselves.

Arriving very early, it was interesting to watch the people as they came in to be seated. Soon they brought ice cream, all kinds of cookies and cakes, and tea. People came crowding in until every small table and chair was filled and no standing room left. The orchestra was playing soft, gypsy-type music.

Finally, the lights went out and an announcer, a woman in red, said something in Spanish. A couple came out and danced all of the South American steps—samba, rumba, and a handkerchief throwing affair—all very good; then a man, Bob Hope type, told jokes in Spanish, and everyone roared with laughter. That's when one wishes they knew the language.

A large girl from Miami, Florida, came out and sang many American songs. She was called back again and again. The last time she sang "Amour" and came down in the audience and sat on the men's laps and rubbed their bald heads, tickled them under the chin, straightened their ties, pinched their ears, and had lots of fun kidding; and the men must have loved it the way they beamed. She was really cute. That music was unusually good, even if it was too loud.

For more than a week now, Santiago has been full of surprises; we're having a wonderful time—grand food, lovely people; we've been everywhere, seen everything there is to see. This is a terrific city, reminds one of Mexico City—noisy and wild.

Today at the Embassy an American Marine who has recently married a girl from Texas—they spent their honeymoon up in the Andean mountains—said they were marooned in the mountains for several days and had to walk out after the storms and snow slides. Such a ghastly experience for honeymooners!! They were terribly sore footed and sunburned from the ordeal, and were thankful to come out alive.

He said, "You can't possibly go through the road pass to Mendoza before Christmas in your car; we saw the avalanches of snow that completely destroyed the railroad tracks, and it will be impossible to get the tracks and road fixed before Christmas, regardless of what others say. Others may kid you along to give you hope, but I say differently, as much of this roadwork is done by hand, a shovelful at a time. These Chilean people have not the equipment and will not work fast, and the continuous rains will be a further delay in the roadwork. Your best bet would be to try to get through one of the passes down south."

The plan had been to go through San Felipe, Los Andes, on into Argentina through Mendoza—he knows what he's talking about, and the thing to do is to take his advice and go at least 1,200 miles further south, through the Lake District, and see everything possible.

This has been an unusually late spring in Chile, so everyone says. There's been a light drizzle for several days now—if the trees were not so magnificently in bloom and the mountains were not so gorgeous with snow, one might be downcast over the rainy weather. But with so much beauty, why bother over a little rain.

This pass in the south of Chile looks like the logical way to make it into Argentina in a few weeks; it will entail going to Tolca, then to Concepcion, backtrack to Chillán if there cannot be found a possible alternate road, then to Los Angeles, Temuco, Valdivia to Puerto Montt.

One learns it's best to take each little town, each stretch of road with a philosophical viewpoint—"Let each day and hour take care of itself."

If the pass is open through San Carlos de Bariloche to Argentina, it will be the one to take; if it is not open, it will be necessary to come back to Victoria, Villaricca, Pucon, Curarrehue and try to make it from there on in to Argentina. It is a very narrow pass, following a river, and very dangerous if icy.

It will be bitter cold, whichever pass is taken. Red flannels, and all other woolens one can comfortably put on, will be the best thing to wear, if it takes that to keep warm and to see the Lake District, as well as get through the pass.

Some of the most beautiful paces in the world are to be seen going south, so they say. Black and white pictures of the south of Chile make it well worth the struggle to see. It's foolish to sit around here and wait for this higher pass to open up, or backtrack here after going south. Every inch of this country is worth seeing.

One enjoyable afternoon was spent having tea at the Golf Club with Mrs. Reyes. Tea is a must in

Santiago. This golf club is one of the most magnificent places in the world at this time of the year, with snow-capped mountains surrounding it, then great expanses of green lawn, with all the yellow, pink, and white trees in bloom. There are no colored postcards of this spot, or any other, in South America—someone could make a fortune out of them down here.

Still in Santiago. A change of hotel has been made and with it a complete change in atmosphere. The Crellon, old in years, and still retaining the charm and customs of early days, is a delightful place of abode. Should one want to learn the heart of Santiago—that's the place to stay. All of the older elite and society people patronize that hotel for book reviews and all social events.

There's been a week of joining in these events and watching all the fabulously well-groomed, jeweled women come in the afternoon for tea—their chit chat going full blast as the orchestra would swing into the most beautiful music, with tons of Brahms, Beethoven, Bach, filling the rooms with sweet harmony.

At the dinner hour the most luscious foods, bountifully and artistically served, bring the most particular gourmets of eating and drinking to their dining room each evening—or for the late dancing hours, which continue the whole night through and would make the "Lullaby of Broadway" a nursery rhyme, by comparison.

These Santiagans are fond of singing all of the good old American songs, indulging in harmonious groups of four to a dozen, and singing such songs as "Let Me Call You Sweetheart," "Mill Stream," "Home on the Range," "Way Down South in Dixie," and "Deep in the Heart of Texas." The amazing part of this is all these songs are sung by people who could not carry on a normal English conversation at all, but they could say the words of the songs without the least brogue to the English words. It was remarkable in many ways to hear this, and gave one the feeling that songs could bring about a universal language.

Two wedding parties have been watched from the sitting room and what wonderful affairs they do have—with orchids and other magnificent flowers decorating the rooms in gorgeous array—and the dancing most of the time a hippity-hop affair with partners facing each other. These have, indeed, made the lengthy time necessary to stay in Santiago much more worthwhile.

This rain is getting very serious. Most of the time it's just a slow drizzle or mist—just enough to keep one uncomfortable. It has been raining like this every day now for ten days, and now the Automobile Club has said one should not try to go south for three days after it quits raining.

It's tempting to disregard their advice, as was done in La Serena and go on, but somehow each morning finds a new experience; but it's getting tiresome, this big, noisy city.

It was a beautiful clear day yesterday for the first time, and a drive to San Antonio, about 70 miles away, near the coast, was a new experience which had been put off due to rains. Everything looked washed so clean and the flowers were out in their brightest array.

The peach, cherry, plum, mimosa, jasmine, wild mustard, iris, calla lilies (the largest and most beautiful we've ever seen) were all along the highway and around fence rows, and near the homes.

Children were selling rhubarb, watercress, eggs, oranges, apples, cherimoyas, and other farm products, as they do in wayside stalls in the USA.

The small foothills and mountains were beautifully green to the top, with low bushy trees to relieve the monotony; many thousands of cattle and sheep were grazing all over the fields and hills. It was a sight to see these lush pasturelands and farm homes so well kept and so plentifully stocked with fat, well-groomed animals.

The road was paved all the way into San Antonio; traveling north to Cartegena there was to be seen favorite beaches and hotels; the stalls for snacks and seaside novelties, abalones, shellfish, dried oysters (strung on long strings), sea urchins and crayfish. They were tempting and it was hard to say "NO" to the many bargains.

Then following the coast south, watching the docks for fishing ships in the bay—one could not recognize any of importance as the flag wasn't flying on them—continuing to follow the coast to Lio Llioe Rocaede, then on to Santo Domingo. Everything, including trees and shrubs, were beautifully in bloom all along the way.

Santo Domingo is a somewhat new summer colony—a point of land jutting out with a river in between it and the mainland and connected by a long bridge. This bridge looked in terribly bad shape, and the water was coming in billowing rapids under it from the mountains in the distance and emptying into the ocean nearby.

There was deep mud on either approach to the bridge, and it looked most unsafe and wobbly going across, but the marvelous views made it worth the risk.

Going up one street after another street of these summer homes, all built with ocean views and with yards and lawns so bright with color, was indeed a spectacle.

One place on the crest of the hill had a rounded point covering more than an acre of ground, all covered with a sea plant with red blooms massed like the American bluebonnets. At focal points there was a yellow cactus plant, about two feet tall, that shot up into yellow blooming spires over the upper part of the yard, and seemed to top off the other blooms into a crowning glory.

Santo Domingo has its own big clubs, swimming pools, horse racing tracks, bus service—everything, including hotel, for comfort. A wonderfully delicious meal was served at this hotel tucked away on the side of the mountain, overlooking the bay, surrounded by a lovely park of eucalyptus trees, castor bean trees, and many kinds of deep, dark, and big foliage plants, too numerous to recall their names. This combination of sea, desert, and wild plants and flowers around the hotel was most restful and exhilarating.

This exceptionally good meal is worth talking about. For an entrée a cold, boiled fish called locos, plastered with a mayonnaise sauce sprinkled with parsley, chives, and such was served; then they brought in big bowls of a hot fish mix, similar to clam chowder; corn on cob, cut in inch slices through cob, sprinkled with cornmeal, and mixed with red and green peppers, pink snails, small crayfish, and oysters.

In the hot fish mix were two large servings of a

most delicious boiled fish called *congrio*—there's never been anything that tasted any better—it was fit for the Gods and is one of the Chilean national dishes. The same fish fried is wonderful, too.

This place and all the surrounding country is easily the most paintable place to be seen so far; the soft, muted colors, the rush of sea into sand, and not so many overwhelming rocks, makes it most restful—the general quiet atmosphere made one want to stay there forever.

But thinking of those awful muddy approaches to the bridge, the ramshackle, quivering bridge itself was enough to put a crimp in one's soul and made one realize the best thing to do was to get off that bad road as quickly as possible, swing into the main highway, and get into Santiago before it got too dark.

Sleeping late next day, trying to think of something to do, but there was an anxiousness and a goal set to get into Argentina by the 14th of September; however, it looks now as though it will be much longer than that.

The most difficult part of the entire trip will be crossing the Andean mountains. There's supposed to be good roads in Argentina, but from past experience, it's foolish to count on that. It is wise, however, to face these forbidding snow-covered mountain passes with caution—one must listen to reason.

It could be pretty bad if caught in a landslide, or stuck in the mountains in snow, sleet, and ice, and unable to move one way or the other and just left to freeze. That's crossing bridges beforehand, and the officers watch these roads so carefully they would not allow a thing like that to happen.

Of course, the trip south to the Lake District will take a week; lots of changes in the weather can be brought about in that time. Chile's national holidays start the 18th of September and the highway officials try to have all the roads open by then. It wouldn't be fun to put the car on a train to go across the pass, if it was open—they keep saying it will be Christmas before the railroad pass is opened—so that is out of the question anyway.

In a garage in Concepcion—the gasoline tank on the car is being fixed again. For more than an hour now, they've been trying to find the leak. It looks like the connecting nut was loose, but one can never tell with these roads. It's so wise to take every precaution, especially now, with so few places to get repairs, and fewer gasoline stations. In fact, if something should go radically wrong with the car, the nearest supplies would be in Buenos Aires, or back to Santiago.

Left Santiago Wednesday morning and had to detour near Paine for several miles on the way south due to a washed out bridge, which made it necessary to drive in a muddy field for ever so long, and barely made it even with the road men pushing. After that, the road was good on into San Xavier.

A wonderful meal was enjoyed at Curico—the main course was a half of a chicken, stewed with vegetables, and cornmeal used sparingly to thicken the mix. It's a complete meal in itself, served in soup plates. After the soup is eaten with a large spoon, the meat is cut up with knife, and one finishes with a fork. It's a simple way to get a wonderful meal with few dishes and will be a must when and if the USA ever looms on the horizon. They fix a fish dish similarly and it is delicious.

The rivers are all swollen and many are out of banks. Near San Carlos a swift stream went swirling over the highway. Some boys insisted it was too deep for the car, and it did look bad, but determination not to turn back, plunged the car in, made it across with the water seeping through the floor of the car, and barely reached dry land when the car stopped. There was a wait of about ten minutes before the car dried out enough to start again.

Three trucks were in the middle of the stream back behind, waiting for the car to get started. They looked daggers at us, but it was easily understandable how they must have felt about the low slung foreign car, with just two people in it, when men, women, and children were standing up, packed solid in one truck—with household goods piled in, over, and underneath another truck, and a third truck loaded with hay.

As darkness descended, a freshly painted hotel at San Carlos was a welcome sight. The objective had been Chillán, where a new hotel with hot baths and a comfortable, steam heated room awaited us. Refugee French and Spanish people run the hotel at San Carlos and the best food one could ask for was provided. Long spears of fresh asparagus, cold with mayonnaise, spinach omelette for entrée, roast beef, lettuce salad, fruit parfait—it all tasted so good after the hazardous afternoon.

They did not have hot water for baths, and very little heat in the rooms, so to keep warm, slept with clothes on. This was the only fly in the ointment, and very early next morning rushed on to Chillán, a new and modern city.

About twelve years ago, 5,000 people were killed by an earthquake at Chillán, and the city was almost completely destroyed, which accounts for its being rebuilt into a completely modern place. At the same time, Concepcion was terribly damaged, and about 1,000 people were killed, which will be told about later on.

All along the highway there were to be seen tall, paper white magnolia trees—they were something new in trees, so startlingly different from anything seen before—some were as large as an old elm tree, and they have large, raggedy, white blooms that resemble white tissue paper strips tied into clusters. All the blooming is done before the trees leaf out.

Then there were some other most unusual trees—a complete mass of pink, red, or white blossoms. On closer inspection, they were found to be camellias—it was unbelievably fantastic to find these trees so large in size, with such large blooms, and so completely covered with bloom. This part of the country is a fairyland of magnificent flowers, in their spring, which is September and October.

We arrived at the City Hotel in Concepcion about 2:30, parked the car by large windows near the dining room, and had a good lunch in the dining room. The car, with the Texas license, caused a flurry of excitement, and many people came right in the dining room to look at the couple who had traveled so far; and when the people, who had gathered around, were shown the maps of the trip from La Guire, Venezuela, where they had started from, there was much comment and shaking of hands and patting on back. Lots of young men hung around the car constantly, looking it over and wanting to talk English. These are the friendliest and kindliest of people, and are outdoing themselves to be nice.

The gasoline tank, plugged with airplane cement, had sprung a leak, but the garage could not get it fixed until the following morning. With gasoline so cheap, and a temporary plug of nail polish, started sightseeing with little worry. First out to the naval base and the big steel mill, which is the life of this section of the country; then followed the large river, Bio Bio, which empties into the ocean near this point.

Later stopped at the AAA Club to get information for the trip south, trying to find a shortcut to Salta del Laga, a very beautiful falls, which had been suggested as well worth seeing.

An English girl, in the bonds and real estate business, across from the AAA office, helped in translating. She was born in Chile of English parents. For five years during the war, she served in the Women's Organization in England.

She proved to be an exceptionally wonderful girl, and with the attractive Chilean girl who runs the Auto Club, but could not speak English, struck up a nice friendship and had much fun together. They knew the better places and suggested a drive out to a magnificent point where the river meets the sea. It was a glorious evening to watch the sea pounding and fusing the river into submission, just as the sun was sinking in the west.

For dinner, an entrée of congrio fish was served; then steaks with poached eggs on top—Bifstek a la Sabre, called a poor man's steak—with the platter full of beef, onions, and potatoes, it would be called a rich man's steak in the USA. They served nine mixed vegetables lightly cooked together—asparagus, beans, peas, cauliflower, carrots, corn, potatoes, squash, butterbeans. These vegetables are served this way so much down here—maybe it's to save cooking pans.

Upon returning to the hotel about 12:30 that night, the maître d', who spoke English, said that all the hotel people had been phoning around, police were hunting and looking for us, they were so worried and afraid something had happened, since there had been no message left at the desk saying we would be out late.

The young people of the town had gathered at the hotel to talk English with us, and must have put the fears into the hotel officials' minds, since we were not there.

The food that night, described above, cost 75 cents each in American dollars. The Chilean peso has gone wild. On Saturday, the American dollar was worth 240 pesos—as long as this lasts, Chile is the place to live.

Having learned to stay away from the large city tourist hotels, the money goes twice as far—it's remarkable just what can be done with an American dollar in Chile.

After getting the gasoline tank fixed the next day, we were driving down a one-way street, trying to find the way to the Auto Club again, when a fellow on the street kept pointing at the front fender or wheel of the car, which left the impression that there was a low tire.

Stopping the car to see what was wrong, a tall young man walked up and said in English, "Is there something wrong with your car?" We said, "A man down the street kept pointing and we were just trying to see if something was wrong." "Oh, believe me, it was that Texas license—that's enough to attract plenty of attention and cause a person to point at it," said the young man, a Mr. Graham.

He invited us down to his office, a block away at 81 Caupolican, where he is director of the Institute Chileno North Americano de Culture. It's an organization for the promotion of interrelations between countries.

They were having classes of English for housewives, professional men, and children. They had a large library of American books and, all the better, late magazines.

Lots of nice-looking young men were there—some were reading, others playing American songs on a record player; there was checker playing, card games; others were looking on, trying to absorb what was being done.

It was fun chatting with a housewife group of cultured women who were studying English. They seemed to have no inhibitions or reluctance whatsoever in trying to use English words.

They asked many interesting questions relating to life in the United States, and they kept saying that they understood what was being said in English, better, since the words were being said slowly. It's that slow Southern drawl cropping out again to good advantage!

These ladies were eating the first apple pie they had ever tasted. It had been cooked by Mr. Graham's wife, and brought to the school to show them what a pie was like.

Then the US Consulate of Concepcion, Mr. Cortlandt R. Sweet, came over and said, "I'd heard of some wild Texans being in town and the woman doing the driving, and I wanted to see just what you were like."

The answer given was that anyone was wild or crazy to attempt what we'd been through, and it was perfectly okay to add anything he wanted to, to what he thought of us, if he would just call us Texans.

By profession he is a road engineer, Kentucky his native state, but he has spent many years in Mexico building roads before he came to Chile to build roads.

He owns a 5,000-acre strip of land, north of Concepcion, where his home is located on a peninsula called Punta Tumbes. He invited us out there for the weekend, so we checked out of the hotel about three o'clock, and went out to the Naval Base in the car. There was a pouring rain, but the car took the muddy mountain road after some difficulty. After climbing up a steep pass, the car was left in the garage at his son's home, then the overnight bags were loaded in Mr. Sweet's jeep, everyone piled in and started off, down this muddy road with water up to the floor of the jeep, and the jeep got stuck twice—can you imagine ruts that will stick a jeep? Everyone had to get out and push through the slush before they pulled it out.

Mrs. Sweet was very kind. She is of American extraction, though she was born here in Chile. She is a Delano and a cousin of the late President Roosevelt. Her grandfather, a Dr. Delano, came down here in early life and married an English woman.

Her mother, one of thirteen children, was born at Tumbes. The boys in the family were registered and sent to the US for their education. The girls, six of them, were not registered, but were sent to a Catholic school here, so her mother was a Catholic. When Mrs. Sweet was married, she had three weddings—civil, Catholic and Methodist.

When they had the terrible earthquake at Chillán and Concepcion in 1949, it killed both Mr. Sweet's and Mrs. Sweet's mothers, a five-year-old son, and seriously injured their oldest son.

There were pictures of the beautiful two-story rock house before and after the ground just cracked opened and it caved in. After the earthquake, they moved on out to Point Tumbes, the old family home, which has a commanding and marvelous view.

Just two years ago, they had another light earthquake there, which badly damaged this old family homestead they are now living in, completely destroying a large porch, and cracking all the walls of the main house.

Mrs. Sweet spends her time growing very lovely flowers. Sunday morning we walked all over the place while she inspected hotbeds of rare flowers and choice vegetables, such as artichokes, asparagus beds, rhubarb and cauliflower.

Her fragile white camellias are the dream of a bride's bouquet and are used in many weddings. There were violets so thick the green leaves were hidden—huge bunches of these sell in the flower shops for an American dime.

There were jonquils by the hundreds, larger than the King Alfred; calla lilies were growing wild in massed clusters; capihues, the national flower of Chile, straggling over arbors and tree trunks with a waxy red bloom dangling down—these blooms are shaped similar to the trumpet flower; then there were many other kinds of exotic blooms unknown by name.

Mr. Sweet, the Consular of this district and on to the South Pole, came on south to Angal with us—he insisted he had to show us the best way to get there—lucky for us he did come along. He was wonderful to show us all the better back roads, some looked like country lanes—we would never have dared travel them unless he had been along.

One time this back road was the only way left to get through; it was a deep sand road, full of waterholes, which could not be traveled on unless it was wet, as one would bog down in the sand when it was dry—sounds crazy, but it's true.

Mr. Sweet's a good fisherman and knows this country like a book. He told plenty of good fish stories and kept us in a laughing mood most of the day, which was relaxing with such bad roads.

Then he took us out to El Vergal, an agricultural experimental station near Angal, and introduced us to the directors of the institution. Then he said, "This is as far as I can go with you now. If you had arrived here in the summertime, I would have gone with you on into Argentina." Later, when he made preparations to return home, and we thanked him for coming with us, showing us the Falls Salta del Laga and the best way to get through this rain drenched land, and appreciating his being so kind, understanding, and patient with us, he replied, "Well, if you fool Texans were fool enough to come down here in a car, at this time of year, I guess I'm fool enough to help you try to get through these roads."

One entire day was spent out at El Vergal, looking

at the beautiful flowers, fruit trees, and vegetable gardens. This Vergal (Verhal) is an experimental station, owned by the Methodists of the US. If the Methodist members could see just what all they do and have done here in the last 50 years, to bring about a Christian religion, as well as improve living conditions of these people, they would be very pleased.

A small portion of what every member pays into the Methodist church in the USA goes to the men and women who work, preach, and teach in Vergal; it was amazing to find out about it all. When the word "mission" is mentioned, one takes so much for granted.

One must see this place to fully understand it is more than a mission—it is a highly organized, paying, agricultural accomplishment, with the Chilean people benefiting from it.

The history of Vergal is inspirational and worth delving into. They have contributed much to the agricultural interests of Chile, especially in the development of hardy apples and other fruits; and it's remarkable what they have done with protein vegetables, such as lentils and big beans.

The most wonderful flowers seen yet have been developed in this station. There were extra large, paper flower white magnolias straggling down over limbs—this was something entirely new in flowering trees and, as had been mentioned, had the appearance, on first glance, of white tissue paper cut in one-inch strips, about four to six inches long, and tied and crinkled together. It's amazing in its shagginess—this tree has to be seen to be believed.

There were also some light purple trees, similar to the Japanese magnolias in the States; also there were deep purple ones, so thickly clustered one could barely see the limbs of the trees; then there were sparsely scattered ones, almost like orchids, but in a delicate pink.

Propagating rhododendrons was one of their chief occupations at that time of the year, and they were to be found in the most gorgeous colors—deep to light cherry—with boxes of dirt built at the top of the trees for the propagating work.

There were to be seen, along with all these other above-mentioned plants, some of the most delicate camellias in formation and color, completely covering huge trees; the trees were 12 to 14 feet in size—they would flabbergast anyone not used to such prolificness.

Weeping cherry trees, of a delicate pink color, were in full bloom. The national flower, the capihue, in a dozen different varieties, was being grown and propagated there—the waxy looking white, a newly developed specie at Vergal, is very popular in bridal bouquets.

The snow-clad distant mountains, and the closer rolling hills of green, blending in with the dark pine, spruce, eucalyptus, willow and mimosa trees, gives this part of the world such a serene, contented, picture postcard look. One can't keep from loving all this country and its people—they stop us on the street, shake our hands, and smilingly welcome us to their city and country.

To see all this beauty and these fine people, who are so helpful and kind, you would never realize Chile is in such desperate straits financially—it will be disastrous if they don't sell their copper soon. It's really deplorable to see such a wonderful country as

Chile have her economy uprooted and her future jeopardized. Why was the peso going down every day in value? This question was being asked on all sides. It's most grieving that this is happening to Chile, the one country out of all the South American countries, most desirable to live in.

Here are some of the answers to the question, as told by a government official. The devaluation of the peso has been brought about because of Chile's failure to sell her copper (which is the basis of her wealth) to the US government. It is said that Uncle Sam cannot be blamed for this, as Chile turned down the US contract and had hoped to sell her copper for more on the world market. The world market has proven her undoing and Chile has been left holding the bag, so to speak.

It looks like Chile's problem dates way back to when controls were forced upon the people, and her economy was weakened from these controls over farms and small industries having to go out of business. Here are a few statistics, which were copied from government pamphlets, and explain some of her problems:

The Chilean government has in service 123 generals with an army of six divisions. They have 64 admirals for 3 cruisers, 9 destroyers, 1 submarine, and 20 small craft. They have 16 generals in aircraft for only 54 planes. With hundreds of other officers, the generals are retired after 25 years service at full pay; they are allowed to retire as captains with 15 years service, at half pay. If these figures are studied, they will reveal a one-sided situation in the country, with regard to their defense program. Too many men for so few defense crafts.

Chile has more public employees than England. Farm workers get fixed salaries—as a result, small farms cannot afford to operate under these conditions, with wages higher than production, so with a loss, they have been abandoned. A great deal of Chilean foodstuff is imported—wheat particularly—when in earlier days each small farm produced enough wheat to take care of its own needs.

The working class has moved to larger cities, like Santiago, La Serena, Concepcion, Valparaiso, by hundreds of thousands and live in squalor in dilapidated huts and makeshift homes on river banks near the ocean, or near government warehouses, and eke out an existence on fish, snails, and other easily wrested foods from the water.

Both men and women work, but the woman usually supports the family, while the men live a carefree existence and spend their money for wine, women, and song.

The drink problem in Chile is staggering, as wine is given to the children from infancy. One unusual situation regarding the youth of the country is that boys and girls go to different schools and are not allowed to date until approximately 16 years of age—and yet, there's much delinquency among the girls—very few young girls of the middle class are virgins here, so people in the "know" say.

Chile has some very difficult problems to solve, and it will take years to work out their economy. The President is now trying to enact new laws such as: Not retiring men in government work until they've had 40 years service. They are trying to cut down the help in the embassies over the world. They want to cut down on public employees; in fact, these government employees only give about three hours of work each day, from 9 to 12, then two hours for lunch with a heavy meal and much wine, and the two remaining hours, if they return to work, are practically blank.

Free enterprise is another answer, but it will take years to overcome some of their fixations.

Look on the map for Temuco. Our arrival there was punctuated with several narrow escapes from the celebrating drunken populace of the countryside. From Victoria to near Lantaro, traveling was done at a snail's pace due to large rocks in the road, and to the oxen carts full of people lolling over side of post framework of carts held together with rawhide thongs.

Some fellows were vomiting; some were excreting; others singing. Cursing, they would get out of the carts, and some of the men would stagger toward the car. This was enough to scare the wits out of a person. At times the only sober person in the cart would be a small child, hollering and slapping the whip onto the oxen's trunk, as they slowly groped their way along the road, hogging the better part of the road, and the car would have to take to the side of the road to avoid a collision.

The slowly going car suddenly stopped and after repeated checkings, it was found that the motor was not getting gasoline, but the reserve tank emptied into the regular tank did not help to start the car. We were helplessly checking everything that could be wrong, when another group of drunken men came slowly weaving along, cursing, fighting and yelling. They stopped their cart near the car.

We stood, trying to figure what was wrong with the car, trying to decide what to do, talking constantly, with only screwdriver and pliers as our only weapons, as with fear and trembling we watched these men come staggering over toward the car, with what looked to be leering and vicious looks on their faces.

Looking around for a weapon of defense, should they attack, there could be seen in the distance a truck coming toward the car. If we could keep these fellows placated until the truck could get there, was the thought uppermost in our minds, and continuous talking, with pliers and screwdriver waving in every direction, did seem to hold them in amazement.

Upon the arrival of the truck at the scene, it was a relief to find that the driver, a young man, could speak a few words of English. He tied the car to his truck with a long cable, and driving it at a 40 mile clip, pulled the car through deep water and mud holes, around curves, up hills, into the small town of Lontaro, to a Ford station where the mechanic soon found the copper gas line from tank to motor had been broken with a rock.

The mechanic put in a complete new line, much farther up on the chassis of the car, so a similar accident could not happen again in the future.

Upon questioning the young man who had pulled the car to the garage, found he worked for an implement company in Temuco and had been on a service call. It was one of the luckiest breaks so far, that it he came along when he did.

The Ford people telephoned a group of young people studying English to come down to the garage to see us, while the car was being repaired. Much fun was had talking and singing and reciting English sayings with them. One time a couple danced the Chilean national dance, waving their handkerchiefs, while others of the group clapped hands and hummed their national musical score.

This was the beginning of their national holiday and accounts for the drunkenness on the highway, and the gay, carefree spirit of all the people.

After the car work was completed, we bid them a fond adios and started on through a scary, water-logged road into Temuco, and a wonderful new hotel where every courtesy and comfort was extended. A beautiful room, overlooking the snow-clad mountains, was most luxurious and enjoyed to the full after such frightful experiences.

Next day the young man who had pulled the car into the garage at Lantaro came by the hotel and as a reward for his kindness, we took him to dinner and turned the car over to him to drive wherever he wanted to go—a beautiful drive up to the snow-clad mountains, where a famous ski jump, very popular at this time of the year, was thoroughly enjoyed. We would have stayed longer, but the hotel up there was bulging with people who could not get rooms and roads were almost impassable with cars and old jalopies in bumper-to-bumper formation.

So back into the city and another mountain drive nearer in, with a magnificent panoramic view of the countryside. This is indeed a lovely country, and everything so reasonable in price. Food the best ever.

There was a dance in the hotel at night that lasted the whole night through, tons of wine, champagne, cider, roast chicken, beef, lamb with bread, preserves, fruit, olives, nuts. Everything was piled high on long tales where couples were served cafeteria style again and again. They would eat, drink, dance, then start all over again.

Outsiders ate in the barroom, but with a large plate glass window giving a splendid view of all that was going on. Nowhere in the world could they celebrate with more abandon than there.

One interesting thing—most all the music was American—just once or twice in all the night's music was there to be heard an unfamiliar strain; and those unfamiliar had the dash of and brought about the swishing, whooping, and hollering of their national songs.

"The Missouri Waltz," "Let me Call You Sweetheart," "Dixie" (was a favorite), and a skip jump sort of dance with each partner facing each was danced to the tune of "Deep In the Heart of Texas."

All of that American music brought about a nostalgic feeling and a secret promise was indulged in—if Texas and the good old USA could ever be reached again, there's where we would stay!

The hotel people said the roads south are impassable due to the excess rain, and one should wait another week before attempting going on. It's been difficult to decide just what to do, as the young man who has been driving us around says it's passable, as a bus had come through. There's a strong suspicion this hotel wants to keep their guests as many days as possible, as there are so few right now.

Hearing of a group of American Baptist missionaries in the city, it was decided we should pay them a visit, and they in turn could and would get the lowdown on the roads. They were very kind and hospitable and seemed very happy to see North Americans.

They have good schools, fine churches, nice homes, and appear to be doing a great service to the people of the city. So many people of Temuco speak English, and these mission schools are given the credit for their achievements in cultural things, and that probably accounts for so much American music being played and sung here.

Through phone conversations, they found that several jeeps and a bus had come through this bad road going south—they had had to go slow, but had gotten through. The slogan up to now had been, "Anywhere a bus could go, the car could go." So after another happy day with the young man, going out to the airport and watching his brother fly a Cessna plane, then a trip into the country to see just how the *granja* (farm) people live, with good steaks cooked over open fire in the yard, vegetables and salads fresh grown; then walking over lovely estates surrounded by green fields full of sleek fat cattle and all the beautiful horses one could wish for, with well-kept barns, pens and fences for these animals. It was indeed a pleasure to see and enjoy such hospitality, and they will always be remembered as very gracious people trying to show appreciation for Americans.

Their remark was, after being thanked, "People in the United States were so kind to us when visiting there, we try in every way possible to return those favors when Americans come to Chile."

On the return journey through the backwoods, the car got stuck in the mud twice, but jacked it up, put rocks under the back wheels, and pulled out with very little difficulty the first time.

The second time a pair of oxen pulled the car about ten feet—a bend in a swollen river had washed the road to a dangerous, narrow edge, which looked like it would cave in any minute, and staying in the ruts on purpose was the safest way to get through, and the oxen were there to help.

It was grand to get back on good roads again—ordinarily all these roads are good, but it's just this excess rain they've had this year, the most in 15 years. One could be here for weeks, if it continues to rain, then again it's possible to be in Argentina in two days.

Tomorrow the car starts nosing its way south again, down to Villaricca, a great fishing village, if the roads are passable; if not, a turn back and a stay here in the Temuca Hotel will not be bad at all, until they have time to repair the road.

It's terrible the way women are treated here in this country. By law a woman cannot have a bank account by herself. It's unheard of down here for a woman to drive a car the distance this car has come. The men seem shocked when they see a woman get down in the pits to see the condition of the car when having work done on it; but to be sure and feel secure to continue on, it's absolutely necessary to check everything.

In a garage again—the same old trouble—the gasoline tank. They have taken it off twice to find all the leaks. It actually costs just about two dollars, American money—if they didn't take up so much time taking it off, it wouldn't be bad to get it fixed, and would be foolish to put on a new one, if a new one could be found.

If one had to be stuck in a place for a good length of time, this Yachting Club Hotel here in Villaricca would be better than any other place in all of South America seen so far.

The volcano Villaricca is in full view from the hotel windows, and in a foreboding but majestic manner, dominates the lake and the countryside. Four years ago this volcano erupted and did a great deal of damage to the land between here and Puccon, a summer resort town at the other end of the lake; it belched up rocks as large as houses and lava, which poured down the mountainside, destroyed a large skiing club, and many houses in its path were buried in the black, hot volcanic ash, as it spasmodically ejected itself into the lake.

There is a great deal of destruction visible yet; especially forests of huge trees uprooted and piled along the water's edge. The road has been restored through this tragic spot and gives one the creeps as they drive through.

At the hotel, they keep a wood fire going all the time. With steam heat added, everything is most comfortable. The food is delicious—quail, chicken, grouse, steaks, and lamb are plentiful. Service is excellent and such cleanliness and comfort is to be found in every way, one should really enjoy this to the full while it lasts, as it's all so reasonable in price.

The country gets more beautiful every mile going south. We wouldn't have missed this for anything in the world. Although it clouds up and rains every day, we are thankful to be seeing it in any kind of weather.

A short strip of road just out of Villaricca is horrible. The car made it halfway through when it hit a wet spot in front of an old rundown hut and could not go on. It looked like the man from the hut had deliberately dug drainage ditches from his cow lot into the road, so he could keep the road unusually wet at that place and make [last line is cut off] He had pulled a bus out the day before. It will be necessary to go back over that same road to go on further south, which will mean staying here two to three weeks if the rains continue.

The Chileans are recuperating from celebrating their Fourth of July, and when they go through the recovery stage after celebrating, they really put on another festival that outdoes the first one. It's always been a week affair, but it has taken a few extra days this year for some reason.

I don't believe there were ten sober people in town. On one drive there was a man sprawled in the middle of the road—he looked dead, but one dares not investigate for fear that the person is dead. The law in Chile is something like this—if one turns in a report of a dead person, or picks them up and carries them to a doctor and they die, that good Samaritan is responsible for the dead one and must furnish funeral expenses and such for them.

The country folk and Indians were hanging over oxcarts, yelling, whooping, hollering on the way home after days of celebrating in town. Many were weaving over roads as if in a trance and unconscious of near trouble or danger—all of which makes it so dangerous to travel in car over the surrounding countryside, exploring, with such goings on.

Most town people are extra nice. There are lots of Germans who speak good English, and it's a relief to talk with them. Homes and hotels are neat and clean. Everyone is flying the Chilean flag during the holidays.

Two blocks from the hotel there was a large American flag flying with the same size Chilean flag. When that American flag was seen flying in the breeze, it was with great determination that we decided to find out who owned that flag. A Norwegian took us there in his jeep, as a stream had half-washed out the bridge leading there, and the jeep was the only way left to make it.

A Mrs. Diamond from California, most charming, graciously invited us in and served drinks. She seemed overjoyed to see Americans. Her husband, an Irishman, had died a few years ago and she had moved from Temuco and lived here in her summer home all year. She has the best and choicest view of the lake and the volcano. It was indeed a lovely place to spend restful hours.

While filling up with gas at the Esso station in Loncoche, the Esso traveling representative drove up in his car and said there wasn't a chance to get through to Valdivia on the main highway, as the roads had been completely washed away. He was going the long way around, he said, by the lakes, back to Valdivia, his home. When he said that was the only way to get through, and going that way one could see some of the most beautiful spots in the world, it looked to be a happy streak of luck to have met him and to follow him through these back roads.

Arriving at the first lake about five o'clock, a gorgeous time to see it, so crystal clear in spite of the rains, with the Villaricca volcano predominating the northern view. This lake is called Calafquen (Car-laf-can), an Indian name, and some of these Indian names are dillies. It would take an expert to remember all of them and pronounce them. For instance, the night was spent in the town of Panguipulli (Pan-gee-poo-ee). The lake of the same name begins a hundred yards from the hotel and extends many miles back up in the Andes.

The hotel room had seven windows overlooking this lake. It was very lovely, but the mist had the distances covered from view, so the volcanoes Chochuenco and Co El Mocho could not be seen to the southwest, the focal points of interest at this spot.

This is a very enterprising part of Chile. Two steamers ply this lake, bringing lumber from the distant side down to a large barge, which goes down the river Enco and empties into Lake Rinihue, then to river Calle Calle on in to Valdivia, where freighters take it across the ocean to England. It looks like burl maple, very fine and durable.

These back roads, unused at this time of the year, are in much better condition than the main highway; trucks and buses have dug such deep holes until the main roads are in a pitiful condition. This experience has been a good lesson, and from now on will make a business of finding the good back roads. Then, too, the most beautiful scenery is to be seen that way.

From Lake Rinihue it was frightening to follow the swift river going west—following it all the way into Valdivia. The river is deep blue-green, crystal clear. When fishing, the fishermen can see themselves catching fish—mainly trout, but big ones. It's hard to believe water going so fast can be so clear.

At times the road following the river was almost a 45 degree angle, and with red clay, wet and slick, to contend with, it was with thankfulness that there was a LoLo on the car, and the steep grades could be made without sliding off the high, narrow embankments into the river. Perched on top of a slick, steep mountain, on a narrow road, with the river directly straight down, isn't a very pleasant experience when one thinks they are out of gasoline. Later checking showed the tube inside the tank was not reaching the gasoline when the car was perched at that steep angle.

All this had a happy ending upon arrival at the beautiful new hotel, Pedro de la Valdivia, in the city of that name. While asking the clerk for a room with bath, the manager, who speaks good English, came up and insisted on turning over to us a large suite of rooms (looks like the bridal suite) on the top floor, at the same price.

The view from the rooms is magnificent, with the river making a circle around the grounds of the hotel. It's plain to see all the big boats and small fishing craft plying up and down the stream.

For people to have come this distance in a car, over these roads, is almost an impossible thing to do, so they think, and they want to do everything to make the visit to this city a remembered one. The hotel suite is only 500 pesos a day, which is less than $2.50 in American dollars. This is the place to live, this is the spot one should choose. It is supposed to be the garden spot of Chile, the cheapest place to live, and the most perfect in climate.

It is indeed a lovely city, with the people so friendly and so helpful. However, it's real cold—colder than usual, but with hot water in the bath, steam heat, a charming sitting room, downy beds with rose satin coverlets, huge closets for luggage, a powder room, and a million dollar view, it's like being in heaven.

An anniversary celebration was enjoyed the second night by inviting the Esso man and his wife for dinner. Both speak excellent English. She was educated in Santiago at the American College, a beautiful girl and niece of the President. Another uncle is ambassador to Argentina. A letter has been given to present to this uncle upon arrival in Buenos Aires.

The party was a wonderful success. There were rounds of famous cocktails, as only Chileans with their *gran vino reservado* know how to make them. the service was splendid, there was good bantering conversation with these friendly folk, then a most delicious dinner consisting of fresh mushroom soup, asparagus with mayonnaise, watercress salad with eggs, lamb chops, and mixed green vegetables. For dessert, a mild lemon sponge pudding, served so often down here, beautifully decorated with ground nuts and particles of colored candied fruits.

After dinner, the next thing on the agenda was going into the dance room and listening and dancing to wonderful music. The Edwin Langdons (English and Spanish extraction) are practically professional dancers and they did all the South American steps beautifully.

It was one of the gayest times ever spent anywhere in all the world, and it cost so much less than it would have cost anywhere else in the world. Believe it or not, the dinner for four people was only 500 pesos. These Chilean pesos sure buy a lot right now.

Now at Puella, the last outpost before crossing

to Argentina. Some fantastic experiences have been our lot, and some of the most beautiful scenery to be found anywhere, has been our privilege to see, these last few weeks.

The Langdons led the way in their car going south again. The roads turned into slush pits about ten miles out of the city, and it was a tedious slow process to get through, but with a delightful couple to boost us on and watch out for the worst mud holes, the arrival in La Union was completed successfully, and from then on comparatively good roads have radiated into a most pleasant trip since.

Osorno is a clean, up-to-date, enterprising city; the people are mostly of German extraction and have beautiful homes and farmlands. It's an important distributing point for agricultural products.

From Osorno over to Lake Puychue was an exceptionally interesting drive, with magnificent views of lakes and snow-clad mountains in the distance.

On the way over, it was well worth it to make a 30-minute stop at Salta del Pilmaiquen to view the picturesque falls as they made their mad dash into the river Bueno.

Then when rounding a mountain just before arrival at the hotel, steam or mist was seen to be literally coming out of the sandy earth. Upon closer inspection, the roadbed dirt and mountainside earth, void of most vegetation, was downright hot to the hands, and yet it was a very cold day. It seemed so hot there was danger of tires burning or gasoline dripping from tank catching on fire.

Such phenomena has some connection with the mineral water of this region, as this is a health resort where they give mineral baths, have large swimming pools open the year round, and the carbonated mineral water is bottled and shipped from the place and used for drinks all over Chile.

The hotel at Puychue, a castle-like barny place, is tremendous in size. The entire plant, including the mineral springs, baths and bottling works, covers a complete valley facing the lake and the Andean chain of mountains. What a magnificent setting! What a place to rest!

The place is also famous for its skiing parties, as many nationalities gather here for such affairs. Upon arrival at the hotel, we found many other cars were already there and more coming. Some said this great crowd was for weekend skiing events up in the mountains, and that was something to look forward to, but we finally learned they were having a big wedding that evening—two prominent German families from Osorno.

The actual wedding ceremony (Lutheran) was not seen, but the chapel in the hotel was beautifully decorated, and the reception following in the big parlor of the hotel could be seen by all outsiders.

It was an occasion to see the very lovely dressed women in evening clothes, to note that they were dressed in similar styles as American women would wear on like occasions; and the fur coats they were wearing were especially lovely—there were many Persian lamb, mouton, and mink coats. Orchids and camellias were worn lavishly and set off these elegant dresses and coats.

The bride was gorgeous in a graduated, tucked net dress over [last line cut off] finger length veil, classical bouquet—the bridesmaids, all in blue, of the same type dresses.

At ten o'clock they served dinner in the main dining room, with a six-tiered cake centering the table in front of the bride and groom. There was continuous serving the whole night through to more than 300 guests. Then there was dancing, drinking, and toasting and eating again. In fact, while eating breakfast about nine o'clock on Sunday morning, many bleary-eyed young men, still in their tuxedos, were trying to keep awake with black coffee.

Though it had rained, sleeted and snowed most of the night, the sun popped out early to give crystal clear, fresh views of snow-clad mountains and glaciers, valleys and lakes. It was a temptation to stay there several days, but when the sky and ground cleared up so beautifully, with so much to see it was impossible to sit in a big cold hotel. So our minds were set on seeing all that could be seen on such a gorgeous day, traveling south.

Then, too, the hotel officials had been so busy with the wedding and wedding guests, they had put us in a third floor room a half mile, it seemed, from parlors and dining room, which made it necessary to do a lot of walking up and down stairs.

It was bitter cold and, being such a monstrous, barny place, it was enough to make anyone unhappy, to have to walk up and down those stairs. Hot water bags were furnished to keep feet warm during the night, as no heat was on in the third floor wing.

All the way going down south to Lago Llanguihue, there was to be seen one beautiful spot after anther, so lush with wild vegetation in spots, then flowers, gardens, and farmland growing wheat, oats, and other colorful grains; and there were native pastures, well-built farm homes, fine cattle and sheep—everything to indicate these German people are happy and prosperous.

The volcanoes, Osorno and Colbuco, on either side of the lake, were striking with sun and clouds intermingling. They looked as though they were coming up out of the water, which they were. It was a marvelous and fantastic sight.

Following the lake from Octay through steep winding roads, by magnificent farm homes, every kind of tree imaginable was to be seen in bloom. The green pastures were thick with herds of fat cattle and woolly sheep. The views of the lake, snow-clad mountains, and beach—all in conjunction with the farms—gave out a spectacle never to be forgotten.

Arriving at the quaint little German town of Fruitillar in time for lunch on Sunday, it was just luck that the eating place was chosen. A wonderful lunch of oysters with sauce, soup with a half breast of chicken, roast leg of lamb, vegetables, wine, and peaches dried whole, similar to peaches at home. While eating, it was noticed two fine looking couples at a table across the room were eyeing us; before coming into the dining room they had stopped and looked over the car outside with the Texas license.

One man ventured over and asked, "Are you really from Texas and where are you going in that car?" Taking a South American map out of the big pocket of the black coat, we showed the man just where we had landed in Venezuela, and penciled the trip on to their village.

He called his wife and the other couple over to introduce them, and from then until 4:30, all they did was open up bottles of champagne, pour in glass and hold glass up and say "salute"—that's what all Chileans do when they think some feat is extraordinary and they are drinking. Drinking wine down here is like drinking water in the United States. Champagne is very mild and costs only one dollar a bottle, but is supposed to be very refreshing.

These people were so kind and friendly, it would have been most undiplomatic to refuse their hospitality.

There was a Lion Club emblem hanging in the hotel, stating the club of that little town was there every Thursday—and one of the men was wearing a Lion Club pin in his lapel.

When he was told that Earl was a life member of the club, this fellow got up and called the president of the Lions Club to come down to see us. In a short time, the president and his wife came in—she a beautiful blonde and most attractive—he a big, handsome, jovial fellow. They were so friendly and likable.

There was a new round of champagne upon their arrival, and with each glass held high, they would say, "salute." They tried to induce us to spend the night there with them, but since reservations had already been made in Puerto Varas, it appeared to be the wise thing to go on.

Exchanging names and addresses, followed by goodbyes, we bundled into the car and, slowing driving through the magnificent views of the lake, over mountains and countryside, we reached the attractive little town of Puerto Varas.

There was still a couple of hours of daylight left, so it was decided to drive on south to the little town of Puerto Mentt and see about a boat that makes the trip through inland waterways down to Arenas, the south most city of Chile.

On this Sunday the ship's offices were closed, so the information was obtained from a hotel clerk who said that was no time of the year to go as the boats were very small and cold and not very pleasant to be in at anytime of the year, much less at this time.

Going over the mountain into Puerto Mentt is a beautiful sight, and gives one a weird feeling to see the land stretching out into long peninsular hands as it reaches out into the sea.

These juttings and our usual curiosity sent us all up and down this strip to see the port and the fishing villages; and many men were mending nets and preparing stalls for selling fish and other things, such as shells, strings of dried fish, shrimp, oysters—just hanging in the open with flies all over. They take these dried sea foods, soak in water for some time, then boil them.

There were several large ships in dock, and we tried to get information about them, but they looked like they were tied up until summer.

We made our way for a long distance down the ribbon coast, past a large island, then back into town. Another road on the west coast was followed to the airfield, where there was a good view of the Pacific inland waters.

Then back to the beach road, which leads upstairs, as so many call up top of the mountain; looking back to view all the lights, the church spires, the inland bay—so busy with activity—and the deep,

deep blue of the water. It was a picture to be long remembered.

They never serve dinner down here until 8 to 10 o'clock. So it was long after returning to the hotel and getting washed up before the food was ready. But such good food they serve is well worth waiting for.

In all of the South Lake District hotels, they always include food with room, and they serve their food so beautifully and bountifully, it's a problem to keep from overeating and gaining weight.

This huge, cold hotel overlooking the lake is bound to be wonderful in the summer (in December) with several volcanoes in full view; boats, sail and steam, plying the lake; nice cool beaches; and everything to be thought of that's lovely and restful for this holiday land.

Up early for a leisurely start to Petrohue through La Pazo, a small but quaint place; then on to Ensenada, one of the most attractive, but old-fashioned hotels—a restful place with excellent German food, as good as can be found anywhere. This hotel is right at the foot of the volcano Osorno. It would be a wonderful spot to spend a long vacation, as there are many walks, drives over the surrounding country, good fishing and boating.

From then on it was driving through one dry lava bed after another—at one time stopping to watch the eerie falls and dashing waters of the river Petrohue as it pounded over rocks from one lake to another in its mad rush.

Petrohue looked to be a town on the map, but proved to be just a hotel with all conveniences—and the last outpost before Argentina.

The barge to take the car across the lake was not in the dock and would not be for several days, so it was decided the sensible thing was to lock the car in a garage and cross the lake on this old time, wood burning steamer, *Esmeralda*, and see what the situation was near the border. The officials had already said we could not make the pass in the car to Bariloche for at least two weeks and possibly a month.

Steaming over on this emerald green lake, Lago Todes los Santos, with the snow-covered mountains hemming in the lake on all sides, was certainly a never to be forgotten sight. The volcano, Osorno, most beautiful in its gradual slopes, is on the left side going, and is similar to Mount Fuji in Japan. The Co Benete on the opposite side of the lake is very nearly the shape of the Matterhorn in Switzerland.

The greenest of green trees, and other native foliage and bramble, came right down to the water's edge—this all looked an earthly paradise and something to dream about.

The Swiss chalet type hotel at Puello is nestled at the far end of the lake on a small stretch of valley that has been built up of washed volcanic ash, very fertile and productive. Tree studded mountains, covered halfway down with snow, and mammoth waterfalls surround the place. They get their water supply, as well as power, from one of the falls, which they have harnessed.

This place belongs to one family, Roth by name, of Swiss and German extraction. The story goes that this fellow was fishing up on these lakes 60 years ago, explored the place, and saw its possibilities. He and his young bride came up and settled on it, built a home, had four children and, with them, have developed a huge empire.

They have Grumman planes, yachts, steamers, buses, trucks, other hotels, garages, planing mills, furniture plants, and carpenter shops—everything but hardware and nails and glass for building homes is produced here in this valley.

There is a magnificent villa on an island midway in the lake; the founder and one son are buried there. Several miles up the valley is some lovely farming land, with a substantial home belonging to the widow of the founder of this estate, commanding a view of the entire domain in all directions. Here they raise large boned Holstein cattle, pigs, and chickens, and have wonderful flower and vegetable gardens.

Everything, including many homes for workmen and schools and this hotel, has been built with wood from these forests—hand hewn shingles are used mostly; polished wood, some rough and showing knot holes, predominates in the finishing of this hotel, simple but very lovely.

In the hotel they make their own bread and jams—blackberry especially, by the gallon—the blackberries grow wild and are a menace to the countryside. Their cabbage kraut is unexcelled and, with pig sausages, is out of this world.

They raise apples, pears, choicest of vegetables—such as asparagus, artichokes, mushrooms, and serve them most every day. Their beef, pork, fish, snails, chickens, duck, and deer meat, and everything else for the table, is produced on this place. It's really wonderful how self-sustaining this place is.

Today they had for the first course molded head cheese with potato salad and extra slices of ham and (crazy) lettuce, a lettuce growing on the lake banks and looks like celery leaves, only larger, and it sure has a wonderful flavor.

Then barley soup, with a beef broth flavor, very excellent—soup is a must for lunch and dinner. Then they served the Chilean national dish, empanadas, a sort of fried pie with mussels for filling—they also make them with chicken and olives, fish with rice, and beef with onions—but these with mussels are the best yet.

They then served a beef roll, thin slices of beef rolled around a long carrot, filled with a little onion and celery cut up fine—all this baked to a turn. It was round steak cut very thin, and it looked like it had been tied with string to hold the onion and celery around the carrot during the baking process.

There is a regular bus trip to the Argentine border, Puerto Alegre. Each day the tourists go through both ways, spend a few days, then return to Bariloche in Argentina, or take the boat over to Petrohue, and the bus to Puerto Varas where they can get the train, plane or bus to Santiago and other northern places in Chile.

Lots of newly married couples from Argentina come here. There are many secluded retreats, some have the sign of the cross near the most important waterfalls—there lovers, or anyone else, can go to say prayers or commune with nature. It's a perfect setting for honeymooners with its paths into the deep wooded sections where beautiful tropical ferns and flowers of all description can be found.

Strange as it may seem, it never freezes in these valleys, and yet there is deep snow and ice a hundred feet up. Red flannels have been donned for comfort, as the hotel is bitter cold, even though steam heated.

A bus trip up the pass to the Argentine border has been indulged in, just to see if conditions are as bad as they had said. The snow is so high, 15 feet to be exact, that the snowplows can't throw the ice out over the top of the deep trench being cut in the snow for buses and cars to go through.

They say they will have to literally dig the ice in big blocks by hand and form a human chain to get these blocks off the road. That is something to think about.

Up there for hours, we tried to walk around but bogged down to waist in soft, deep snow; then part of the time sat amusing ourselves with "Spite and Malice"—waiting for the people who were in the bus going up to walk to the Argentine bus a mile away, and for the Argentine tourists to walk through to the Chile bus.

Some of the time we hovered over an open wood fire where the snow has been dug out in front of a midway shelter, in the process of construction, but the roof had caved in due to terrific pressure of the snow on top. It was being built so that in the future snowplow men can live there during the winter months and scrape the pass each day to keep it open.

An Indian woman was preparing a mulligan stew on an open wood fire for the men working on the ice. She offered this food to us, but the hotel had prepared sandwiches and a thermos jug of hot coffee for us.

After these workmen had finished the stew, they started this mate drinking—the foreman got a gourd and packed it full of dry, ground, gray-green leaves, then added a teaspoon of coarse brown sugar, pouring boiling water, melted from snow, from a blackened teakettle that was kept steaming on the coals of fire.

He reached in his pocket and got out a bright silver and gold tube, called a *bombilla* tube, with perforations, or strainer-like holes at the bottom of the larger, rounded end, and shoved this down in the gourd cup. Bowing low, offered this contraption to me, but I did not know what to do with it, so shook my head. Earl did likewise.

Then the foreman sucked the liquid out of the gourd and handed it to the next fellow, who added sugar and boiling water to the same gourd, without changing the leaves or the *bombilla* tube; and he, in turn sipped it up. Then this fellow passed it on to the next in circle until the dozen men had had a fill.

Again it started around; and these refills of water and sugar, using the same leaves, continued for about two hours. It was interesting to study the personalities—some happy and singing, others moody—several watching the reaction of visitors with us trying to keep a not too curious, surprised look.

It was a relief to hear the tourists come crunching through—one handsome, big fellow, as he came climbing into the bus, started singing "The Eyes of Texas Are Upon You." Then we yelled out, "What part of the state are you from?" He said, "I knew that song would get a rise out of any Texan in this crowd."

We shook hands with Bishop Martin and his wife, from Little Rock, Arkansas. They were on a tour of the Methodist churches and mission schools of South America. It was like "Old Home Week" to see them.

Next day our leftover Chilean pesos were passed over to them and they, in turn, let us have their leftover Argentine money. Their many points about how to act, what to do and see in Buenos Aires proved useful later on.

After having gone up to this pass and seeing the deepest snow ever seen, there was nothing left to do but wait the weeks necessary to get the pass opened.

We've been here for more than a week; it has rained or snowed nearly every day—just today there was a fresh snow coming down very low. It's unusually beautiful over the mountains and trees, but it's enough to make one glum, as each new snow means several more days of waiting, waiting, waiting.

By this time the long wait was becoming rather boring and, just for something to do, the lake was crossed back to Petrohue to see about the car.

The hotel manager there came to us and said, "There are some more Texans here on motorcycles and they are planning to go back across the lake today with you." Lead us to them, was our first thought.

Two boys came up wearing bedraggled hunting coats with the back and sides of the coats burned to the waist, exposing checked wool shirts and blue jeans. They were the Dealy boys who had been at school at SMU, but originally were from the State of Washington.

They had ridden by motorcycle to Honduras, got a boat there, and had come down through Panama by boat to Buenaventura, then had crossed on to the Pan American Highway and had come a similar route to ours. Some of their experiences are terrific—further details about them and their burned jackets will be mentioned later on.

There were three other people, all in blue jeans—two men and a girl. They introduced themselves as Frances and Jerome Constantine, and Elmer Olhaber, all three from Chicago. They had entered South America at Barranquilla, Columbia, and they had traveled a great deal of the same route in a jeep.

It was great to be on the same boat going across the lake with them, talking the same language, watching them take pictures, and swapping experiences. They have had it pretty rugged, having slept in the jeep and cooked out in the open on the entire trip; but with the bountiful fruits, meat and bread down here, that should be much better than many of the off-grade, slovenly hotels one has to put up with in the small towns.

One just has to see to realize how primitive these small town hotels are, in all of the countries of South America; the crude method of cooking; the danger of disease from such; the almost impossible chance to get hotels to prepare special foods—one has to eat what they are cooking on these charcoal grills or do without.

Many times a can of tuna and some fruit were eaten, rather than stop to look the situation over; so often the conditions would make one sick.

It was easy to envy the Constantines who were lucky to be equipped and able to find and prepare good food for themselves. Of course, upon arriving in the large cities, they could very well envy us the good baths and rooms of hotels, choice foods and service and the hard times could be forgotten while enjoying the luxuries. It was even bitter cold in the hotel and there was an uneasy, guilty feeling when thinking about these Americans sleeping out in the open in the hotel parkway. It was nice to have them come up to the room, take baths, play games, and rest.

The Dealy boys had had their money and papers stolen in Santiago and were trying to get to Buenos Aires as quickly as possible to get checks they were expecting from home.

The following day after arrival, and after much persuasion, the officials decided to let the boys try to get through the pass, with the workmen and Jerome Constantine helping to push those 700 pound motorcycles all the way through the ice and snow of the deep pitted pass.

Jerome wanted to help, with a two-fold purpose in mind. He was anxious to see the condition of the road and their own chance of getting through in the jeep. Two days later, the Constantines made it through the pass, but sent a note advising us to wait until it was completely cut through, as they had done considerable damage to their jeep when going across avalanches of ice.

There were two groups of basketball players who have come in to the hotel, one from Puerto Montt, and the other from Osorno. They sure have livened things up the past two days. Several of the boys can't cross the border into Argentina until they get written permission from their fathers, as they are under the age limit, and the border officials require that of the boys.

They were going to play their national championship games at Bariloche on Saturday, Sunday, and Monday, but have had to postpone these matches until they could get these signed papers from home. Through many phone conversations, the signed papers will be flown in by air in twenty-four hours. Then the boys will proceed on.

The boys from Puerto Montt have been lots of fun and extra nice. They sat next to us in the dining room and, when they found who owned the Cadillac, they introduced themselves, and from then on have been allowed to drive the car around over the comparatively good roads of this little valley.

Lots of singing and talking and dancing has been enjoyed with them, when otherwise these could have been dull and uninteresting days. The only other thing to keep the long wait from being too dull is sketching these lovely mountains.

One boy named John could sing many American songs, every word of the song, though he could not always carry on a conversation or completely understand English. Their English teacher was along, and he understood better; but his pronunciation is very much like our Spanish pronunciation. He was extra nice, autographing a book of the doings of Puerto Montt, their schools, churches, and their shipping interests.

When asking about taking a boat trip down to Punta Arenas, the south most city of Chile, they said the ships were terribly cold and dirty and uncomfortable at this time of the year and advised against it. When one's been freezing for weeks, with heavy red flannels next to the skin, sweaters, wool dress, and heavy topper on top of that, seems like it's no time to go into a colder place.

There were some fantastic pictures of the inland

waterway leading to the glaciers coming right down into the water—it's bound to be well worth seeing.

One can really get enough of this cold and damp weather and, with so little heat in the hotel, it's necessary to go to bed to keep warm. They do build a wood fire down in the club room late each evening, and that is something to look forward to.

There are some of the most beautiful native wild flowers in bloom here. One most interesting kind of bush, called nachai, which grows in abundance around here, has small holly-like leaves and is covered with the most beautiful delicate yellow blooms, similar to a miniature jonquil. The buds are red underneath and have red stems. Wonder if they could be transplanted to Texas.

There is another yellow blooming plant called calasbate, the flowers spring from a cluster of leaves. This flower also looks like a jonquil, but the bush and leaves have a jasmine leaf appearance. In December it prolifically develops little red berries, which are good to eat, and the natives use them for jam and pies. This jam is the berries, it's that good!

Another week of impatient waiting—the officials said the pass would be opened the following morning and it would be possible to get through. The Chileans and Argentineans had literally cut the ice out of the roadbed with pick and shovel and were planning a joint celebration on the Argentine side over the completed job.

That Sunday morning as preparations were made to leave, they insisted a pick and shovel should be taken along as the Cadillac would be the first to go through and a snow slide might have developed in the night. Sure enough, they were right. Some time was spent clearing the road again of a fresh snow slide that had fallen during the night.

7

Argentina: October, 1953

Near Argentine customs a great group of workmen were hilariously gathered around a campfire, where large sides of beef were pierced with wooden sticks or crosses, and these crosses were wedged into ground to support these hunks of bloody meat, standing upright near and around a big open fire. There was good banjo music and much singing, whooping, and hollering as they were drinking continuously from big, wicker covered jugs of wine—one or two fellows drank from mate gourds with the bombilla straws, which they carried around constantly in their hands.

It was fascinating to see how little it took to keep them in a buzz of happiness. The three feet of snow did not seem to dampen their spirits or worry them whatsoever; they swished back and forth in their heavy woolen ponchos, in a constant chatter. Some pretended fighting, others sat hunched between meat over fire.

They are all wearing rakish hats, high, crinkled legged boots, bloused pants, loud scarves tied in knot around neck with streamers flying as they continued to stomp and tromp the snow as it turned into a flattened mire around the fire.

The blood was oozing out of the meat as the men took large, sharp knives from their belts and whacked off big hunks from the side of meat and gulped it down. This kept up for hours, this drinking, eating, singing, yelling—then repeating the whole thing over again—and was their way of celebrating the opening of the pass.

Upon arriving at Puerta Frias, the first thing seen to attract attention, as we entered the hotel office, were two large, framed photographs of Peron and Evita hanging on the wall. Going into the dining room for hot coffee, again there were large life-size pictures of them hanging in prominent places. Back in the powder room, again there were to be seen these pictures on the wall.

On the whole, the people were very kind and solicitous and acted unconscious of the fact that every step they made was followed by those photographs.

A large launch full of honeymooners came in the second day for lunch. They were beautiful, well-groomed, smartly dressed girls in suits and slacks—most of the slacks are tight around the ankles, which gives them a large hipped, or peg-topped effect—and their sweaters, scarves, and coats are so colorful and in perfect harmony.

Lots of these Argentineans speak English fluently and want to help out by phoning the proper officials about the barge. They say the hotel manager will try to keep people indefinitely, as they have so few weekly guests. There has already been a two-day delay in getting a barge to take the car to Bariloche.

This Puerto Frias is a gem of a place, overlooking the deep, mysterious fjord—it was a complete surprise nestled in between snow-clad mountains, with the glacier Tronodor back to the right of the lake. The three feet deep snow down to the water's edge looks like the frosted whites of eggs around a bowl of green jello—the sun is shining, which puts a glistening jeweled effect upon a lovely setting. But oh! So cold – so cold!

It was a relief when, on Tuesday, they told us a large barge would come the next day. The barge was barely large enough for the car, and great trepidation was felt when driving the car over two small, thin planks from the dock onto this barge, and they say the water is very deep in that particular fjord. In the past several cars have gone overboard and been lost there.

As the barge was swinging around a bend of the lake, there was an excellent view of the glacier Tronodor and the mountains all covered with snow surrounding the upper end of the lake. It was a gem of a place, and we felt lucky to be going through the Andes that particular way and to be able to see all this beauty.

The car was backed off the boat at Puerto Alegre on wider boards with side rails, and it seemed safer; then over a one-way road of two miles to Puerto Blest.

On the way, the basketball boys from Puerto Montt were met returning from Bariloche. A happy reunion! It was Old Home Week for a short time right there in the middle of the road, but it was necessary to hurry on, as the bus and the truck with luggage could not get around us on the one-way road, until we arrived at the turnaround.

There was a wait of several hours at Puerto Blest for the barge going to Bariloche. In the meantime, it was necessary to walk about to keep from freezing. So we looked over the hotel being rebuilt into a very modern structure, after having a fire last year. The German builder invited us into the kitchen for coffee, and that helped us to stand the cold.

At Puerto Blest, the car had to be driven onto the barge over 15-foot length boards, with only an oil can supporting the board on the left side. They had the docks tied up with tile and lumber, and this was the only method left to cross—one couldn't turn back—it had to be done. It was enough to make of one a nervous wreck, although the job was done in a few minutes.

The ride down Lago Nahuel Huapi into Llao

Llao (*You You*) was a reminder or combination of the French and Swiss Alps, the Pyrenees, the Canadian Rockies, and the glaciers in the USA national parks.

There were snow-clad mountains with great crevices going deep into the steep, sheer cliffs. Waterfalls from these mountains were cascading in huge gulps from rocks to boulders in their terrific descent into the fjords. There was the glacier Tronodor to be seen from many points; and others, seemingly as tall and grand, rising majestically above all this.

This is the most beautiful country to be seen around Llao Llao. The green countryside, with rolling hills and magnificent hotels, homes, and winding roads; to the right surrounded by all these snow-clad mountains 12,000 feet and higher, and the lake to the left of deep, deep blue—it's something to write home about.

Making several drives through the foothills around the mountains near the city, just feasting on the beauty of the place, we found it so clean and fresh with spring just bursting out all over—the backdrop of snow and ice against the aqua green stone buildings and also fences of this native stone was unbelievably beautiful and had the appearance of so many villages seen in Switzerland. In fact, Bariloche was originally settled by Swiss.

After this drive, arrived at 3 Reyes (*3 Kings*) Hotel in Bariloche, secured a nice room with steam heat and hot baths. Had a wonderful dinner—Otto will always be remembered as a cultured, misplaced person, a German who spoke English so well, and served us so beautifully and bountifully at dinner.

During dinner, some of the better American records were played "softly" on a music box and everyone seemed to enjoy the music. Again, there were to be seen life-size photographs of Peron and Evita, hanging on the wall over the record player in the dining room, in the lobby, in parlors, and in the barroom.

The ski lift to the skiing grounds was not in operation the next day, and it looked foolish to stay three days for that; then, too, there had been enough cold weather to last a lifetime.

The first thing on the agenda the next morning was to go to police headquarters to get permits to proceed through Argentina. The AAA Club produced maps for travel and, when the man was filling the gasoline tank, he tried to tell us by signs and words, "*Peligro, muy Peligro*"—no gasoline, very dangerous!

The driving all morning was bearing toward left around the lake with wonderful back views of mountains. What a picture! What a country!

Then there could be seen a crazy rock formation across the wild running Limay River. These formations looked like hieroglyphics carved by hand thousands of years ago. It would be easy to believe they were done by hand if they had not continued for so many miles.

The road was very narrow in spots, but the car was the only one on the road all day. No homes or people were seen except one time we did stop by an *escuela* building and ask some children the right direction. In the mountainous terrain, there could not be seen any other sign of habitation.

Later in the morning when approaching the desert and pampa country, there were to be found many wild flowers blooming in great patches all along the way, especially sweet Williams and wild peas.

These recognizable by name were growing in sanguine beauty.

There were many different kinds of grasses and low scrub trees and bushes covered with the white, chalky dust of the land, blown on the plants by a mean stinging wind. The road was stifling with this white, chalky dust, which was penetrating into every crevice of the car.

Being aware of the desolate, unfrequented road, there was a lonely feeling of being completely cut off from everyone else in the world. At a calculated distance, there was a gasoline station, the only one seen all day. After being serviced, the car wouldn't start. In trying to tell the young Argentinean who had filled the tank with gas what the problem was, the Spanish conversation book with drawings of a car motor was used, but he kept saying, "*No comprend.*"

There we were in the middle of the pampa, with only two houses—one for the officers to check the people coming through and the other for the manager of the filling station. The only thing left to do was to try to find the trouble and fix it ourselves.

The car was jacked up and, scooting underneath, checked the lever of the starter chain and found it completely covered with mud. Scraping and digging mud out, decided to crawl out from underneath the car and try to start it. Caught hold of the running board to help in sliding out from underneath the car. When doing so, the car door slammed on left hand, cutting thumb to the bone. A mean wind blowing at a terrific rate was responsible for the door slamming. The wife of the filling station man quickly rendered first aid, wrapping large wads of bandages over the hand to catch the flow of blood.

It was getting very late and it was nearly 200 miles to Newquen. It looked like it would be necessary to get a mechanic to come to the car from there, but without giving up completely, for more than an hour kept trying to explain to the man about the Hydramatic and starter, by showing him the Cadillac manual and making crude drawings of a starter chain.

He got under the car, checked the lever, dug out some more mud, got out from under and checked the switch at steering wheel several times, and finally got a spark and then got it going.

The starter was stuck with mud and the long wait had dried it out. The car had come through a deep and swift running stream about ten miles back, which had killed the motor at the time, and there had to sit with water coming up to the floor of the car while frantically grinding on the starter until it started again.

When driving along in the deep sandy road, the dirt must have collected on the wet surface of the starter and stuck the chain. It was with thankfulness we got going again after what looked to be a desperate situation.

The filling station people said a doctor, or *medico*, could be found at Picun Leufu. It was off the main highway and, as darkness had closed in and only a few lights were visible, it was difficult to realize it was a village, until after having passed by. It seemed foolish to risk turning back to so small a place.

Arriving at Neuquen about ten o'clock that evening, saw a policeman in front of a theater and asked him about a doctor. When he saw the hand, he got in the car and gave directions to the hospital.

When asking for a doctor, the nurse was thought to be saying "No, no *medicao*, not bad enough to get *medico* out of bed." A nurse in training brought a graduate nurse and the two together dressed the hand, putting sulfa and a black looking syrupy stuff on it, with much wrapping of gauze over it. When trying to pay them, they refused to take money.

The policeman showed us to a nice hotel, helped get out the bags, parked the car, and shook hands. It was a relief to have a comfortable clean bed for the night, when a few hours before it looked like the night would be spent in the car.

Next morning checked the car at the station and found nothing wrong. Drove over town and suburbs to find it an oasis in the desert. There were Lombardy poplar trees lining the streets and highways leading out of the city. There were hundreds of orchards with pear trees in bloom. Yellow broom weed flowers were in profusion everywhere, wisteria in full bloom covered many homes. This was a beautiful spot to feast one's eyes upon after the desolation and lonesomeness of the day before in the desert.

Pictures of Peron and Evita were plastered over the walls in the hospital, hotel, restaurants, and in the filling station. A bronze statue of Evita was centered in one of the loveliest parks filled with blooming flowers.

She is supposed to be most loved in this part of Argentina, as labor organizations are most active around the fruit and berry picking centers.

Going toward Bahia Blanca, for miles and miles were these beautiful orchards, vineyards, and neatly kept homes. The roads were gravel, terribly dusty, but fairly smooth.

While driving along over a hilly road, were amazed to see, perched on this high mountain, a tremendous statue of Evita, with hands outstretched and a serene look upon the face. The red granite rock of the statue seemed to flow into folds as it diffused into the mountain.

Bleak and desolate was all of the surrounding country; this is bound to bring about a permanent imprint on the minds of people. Then for hours in pampa country again, with the only signs of habitation a group of poplar trees dotting the distant slopes about every ten miles, which indicated a small hacienda.

Straying cattle or sheep could be seen in sparse numbers; cattle guards across the highway and fences were proof that people did come that way, but it was really lonely not seeing a car for more than 200 miles.

Twice that day crossed over the river on unusual barges. The old man in attendance propelled the barge by hand, with car and occupants on it. In this manner, a large wheel, grooved out with cables around it, was turned for a few minutes against the current, swinging the barge wide into the middle of the stream as it rounded a bend, when the swift current of the river took hold and finished the circle to the other side. It was very simple and so easily accomplished and was all free Argentine service.

There was a wonderful new pavement about 20 miles out of Bahia Blanca, which was certainly nice to be on.

Soon after checking in at the hotel, went to the drugstore for clean gauze for the hand. The druggist insisted on fixing the hand himself, when he saw the condition of it. The gauze the nurses had put on had stuck to the thumb, and he had to boil water and douse the place to get it free, and wouldn't charge a penny. He got out his Spanish-English dictionary to convey his meaning of words and let us know he liked Americans.

The next day was to have been spent in Bahia Blanca to do a lot of shopping, as reports were that the city, being a coast town and an open market, had merchandise cheaper than any other place in the country, as ships bring in goods duty free.

Upon going to the car at the garage, found a stiff, cold wind was blowing over the city, and it was hard to stand up when walking along. Since the weather was so severe and my hand so uncomfortable, it was decided to drive on toward Buenos Aires.

The countryside, soon after leaving the coastal area, though sort of flat with gradual slopes, was lush with wheat, alfalfa, flax, and other grasses and pasture lands.

There never have been seen more beautiful cows, all rolling in fat—it seemed like there were millions of them. Other pastures were full of sheep, thick as flies; pastures of horses grouped together in units of a dozen or more; then there were bobtailed horses, eight to a big farm wagon, leisurely pulling great loads of hay.

Small but neat homes, surrounded by poplar trees, dotted the landscape. Many gauchos in bloused plants, heavy boots, black hat cocked at a rakish angle, and sashed sort of belts, were riding horses up and down the highway. They would often stop and salute, then wave us on.

Every time we stopped for drinks or a comfort station, there was the feeling they were expecting us; at least we were conscious these people were phoning ahead to say we had arrived at this place; and then we realized our progress had been continually checked by police officials all along the way since we had entered Argentina.

In Azul, an important cattle center, they served lunch at the Auto Club—a complete dinner from soup to nuts, which took two hours to eat. Many men, dressed gaucho fashion, were eating there. They were not in the least bit of a hurry—very jovial; but when we ordered lunch, they got very quiet to listen to the choice of foods.

They served blood scrambled into a red mash for the first course—it was pretty hard to look at, much less to eat. They do have good soups and unusually good bread.

It was wonderful to be on pavement and to make good time. The Evita Peron Highway—most everything has her name attached to it somewhere. It was always wise to slow up through small towns, but mostly kept the gauge at 60 mph.

The people were very friendly and kind, so much like Americans—though they were watching us. They have good clerks in the shops, just as aggressive as Americans—it's nice to stop every so often and get drinks, especially is it wonderful now that last we can get Coca Cola again. They were not to be had in Chile and most of Peru.

After three days of hard driving in Argentina, we arrived in Buenos Aires on Friday evening—this was the fastest driving done in all of the South American highway. This Eva Peron Highway was very good all the way in from Bahia Blanca; nevertheless, fast driving made it necessary to be careful, and so we were very tired upon arrival in the city, fell in bed, and went to sleep before dinner.

This is certainly one big, beautiful city. It took more than two hours to get into the central part of the town, it was so completely jammed with cars going pell-mell and every which way—people were striding and criss-crossing up and down the streets in the most nonchalant and careless fashion. It was amazing to find that no one was struck down, though several were barely missed by cars.

Had planned to stay at the Plaza Hotel, the swankiest in the city, but found it too expensive. Then tried to get to the Continental, where the Martins had stayed, but found a traffic jam in front of it and would have had to wait for a long time, so settled for the City Hotel, which fitted our needs perfectly. They gave us a beautifully appointed suite of rooms and have been most kind, furnishing an interpreter to help with car, seeing city, helping get glasses fixed, and good buys in leather goods, etc. It's within two blocks of the American Embassy, the shopping center, and just around the corner from the Plaza de Mayo where the Argentineans have had their rally and have been celebrating all day.

This is the anniversary of Peron's presidency and, from the large demonstration going on, he is as well liked as ever. His speech was heard on all the loud speakers, but of course we couldn't understand but few words of it. They will have English translations tomorrow in all the papers. Pink and blue printed pamphlets in Spanish words meaning "Peron and Evita fulfill their promises" were strewn on the streets by the millions. People of all walks of life were marching in groups, carrying banners, singing, chanting, yelling, and lifting their arms in salute. Peron and Evita's pictures hung in every business building passed along the way. Then followed army and navy officials goose-stepping down the street like SS troops of Germany before the war—these men were in the most military dress and fashion.

One could not help but look around in the crowd for Hitler's face, this was so in keeping with pictures seen of his SS troops; and there had been so many Germans in every walk of life in the south of Chile, and hundreds of them had already been encountered in Argentina. It was easy to believe or think all of the most important Nazis had escaped from Germany during that last stand to find a haven in this large and dictatorial land. They could live here for years without being found by anyone outside of the men in authority.

Radio programs were going full blast all day—big life-size pictures of Peron and Evita were displayed in every window and shop—it's a must to display these pictures or the businesses are closed up, so people say.

Labor organizations were banded together by the thousands; their union cards had been taken up the week previous and the only way the members could retrieve their cards was to appear on that plaza that day. After reading of it in the past and seeing it in pictures, it was something extraordinary to be there and to see all this in person.

The famous Pink Palace was at the end of the square down the street, where the mob of paraders and troops gathered—they were wedged in so thick, it was dangerous to be in the throng.

We were right down in front for a while and held together for dear life. Peron, with all his dignitaries, came out on the balcony of this building—the ovation was tremendous—his talk, with the assistance of a loud speaker, was loud and long.

Huge pictures of Evita and Peron were above this balcony, they were stretched on canvas, backed up with wooden frames, and they kind of swayed in the breeze as he talked. There were banners flying and every so often, when Peron made an important statement, the people would raise their banners, flags, or colors higher and yell, whoop, holler and cheer in ten-minute ovations.

The square was jam-packed; it took an hour to go from one corner of the sidewalk to the next block. It would take a long time to describe the seriousness of all this—the power that could force, or willingly cause that many people to stand half a day listening to the oration; the other half of the day having been spent marching to the place—it was beyond comprehension.

There seemed to be a lot of people just following—big, husky, domineering fellows in the crowd who scowled and watched others, as though they would punish those who did not cheer—which showed the great amount of power displayed.

The curious mixture of contempt, wonder, amazement, disgust, courage, resignation on the faces of some native standbyers and onlookers was plain to see. Some seemed to be praying with heads held high, "Oh! God, how long can this last?"

The first thing on Saturday morning was to rush over to the Embassy for mail; letters were lost in a maze of other letters and were found only after much and constant searching. Other letters will probably turn up the same way tomorrow (Monday), as they had only a skeleton force due to its being a weekend and a holiday combined.

Argentina must be very rich in its own resources—after seeing the thousands of miles of lush pastures, the fat cattle, and the fields of grain, it seems like they could feed the whole world.

All the people in the city of Buenos Aires look good, no beggars have been seen on the streets, no real poverty has been noticed anywhere. Homes are substantially built and, in the newer sections, are charming in their patio settings.

This whole city is terrific, is the opinion formed after returning from a guided drive over it. There miles and miles of lovely, well-kept parkways with blooming flowers growing abundantly, such as roses, geraniums, azaleas, just massed in borders around beautiful statues depicting the history of the country, were seen and enjoyed.

The river La Platte was followed as though going to Cordoba. There were yachting clubs with thousands of sailboats breezing down the river and canals dredged from the sandy refuse collected at the river's mouth. There were golf clubs with well-kept turf, and many people were taking advantage of the good weather to play. There were huge swimming pools with loop-the-loop slides that would delight all ages of swimmers.

The magnificent trees surrounding the parks gave a very pleasing effect, and again in every direction turned were to be seen wonderful statues on the plazas and important streets.

The Labor Building, under construction, shows life-size metal figures of Eva and Juan Peron on top of the building, over either side of the entrance. Without exception, every public building, all business houses and clubs had large pictures of the Perons placed in conspicuous places in the establishments.

There were many new wonderful buildings under construction, such as apartment hotels, cathedrals, office buildings—showing that the country is in a state of progress. Many drives down these wide avenues of the supposedly widest streets in the world helped to show off these buildings to advantage.

One can look right out of the windows of the hotel upon *La Prensa*, the once free press newspaper that was confiscated by the Perons, and admire it glittering in jewel lights of the many light bulbs strung over its façade. In the windows of this building are very large, painted portraits of Peron and Evita—he is dressed in a dark suit with official emblems of state across his shoulders; while she is wearing a magnificent evening gown of white satin caught up with blue ribbon.

On Monday had lunch with a doctor from the States at the American Club, which is famous for its food. A Marine sergeant at the Embassy gave us the name of this doctor. Found he had been with Halsey on the *Enterprise*, which gave us so much in common to talk about.

We went without food Tuesday so we could enjoy the food at La Cabana, another famous steak place known all over—it's been written up in *Life*—those steaks were as good as we had anticipated them to be. They were almost half a cow, charcoal broiled to perfection over a hot grill while the guests looked on.

The waiter of English and Scotch extraction showed us all over the place and talked about the labor problems of the country—what a good job Peron was doing, that he actually was fulfilling his promises to the people. The paramount feeling was that he was trying to get us to give an opinion of Peron. Nothing but praise can be said of the average people down here.

A full day of new interests starts each day early, with the first thing on the agenda a trip to the Embassy for mail—letters from home are like a shot in the arm to boost one on.

The Embassy officials here have been more than kind. They have treated us like home folk. Sergeant Morris and his wife, originally from Fort Worth, Texas, have had us out to their apartment for dinner and have interpreted when getting the car checked over at an Olds agency. They shall always be remembered as the nicest couple in the world.

At last have arrived in Montevideo! In a garage having the water pump fixed. Peron should be shot at sunrise for causing all this trouble. The tourists have suffered, along with the native Argentineans, over his diabolical attempt to keep people from crossing over into Uruguay. This situation has been brought about because so many Argentineans have disagreed politically with Peron and have sought and received refuge by the Uruguayan people.

The Embassy at Buenos Aires had tried so hard to get us on the boat across the Rio La Platte to Montevideo, but Peron has slapped outrageous prices on all persons, cars, or merchandise to Uruguay—$70 per car, $30 each for us—and a handling charge of more than $25 for workers for car on the Argentine side, as well as an unknown amount at Port of Entry in Uruguay, which definitely would add up to $175 or more.

The Uruguayan officials are suspicious of anything and everyone allowed to cross over, so they say. Some have said that many times things that were sent over never arrived, were dumped overboard, lost, or confiscated. So it looked to be a bad risk.

The smart thing was to make the best of the situation and try to go up to Iguazu Falls; anyway, that amount of money would more than take us there. These falls are much wider, but not deeper than Niagara Falls.

Later, when crossing a tributary of the same river, the Rio La Platte, 40 miles up from Buenos Aires, going through canals and staying on the Argentine soil, it only cost $2.50 in American dollars. It took five hours crossing, same as near Buenos Aires, which shows the inconsistency of the whole situation.

There was a pretty good feeling about going this way, as there were so many interesting things to see—the ferry had cut across delta land where natives living in grass huts along the canal were seen doing reed and raffia work. There were many birds of all colors and descriptions seen in their natural habitat, clustered in trees or winging their way in formation in and out of the forests and near the boat.

Saw the planted Alamos forests in all stages of production, from freshly planted seedlings, trimmed sucklings and limbs, to cutting timber being barged down the river to the pulp mills.

The crude dock facilities and this, the people's only mode of transportation, was adjoining these canals, and the boats would stop and take on or let off passengers and cargo.

People looked clean and wholesome, and most of them were wearing casual clothes, such as shorts and gay colored dresses. They were mostly barefoot and some were rowing on the river in dinky little canoes or sitting under arbors sipping mate tea with bombilla straws from gourds.

There were dogs, cats, monkey, parrots, chickens, ducks and geese all over these little shack-like places, seemingly living a carefree existence out of doors.

Disembarked at Port Constanza about seven o'clock, then a short drive to Gualeguaychu, where there was found a nice hotel for the night. All along the highway coming into town, we had passed many truck drivers who had first preference in getting off the boat. They had been very friendly on the boat, but had seemed hurt when we refused to taste or drink their mate with them as they sat near us on the boat; however, as the car would come over the hills, and they would see us in their side mirrors, they would move over and wave and honk us by in the friendliest fashion. All truck drivers down in South America are a splendid breed of men—they have helped out many more times than one could possibly remember to mention.

The boat purser was also exceedingly nice and explained, in a subtle way, that he would like to practice his English. He said he had been in the United States many years ago, for a short time, and had found the Americans very kind to him.

He took it upon himself to explain in a most convincing and friendly fashion why Peron wanted to keep the Argentineans out of Uruguay. First, he said, "There are so many beautiful and wonderful places here in our own country—Cordoba, Mendoza, Bariloche, Llao Llao, Iguazu Falls, all of the National Huapi Park region, Mar del Plata, and many other places for the Argentineans to see, and they should see their homeland first."

Then he said many people criticized Peron, but Peron lived for the common people. He said, "Look what he's done for the worker." He explained that a worker can't be fired if he's been with a business firm one month or more, without getting an extra month's wages, if dismissed. He gets two weeks vacation—he gets a month vacation if he has been with the firm long enough.

He bragged about opera houses, dance halls, and picture shows having to play 50 percent Argentine music or they will close the establishments, which gives the native Argentineans a chance to sing their own songs, write their own books—this also applies to painting their own pictures.

He said the country is in much better shape than Chile, Bolivia, Peru, or Brazil. Not once did he say they were better off than Uruguay. Little Uruguay is in better shape politically, financially, and with better roads all over the country, and with all of the waterfront, marvelous sandy beaches, than any of the other South American countries.

Montevideo and other coastal towns of Uruguay have suffered considerably over Peron's attempt to keep Argentine people out of the country, as many of the resort hotels are closed and will stay closed all year, as a result. Uruguay has miles upon miles of wonderful beaches, while Argentina, with the exception of Mar del Plata, has almost no beaches whatever in a warm zone, and the Argentineans must have missed these beaches as much as Uruguay has missed having the Argentineans come over.

The pursuer went on to say, "Peron is a smart man and is trying to keep his people at home in order to build up the economy of the country. The country is in better shape now than it has ever been in past history."

The following morning, traveling north, made it in to Concordia by noon, with hopes of crossing the river into Uruguay at that spot. A telegram to the Dealy boys, seen in Buenos Aires, lead us to believe the Constantines were going to try to cross there.

All the way through this part of the country, it was very warm; but being busy viewing the lovely countryside and seeing and watching the habitation of the place, the heat was of secondary importance.

Palm trees predominated over the landscape and broom wood was magnificent in yellow bloom. Many species of birds were to be seen fluttering near the car—one time a game of hide and seek was played with some yellow breasted blackbirds.

While driving along, a funny continuous noise of tweet, tweet, chatter, a sort of laugh, then squeaking calls, could be heard following the car. After continued gawking and searching, by lowering our heads we found the flock of birds in formation about three feet above the top and following the car.

When the car stopped suddenly, the birds made a circle and came back to the car and seemed to stand in flight until the car was started again, then again they kept up with the car. This was tried out several times and each time they would make that circle and start again. It was most amusing.

Then a drove of ostriches came into view, racing to keep up with the car, and a game of trying to outrun them distracted our thoughts from the smaller birds.

There were condors, vultures, flamingos, and partridges by the thousands; iguanas, snakes and long tailed lizards were plentiful. At times there could be heard the bark and chattering of monkeys in the underbrush.

The armadillos took their time in crossing the road; scared rabbits would leap out of the way; and it was a simple matter of smell to know that skunks were near at hand.

There were long snouted pig looking animals, one didn't dare get out of the car through this section, for fear they were wild hogs. One time a wild cat perched on a tree limb and looked like it would jump on top of the car, so the window was hurriedly raised when passing the cat.

On arrival at Concordia, it was found it would cost as much to cross there as at Buenos Aires, unless we could see the right man, and we would have three hours to wait before he would be back at the docks. Since the possibilities of getting across were so slim, it was decided to go on to Pasa Los Libres and be that much nearer the Iguazu Falls.

The roads from there on up to the falls were supposed to be very good, unless there was a hard rain. On to Chagari, which was made in good time. The filling station there said the roads were *malo* going north.

Paying little attention and acting as though we were going on, he insisted on taking us to see an Englishman who brought cattle there to interpret for him.

This Englishman was hard to take seriously with his "rath-er," "carry on," "You'll jolly well have a tough time of it"—typically English in voice and pronunciation of words, but dressed gaucho from the crinkled boots, the big baggy pleated, checked pants, red kerchief, coiled rawhide whip rolled and tied to his belt, to the flat topped sombrero. The contrast in looks and talk made the situation a laughing matter.

He said the station man was trying to tell us the roads were extremely bad and insisted on taking us a short way out of town to prove his point. Now the road, being so near the town, with some traffic, had dried up considerably.

After talking it over, it was decided to chance it on north, rather than stay in such a dinky hole for three or four days, as he said we should do. So, against that advice, we went four or five miles out on a good highway where the inspection officials refused to fix our papers and told us we would have to turn back.

We did turn back a couple of miles to where some young men were fishing from a bridge. We asked them to go back with us to the custom officials and help us get our papers fixed—which they did. These men tried to get us to wait until the next day, at least, but determination kept us going on.

About five miles further on, this horrible gumbo mud got on the tires and would cling there until they were covered to the fenders, when the car would stop and could go no further until the mud was scraped in big chunks off the fenders, tires and bumpers, with a walking cane carried in the car—then with so much less mud, the car would start out again.

An old Chevrolet car, with small tires, came along and in a short while got in front of the Cadillac, and it was surprising how well the tire treads from the Chevrolet helped the larger car along. The car seemed to take the road much better when going faster. But finally the Chevrolet got way ahead—knowing the road to have a deep, muddy hole, they had bobbed out of it and onto the grass to side of the road for some distance.

Getting into this unusually deep mud hole, we got stuck and could go no further. It was a horrible spot. The car was bogged knee-deep all around and to try to just get out of the car to look the situation over, we would have to literally wallow in that mud. It was about sundown. There we sat in the middle of the road, blaming ourselves for not listening to the Englishman.

A can of tuna fish, an apple, and a pear was the evening meal. Then preparing the car for sleeping in each seat, as darkness fell, we turned in. Earl slept and snored long and peacefully, but half the night I reproached myself for being so fool headed, and not believing these people.

So many times in the past people had said we could not get through places which trucks were going through, it was easy to believe this was just another one of these fantastic tales to keep us in this small town for a few days.

This was broad, open pampa country. It looked to be hundreds of miles from anywhere. It was logical to think one would have to stay there in a mess like that for days.

There was only one can of tuna left, two apples and a pear, and only a fourth of a jug of water. We were least prepared for this experience than anyone up to now.

Sheep, horses and cows were milling in pastures, and gave one the courage to believe that a house was not too far away. Lying there in the car, a million fireflies kept us company. They were the largest and most unusual ones we'd ever seen.

There was a definite glow in the center, then a circle with continuous lighter glows, nearly the size of saucers. They seemed to stand still or move very slowly like distant stars. It gave one the feeling of being lost in space.

Finally, a herd of sheep rushing by broke the spell and all the fireflies scattered for a hideaway, all but one bobbing up and down by the car window as if to say, "When you gotta glow, you gotta glow."

Then the rain came, heavy and depressing. There was a certainty we were lost for days. No human would venture out in this muck. As it continued to rain, it seemed the car was bogging down deeper and deeper in the mud. The water was now swirling up in a lake surrounding the car.

Such an experience finds one talking to one's self, and promising if ever this situation is gotten out of, they will listen to advice from then on.

Morning finally came, in clear, dazzling beauty, and there was spied, on a distant hill, a tiny house nestled behind an avenue of trees. It was decided to lock the car and walk to the place.

On the way the mud was so deep we bogged down, fell down, and lost our shoes many times in the sticky mire. We looked awful and felt worse, but kept pepping ourselves on with talk about the nice breakfast these country folk were going to give us when we arrived at the farmhouse.

Climbing the hill and starting up the long road through the trees, many colorful birds swung down around us and chattered and sang continuously. A great big, black and red bird, with most ferocious bill, would swoop down at a dangerous angle, perch himself on a low limb, then sail to the highest treetop and fuss as if to say we were interlopers in that neck of the country.

Continuing on, there was to be seen a large outlay of houses; one with wiring similar to radio lines. There was a large truck loaded with gasoline drums, a couple of water towers, horses saddled and tied to posts.

Dogs began barking and rushed out growling. One with a half circle on his left hip and a band of white around his neck—a collie, the spitting image of a dog once owned and named Lindy, blunt nose and all—came whimpering up in a friendly fashion. It was enough to make creepers run up and down one's spine to see, in another land, a dog which looked so much like our son's dog.

Surely these people would take care of our needs, and having worked up such an appetite in imagination, what was seen was such a complete letdown, it will never be forgotten.

Two of the better looking homes were closed and boarded up, but we followed where the dogs led, over to the side of this open plaza, where a group of men, barefoot, were sitting around a table on an open porch.

Cold and wet though we were, the tromped rank mud and filthy odors were hard to stomach as we stood and watched these people savagely giving all their attention to a large, half-cooked animal on a big board in the center of the table.

Each man had a knife, larger but similar to Boy Scout knives, and was slicing off big hunks of bloody meat and literally gobbling it down. There was no bread, nothing on the table but the meat. Women and children and dogs were standing around looking wistfully for the smallest crumb, it seemed.

They did not pay us the least bit of attention until they had scraped the meat clean and given the bones to the dogs. One dog jumped on the table and started licking the blood, but was cuffed off.

Then and only then one of the men came over and stood nearby and just looked at us without saying a word. Using the conversation book, we tried to explain that the car was stuck in the mud several miles back and asked if he would bring two oxen to pull the car out.

From where we were standing on this hill, there could be seen in the distance what looked to be a ribbon like new gravel highway and, with many hand motions and all the Spanish words that would come to us, we tried to convey to these men if they would get us to that point, it sure would help us out. This fellow nodded assurance as he motioned to the other men to follow him.

We started walking back to the car through pastures. In the meantime, these fellows got on horses and started down the lane to the car. It was terribly upsetting seeing these men ride off on horseback; the thought was they could never get the car out of that mud with horses.

But when we got to the car, they already had rawhide ropes tied to the car and fastened to the belly bands of the saddles and were just waiting to get the motor going. Those three horses pulled that car just like a sleigh, through the watery mire for about five miles.

These men were real, down to earth, gauchos—they wore old baggy, pleated pants, flat topped hats, and crinkled leg boots were tied to the saddles to keep out of the mud. Two were barefoot, one in sandals. They were so kind and grateful for 10 peso notes (equal to 30 cents each), and they bowed very low in thanks.

This new gravel road, which was fenced in, had been deliberately cut with wire pincers they carried to let the car through. It was a strange feeling not to know for sure where we were going, but we cared less as long as we could stay on this gravel road.

After half an hour's driving, we came to another fence across the road, and big construction machines, with men in attendance, were nearby. A German speaking fellow came up and said no one was supposed to be on this road and said for us to turn back—but we refused, saying we were tourists, lost, and didn't know where we were going.

We insisted he should cut the fence wires to let us through, but with much gesticulation, he refused. He finally made us understand that if we would deliberately go through a large ditch by the side of the road, he would have a tractor pull the car to the other side. After much deliberation, it was decided to do that, rather than go back. The car almost turned over in making the slide, at a cross angle, as the ground was so terribly wet and muddy.

After a half-mile stretch we continued on a muddy and slick road, one time turning the car completely sideways on a high embankment, with big lakes of water on either side of the road. It was too dangerous to try to steer the car without help, as it could have easily slid into the water.

A gaucho on horseback came along and righted the car, with the help of two natives to hold the car on either side; then a doctor came along on a Ford—the Ford was a 1918 deluxe model, all brass shining through the mud, wire wheels, narrow rubber tires, with an old-fashioned canvas top.

He offered to push the Cadillac after the car was righted in the slush, and it was amazing to see that little bantam Ford push the big heavy car through the deeper section of slush and mud to the top of the hill and the better drained road. But no sooner did the Cadillac get into a valley of muck and it would have to be pushed again.

Finally arrived at the small village of Mt. Caseros, where the doctor led us to a large, ugly looking hotel, but we were thankful to be there. Anything was better than the middle of a muddy road.

The hotel turned out to be much more attractive inside than it looked outside, and the owners outdid themselves to make us comfortable. This hotel formed a large square of buildings with beautiful flowers blooming in the enclosed patio. The flowerbeds were in the shape of two perfectly formed stars—made of small rocks put together with cement. From the center of each grew large grapevines, supported by wire netting at the rooftop to hold the branches and clusters of grapes hanging down, also giving shade to a great portion of the enclosure. This made the place restful and cool appearing.

Most of the meals were very good. They did serve raw ham and blood bologna as an entrée, which was hard to stomach as it hung outside in the open air all the time with flies covering it. Before each meal, they could be seen slicing the thin slivers with a knife. Most of the gauchos ate it with gusto. There were many men marooned there due to the heavy rains.

The car created a lot of excitement for the small town—people gathered around it in droves. A good number of the men were allowed to drive the car. It being the first Hydramatic car they had ever driven, they would beam with admiration when they didn't have to shift gears and would say, "How you say *marvillaso, esplendoroso, neto, fino?*"

When we first arrived in town it was raining, but we took the car down to the garage and asked them to wash it—especially did we want to get all the gumbo from underneath. I'm sure everyone thought it extravagant or crazy from the way men, women and school children hung around and gawked at us. But the car was much lighter and easier to handle after it was cleaned.

The garage man drove us back to the hotel when we discovered we had lost two one-hundred peso bills. He drove us in a new, late Chrysler car from the United States. He was asked how he went about getting the car, and he said he had to go to the Peron government to get a permit.

He got out the papers, which he had in the glove compartment, and showed where he had paid 174,000 pesos for the car. In other words, he had paid $6,000 for a car that ordinarily would have cost him about $3,000 in the States—so Peron and the Argentine government seem to be in the car business in South America, and they let those, who can and will pay the price, have cars.

It rained all day Saturday and Sunday morning. Thoughts of being marooned there for a month made the situation glum; however, late Sunday evening a stiff breeze blew in. On Monday morning they said the roads had so completely dried from the wind that it was safe to start north again.

A radio salesman staying at the hotel insisted on going with us to Las Libres. We reluctantly took him along. He had three suitcases and the car was already packed to the gills. But he kept insisting that he knew the roads well and could help out.

Near Curuzo Cuatio he directed us onto the wrong road and the car got stuck again. After a couple of hours wait, we finally got out with the help of another gaucho who came along on horseback. He tied a rope to the back of the car and the belly band of a huge saddle on a big raw-boned hose and pulled the car backwards out of the gumbo mud.

This gumbo mud is different than any mud ever seen before; it can be picked up in the hands and it sticks and clings to the hand as if it had glue on it. This mud was difficult to combat and enough was enough of it.

We finally made it back to the main highway. It just wasn't safe to trust these people about their roads—20 miles from home and they didn't know themselves whether the roads were good or bad, or the right roads.

Gasoline was needed in the car and the Argentine pesos were running low, due to the fact that the gaucho had charged so much to get the car out of the mud. And always, when arriving at the border, we tried to have as little of the money to exchange, as they gave very poor rates when making exchanges between countries. So we gave up the idea of going to Iguazu Falls from the Argentine side, but would try it from the Brazilian side.

8

Brazil: October, 1953

Late in the afternoon, after much palavering and a thorough search of luggage, with agents trying to confiscate the typewriter until record of its entry into the country had been found, the Argentine customs was cleared, and the International Bridge was crossed at Uruguayana, Brazil. The Brazilian customs official said, in a gruff manner, that he did not know where American Express checks could be changed into *cruzeros*—that's the name of money in Brazil.

This same customs official, who knew just a few English words, kept saying "nuts" to every statement made; and he repeated it again when told that Argentine officials, in Buenos Aires, had wanted to overcharge to allow us to cross by boat into Uruguay.

After completing customs and getting our papers intact, when ready to leave, we let him have it good and proper. We told him how stupid he sounded—that "nuts" was not a good word to use around American tourists at any time—that he was not giving us the right assistance whatsoever in trying to get through the border. He had tried to take some of the Chilean money that was being kept for souvenirs; he had tried to take a bottle of American bourbon; and he had acted entirely too fresh; and he was going to be reported to the national authorities.

Then we left without further words. He followed the car on a motorcycle quite a way, stopped once right in front of the car, which scared us. He said, "Let me show you to a good hotel." Then he gave us the name of a possible place to cash the travelers checks. It's difficult to understand why he changed so completely after being bawled out.

The hotel had horrible beds, but fairly good food served on large open platters for one to select from. A nice Rumanian couple, with four darling children, one year up, lived there.

At breakfast time these children were all eating bread soaked in coffee—they looked to be healthy, too!

The rainy season had started in Brazil, and head officials of a garage had said it would be impossible to get to the falls in car directly from Uruguayana, but if we would hurry on and get to Port Allegro in two or three days, then on to Curitybo, there was a good road to take back to the falls, which would be much nearer than from Uruguayana.

There were no AAA clubs in the town to get official information from, but this good garage man said the roads were all hard surfaced all the way, which was found to be true and we arrived in Alegrete in fast time with only one incident to slow the car down. A fast running ostrich, in an attempt to outrun car, swerved in front, and after much honking swerved out again; but for a long distance it kept right alongside of the car.

Had lunch at a small hotel, where they served delicious black beans and a sausage dipped in what looked like meal. Then rapidly going on to San Francisco de Assis, noticed a water leak in the radiator of the car and the car was heating up for the first time on the whole trip.

A garage man in Gal Vargas said that upon arrival in Alegrete, to have the pump fixed there, as he didn't have the necessary parts. When he was told we were going in the opposite direction on to Porto Alegre, he said, "It's impossible to get through as the water is four to five feet over the highway, and it will be many days before the stranded buses, trucks, or automobiles can get through."

Rather than stay there in a little town for five or six days, maybe longer, it was decided to try to make it down to Uruguay, as had been originally planned.

The officials had said it would be necessary to go back to Alegrete, then turn south to Livramento; but when, upon arrival at Alegrete, we started south, the road men turned us back again on account of high water.

Back in the city of Alegrete. A tire was getting low and had to stop in the middle of the street to keep from injuring the tire. While trying to pump up the tire, a garage man attempted to fix the water leak. A well-dressed young man came along and asked, in English, if he could help. When he saw the trouble, he suggested taking the car to the General Motors garage, several blocks away. He kept saying his uncle spoke good English and would help us out, and while the tire was being fixed, he would try to locate his uncle.

Several distinguished men came in to the garage. Introduced to us was Dr. Salathiel Santos, the Treasury delegate to the UN from Brazil. The doctor, acting as interpreter, explained that the leak was in the water pump and not the hose, and by keeping the radiator full of water, we could travel the following day without harm, as the garage did not have the necessary parts to repair the pump.

The Chevrolet agent, along with the young man, insisted we have dinner with them at a restaurant where they served meat cooked gaucho fashion, over an open fire. This meat had a wonderful flavor. Then, we had wiener-like sausages broiled on same fire and served dipped into a dry looking, ground substance—looked like cornmeal, but was found to be a white potato root, dried, and ground up.

A hotel room was the next problem. After a long wait, they took us to this room all fixed up with hand embroidered sheets and pillow cases, and large pink towels—not at all like the average hotel linen. The monograms on these linens led us to realize these people had brought in their family linens for our use.

Next morning when we went to the garage for the car, the doctor was there and said he had investigated the roads, and the best way to Uruguay would be through Artigas.

About that time, two men in a large truck came in; they had been over these roads the night before and they said the river to the south was out of banks, and in one spot it would be impossible to cross, as they, in this high, off-the-ground truck, had had to have a bulldozer pull them through.

Being most anxious to get on, and discounting what they had said, we were about to go on, but the doctor did believe these fellows and rather crossly said, "I can't be responsible for you Americans unless you follow my instructions." Then he added, "There is just one safe way for you to get to Uruguay, and that is to go back to Uruguayana and start south from there."

It was a hard decision to turn back the third time, but again we started back. Two flats, due to going so fast, were our next worry, but we were trying to make up for lost time. While having the flats fixed, the garage man said the road south was good and there would be no difficulty in getting through.

Successfully driving about 50 miles south, we approached a large stream of water. We were just waiting, trying to make up our minds to venture into the water when a man in a Chevrolet truck came up. With honking and much motion of hands, he tried to turn us back. He finally got out of the truck and showed us how deep the water was and how high it would come up on the car.

There were many tracks of other cars having gone through and we kept motioning and asking this truck man to go on through and show us the way, which he did, slowly but surely. It was the last chance to get to Uruguay, or any other place, for days if we didn't try. So we plunged in with that thought in mind, going a circular way, as the truck had.

The gasoline tank struck a large rock, but the car made it across, coughing and spitting, but kept going. Driving as fast as it was safe to do, caught up with a large, high bus, and watched it cross a deeper, but narrower stream. The car barely made it across this time, and the water got well up on the floor; but on it went, passing the bus. All the time there was the smell of gasoline, but we were afraid to get out to look for fear we would have to stop.

Arriving at another out of banks stream, which looked less dangerous than the others, it seemed wisest to make a circle and, as the front wheels reached for dry land, the car stopped suddenly and the rear end actually sank further and further in quicksand.

Men working on the road nearby came over to help shove the car out of the water, but it was impossible to budge it. A man with a horse and cart tried to help, but he broke a rope and the back end of his cart.

Realizing the starter was wet, as had happened down near Neuquen, there was nothing left to do but wait. Along came the bus we had passed up. After much persuasion they agreed to pull the car out with the cable they carried. The motor got started again, but each time the bus stopped, the car motor would die.

The bus, with car behind, entered the tiny, little village of Barra de Quarai. The bus man disconnected the car in front of a corrugated iron building and said *otel*. In the meantime, the whole village turned out to see what was going on.

Several men fooled with the carburetor, the battery and the spark plugs, but we kept insisting it was the starter. We jacked up the car to show how to find the trouble. Crawling underneath, found mud packed solid all over the front motor pan part and the starter box.

We kept asking for a *mecánico* and finally one arrived on the scene. He wanted to tinker with the spark plugs and the carburetor, as the others had done, but we literally pulled him down underneath to show him the starter all covered with mud. He acted queer and kept saying something in Portuguese, which could not be understood at all. Then he got up and, without a further word, he left.

This was upsetting, and it was hard to tell whether his feelings had been hurt or what, so kept asking for another mechanic. After having listened to the Spanish language for several months, it had become natural to understand many words said in Spanish, but this Portuguese mixture was so foreign, it was aggravating.

With the help of the people crowded around, the car was pushed into the yard of the hotel, and a dishpan was placed under the leaking gas tank. This looked like the time to give up, with a leaky front and a leaky rear end, and the starter wouldn't work—and 40 miles from nowhere. Those were the bluest moments of the whole trip.

At last we went into this dilapidated looking hotel. We looked at the dirty old cots, arranged row after row, and decided to sleep in the car rather than there.

On the way to the bathroom, there was this brick portion of the hotel, with a perfectly clean and fragrant kitchen. A fine looking, neatly dressed older woman came out to shake hands, and in a charming way she bid us welcome to her abode. She motioned and led us to a sofa and chairs in a neatly appointed sitting room.

There we sat as all these men on the bus filed in, including one negro man with a white wife and two cute children. They all started this *mate* drinking, offering us the first drink. They would add a teaspoon of sugar and boiling water to the small gourd each time it was passed around—everyone using the same straw, the same gourd, just more water and more sugar.

For at least an hour we sat watching and listening to their conversation in Portuguese and Spanish mixture. We could understand some of the Spanish, but the Portuguese was so foreign to our ears, it gave one a frustrated feeling.

In the yard later to watch the sunset and to think and talk about what we should do in the morning. A man came up pushing a wheelbarrow on which rested a bright brass iron bed and a pair of springs. Two girls came in with freshly stacked sheets and pillow cases.

An elderly person came up with an apron full of garden fresh vegetables. Two children came up with bouquets of flowers, and they all seemed to be watching us in a shy way.

As darkness was fading out the reds and pinks of the sky, the lady whom we had seen in the kitchen, came out and took my hand and led us to a room. They had cleaned this room out, taking out all the cots; had borrowed neighbors' beds, mattresses, embroidered sheets and towels—just for us.

A large bouquet of flowers stood on an old-fashioned dresser, and an elaborate washbowl and pitcher was in a little wire rack with fresh bars of soap, toilet paper, and everything as neat as possible for comfort.

A delicious dinner was served, as good as in the better hotels. Several other guests tried to shower us with wine and other drinks, when they saw we had not ordered wine.

Most of the men were typical gaucho with well-polished boots, wide brimmed hats and, in offering us their *mate* drinks and wines, they were trying to make us feel at home.

After a good night's rest, the world looked brighter. First thing next morning, jacked up the car again and for an hour worked cleaning caked mud from around the starter and finally got a spark.

About that time, the *mecánico* of the evening before came walking up with a roll of tools under his arm. At last it was understandable—he had to have certain kinds of tools to do his work—and that's what he was explaining the evening before. He got the starter off right away and found it soaked in water and mud. The gasoline that had leaked from the tank into the pan during the night was used to clean the filth and mud away. He quickly put it all together again and immediately the car started; then filled up with gasoline and water at a station nearby and headed for what we supposed was the ferry, the mechanics going with us.

The most ridiculous situation confronted us—it would be necessary to go down into shallow water to get on the 12-inch improvised boards to this hand paddled boat, not longer than the car, and called a ferry. The water was many feet out of banks and the regular drive to the ferry was under water.

We refused to attempt such a crazy procedure, so after studying the situation over for an hour, asked the custom officials if we could take the car back up on the hill for loading onto the barge, which they agreed to let us try to do, and which was accomplished.

Railroad tracks and houses were underwater, fast running water; and with debris and refuse bobbing up in the muddy current, this hand paddled barge looked to be so small we wouldn't have given a dime for its getting the car across the swift and swollen stream.

9

Uruguay: October 26, 1953

Finally, after two hours of slow progress, going with the stream most of the time, we did arrive in Uruguay, which was immediately on the other side of the river. The next problem was to get the car off the barge and onto dry ground. The barge men maneuvered it into an inlet away from swirling logs, trees; then waded to shore, and with ropes tied around large trees, forced the barge close enough to shore that the boards could be placed from boat to dry land; and they unloaded the car in a hog wallow, grassy pasture. It was necessary to go through ditches, over railroad ties and tracks to get to a road.

During the preliminaries of customs, the nail polish put on the gasoline tank gave way, and the gasoline was leading steadily. We went from one customs official to another official, explaining that we had been turned back three different places in Brazil, and that it had been impossible for us to get the necessary papers to enter the country.

In fact, the AAA book had shown that a visa, or any other form, wasn't necessary as long as we had passports. So finally they let us go, and we rushed to an Esso garage there in Belle Union (Bel-Un) to have the tank repaired. They had to take the tank off a second time before they got all the leaks.

It was four o'clock by then, but the good roads encouraged the thought of traveling on and making up for lost time, even if we had to travel by night.

Salta, a great fishing resort, was reached about dusk and a lovely new hotel was selected. When the hotel manager found we had come such a great distance in the car, he insisted we take a beautiful suite of rooms for the night and begged us to stay two or three days and go fishing, where the dorado, a terrific scrapper fish, is caught under rugged water conditions.

He spent an hour explaining in broken English the heavy tackle lures necessary to catch this gamest of all fish to be found in "sweet" water, but not being very good fishermen, it was not very clear to us.

When trying to cash some Express checks next morning, a group of high school girls came along. They wanted to practice their English. We had lots of fun with them singing songs, talking about the theatre, movie stars, and looking over the car. They were most excited about the trip, then asked many questions about the United States.

Drove hard all that day, just stopping to add water to the radiator about every hour. Many prosperous villages were passed through, and we were greatly impressed by this beautiful, rolling country and the wonderfully smooth roads, for a change.

The red verbena, the white daisies, purple flowers, and the yellow broom weed, covering the sides of the road in masses of color, were unbelievably beautiful—and the blue flax fields had all the appearance of lakes in the distance.

The gleaming white farm homes, or *estancias*—with red tiled roofs, were set within a grove of tall trees. Nearby were orchards of peach, pear, apricot, fig, plum, and grapes. Many of the trees were in bloom. There were well laid out and well tended flower and vegetable gardens.

Gauchos, covered with white fringed, bordered ponchos and wearing white hats—riding sleek, well-trained horses—were numerous on the highway and in the fields, tending the finest looking sheep and cattle.

Such contented prosperity we had not seen anywhere, even in Argentina. There was a happy feeling that we had not missed this beautiful, well-kept, well-groomed land.

Montevideo overwhelmed us with its big buildings and its prosperity. We rushed to the Embassy to find no letters from home, but talked to some good American boys who helped out in getting hotel reservations.

We called on Major Van Horn, whom we had met in Lima. He and his wonderful wife had us out to dinner on Saturday night. They served the best fried chicken, good vegetables, homemade ice cream with strawberries, which brought a nostalgic feeling for the States.

One of the Marines from the Embassy came over that evening to show on a map the best way to go to Brazil. He kept saying, "Don't let them talk you out of going the beach road—it's 150 miles on sand along the edge of the water. The wind has to be right and no one should go it alone, because if something should happen to the car, like getting stuck in the sand, or having a puncture, then you and the car can be lost in the tide."

Montevideo is known as the "City of Roses," and we found it to be just that. One of our first visits was out to the El Prado where there is said to be over 800 varieties. We have never seen anything to equal the magnificent roses blooming in this park, yet one of the policemen in charge said there had been twice that many blooms the week before.

For miles on miles, we followed the Horseshoe Bay Drives around the "Cerro"—a high point to view the rolling waves and clean white windswept beaches. Such beaches! We can understand why the Argentineans liked to spend their vacations in these lovely guest houses along the seaboard.

The city itself has many impressive buildings—the Cathedral, the Banco de la Republica, the historic Cabildo, and the Palacio Salva were outstanding from an architectural standpoint. One could stay there forever, it's so picturesque and charming. It's like New York—one could spend a lot of money there, too.

Since the officials had told about more bad roads to be encountered in Brazil, and since the rainy season was upon them, it seemed wise to get on the way as soon as possible.

They were having a holiday in Uruguay, lasting three days, and it was said there would be much travel on the beach road, so we started north early Sunday morning, stopping in many places to get the news, and did not arrive in Chuy until about noon.

Missed the custom officials as we drove into town and they came after us. Not realizing who they were—being on the border their Spanish is mixed with Portuguese and it is harder to understand—we told them to leave us alone until after we had had our lunch.

They kept hanging around and telling us to follow them, and we could not understand what they wanted unless it was to drive us through the beach road, as so many people had drivers do. Finally, we found a Norwegian who explained to us that we had passed customs, so we changed our tune right away. After fully two hours delay, due to our impudence, we got our papers fixed up.

We started driving around and looking the place over, trying to contact the bus man who was supposed to go the beach road the next morning. Since it was a holiday, the bus man wasn't going, so we drove down to this beach road just to look the situation over.

Several men came down and warned us to not go until the next morning. One fellow kept saying that he would drive the car for 50 pesos—in American dollars that is about $25. Since we had been 14,000 miles over what we had been through, we certainly felt we could drive the beach road without help and dismissed him.

A sightseeing bus came along. We asked the driver if he was going the beach road and he said no. Then a Uruguayan couple in the bus came to the front and asked in English what we wanted. We told them we would like to take the beach road in front of some other car. This couple took us under their wing and asked us to go to their hotel for the night.

All the time we were with them, this man kept trying to persuade us to not go the beach road in our heavy car. He drives over the country a great deal and knows all the roads, and he outlines the road he was sure we could take and get through to Brazil. He has driven through the United States and the American people were so good to him that he felt he must help us out, is what he told his wife when she upbraided him for being so insistent.

He found there would be no bus going over the beach road for two days, due to the holidays, so again he insisted that we might as well drive the other inland road and see the lovely northern countryside of Uruguay, instead of waiting. Then if we should not be able to get through, we could return and go the beach road.

Early next morning made it to Valasquez, Jose Padro, Vereta, to Treinta-Y-Trez, then on to Melo. The roads were surprisingly good. Crossed the border at Ecugua, without the least trouble, and started over what was supposed to be a very bad road.

10

Brazil: November, 1953

At one spot a small boy waded the stream and showed us just where to go, otherwise we might have gone into a deep hole as a car coming toward us did. Arriving at Eage about four o'clock, we were making such good time and getting over the roads so well, it looked foolish to take out so early, so we continued on to Cacapava de Sul, then drove hard through Lavars de Sul over beautiful rolling country—up one hill and down the next into lovely grasslands—saw attractive farms covered with fine cattle—all the countryside was wonderful to behold.

We got our towns mixed up and thought we had to make Cochoerra de Sul for a good hotel, which we did just at dark, only to find we had passed up a good hotel at Lavars de Sul and there were no hotel accommodations anywhere in this town, as a carnival was playing there.

A young student of English from the Methodist College at Santa Maria tried to help out and find a place for the night, with no luck. She and her mother did show the way out of town.

Being rather tired, we decided to pull by the side of the road and sleep in the car until daylight. Awakening with the first crack of dawn, found we had slept within a short distance of a home. Chickens were crowing and cackling, dogs barking, and all other activities of the farm sprang to life very quickly, so there was nothing else for us to do but arrange the luggage in the car and start traveling.

The countryside was made up of hills and valleys, with quaint, small villages nestled between; and pastel colored churches, with spires gleaming in the morning sun, adding to the beauty of the land each time we climbed to the top of the hills and looked down. The highway, if one could call it a highway, had had very poor engineering to mention, and was one continuous up and down ride like the Shoot-the-Chutes at the fairgrounds.

We had been traveling for two hours or more when, on one of these downgrades, we had a blowout. Things happened so fast one can't be sure about anything, but the car must have swerved to the right when a deep canyon was seen on the left. The car had gone over many rocks and bounced against the side of a rock cliff.

In a short time, two cars and a truck came along. There was not a person in the group who could speak English, but the men changed the tires, and with long cables the truck men tied the car to the truck and pulled us in to a small village nearby.

Taking off the front bumper, lights, and other portions of the demolished part, temporary repairs were made. With the aid of the American Consulate at Porto Alegro, whom we had phoned for help, we found a good doctor who had us feeling able to travel again, after a week's rest.

The accident had made us low on tires, but we hated to buy such expensive ones in Brazil, as we had in mind a complete set of new whitewalls when we returned home. It was decided to risk those left and make it on to Rio, as we were to be in thickly populated country and on good roads.

We left Porto Alegre and started east on a Saturday morning, after Mr. Moncrief of the Consulate brought us our money. He got us 48.5 cruzeros for our dollar—not so bad! We had 3,000 cruzeros in our pockets, surely enough to get us to Sao Paulo.

Realizing how low we were on tires, we were going to go very slow for that reason, and on account of the terrible up and down hill condition of the roads of Brazil—we had learned the hard way that to get a puncture on a downgrade was almost suicide. There are no roads in all of South America as dangerous as these. If a tire went out and you should skid on loose gravel, a hairpin curve on a deep descent could very well be disastrous.

The supposed good roads going north turned out to be terrible. About 50 miles out of Porto Alegre we had to creep along less than 15 miles per hour on account of the large gravel rocks in the road.

On the back right rear of the car was a tire that was more than six years old. If one could have composed an ode to a tire, it should have been done so that day as we wheeled our way along.

That tire, if it could have talked, could have told fantastic tales; it, with three others like it, was bought for a 98 Olds six years before. When we traded for this new car, we had kept the old tires because they were heavy duty, white walls, and we would rather have them than have all new black ones.

That tire had led the way all through the Rockies of the USA, the Grand Canyon, Brice and Zion Canyons, the Tetons, Yellowstone Park, Glacier National Park, then into Canada through Banff, Lake Louise, Kicking Horse Trail, the Big Bend Canyon Road and down to Vancouver—then Washington State and the Columbian River Road, the Pacific Coastal trip from Oregon to La Jolla, California, and the Salt River Canyon pass back to Texas.

And think of all the going it had made in Europe—a complete coastal circle of England, Ireland and Scotland; crossing the Dover Strait to Belgium and Holland; making a circle trip of Germany to the Czechoslovakian border, Munich and down into

Austria; the Brenner Pass into Switzerland, Geneva, Interlocken and through the Simplon Pass.

Then into Italy—Milano, Lake Como, Venice, Florence, Rome and magnificent Vesuvius, Naples, and the Amalfa Drive; backtracking up to Rome again, following the Mediterranean to Genoa, Cannes, Monte Carlo to Marseilles; through France to Paris; through the castle country to Limoges; and back again to beautiful Paris.

From there over the Memorial Highway to Luxembourg, then to La Havre, and embarking for New York; the Pennsylvania Turnpike, the awe-inspiring Courley Mountain Drive, the Ozarks of Arkansas, and into Texas again.

New tires had been contemplated while planning the trip to South America, but after looking them over carefully, it was decided there was too much good rubber in them to throw away, and we had been told that we could get good tires in South America, cheaper than in the United States.

With two spares it seemed safe enough. But the hot, pitted roads through Venezuela and Columbia took their toll on those tires, and at Pasta, Columbia, as has already been mentioned, four new tires and four inner tubes were put on the car, saving three of the better whitewalls for spares. It's easy to see one of our main worries was over tires from now on.

After getting sidetracked about the tires, let's get back to Curitibo, which was the next town of importance on the agenda. It reminds one of an overgrown boy that has grown out of his britches. It is a busy, thriving lumber town, with sawmills and logging camps nearby.

Dozens of huge, dangerous lumber trucks were seen every hour of day and night, swerving around bends in the road and gouging out big holes on the highway, and this has added to the hazards of driving and made our progress very slow.

After leaving Curitibo, we got on a road being repaired and the winding curves being straightened out. The construction people were filling the holes with large granite rocks. These large rocks, sharp and hard as flint, if driven over fast, could do great damage to tires, so going slowly and carefully had been our slogan.

We came to a place where large machinery stationed nearby had broadened a section of mountain to a wide curve, but was a one-way road. Deep mud and slush looked to be all that was necessary to go through, which was done with a running start for fear the car might get stuck—when ping! went the right rear tire. There went the last good tire in the rear.

Fortunately, we were in front of many cars; in just a few minutes all kinds of trucks and cars with people were lined up behind and they helped change the tire. In this deep mire, the last spare was put on—this spare had been run on too long, and the cords had been broken. An extra inner tube had been added to serve as boot. We doubted if it would go five miles.

It was 25 miles to Capao Bonito. We hoped as long as we could keep all these trucks and cars behind us, we surely wouldn't be left stranded, as darkness was closing in fast.

Arriving in the small village of Guapiara, we tried to find the right size tire for the car, but found it impossible, so we had to have the old tire repaired the best it could be with a boot.

A couple from Rio, who spoke English, had been following us in a Buick car. They had offered us 1500 cruzeros, or as much as we needed to buy a new tire. They said they would make reservations for us at the hotel in Capao Bonito, but needed to get on an account of their little two-year-old girl. Everyone else passed us up, as we slowly made our way along, and we practically held our breath with every turn of the wheel, until we got into the small town.

The Rio people were actually waiting for us and had saved us a room. A very good dinner of liver, barbecued beef, black beans, mixed salad, rice, potatoes, and delicious squash pickled like we pickle beets—with green onions and parsley sprinkled over it—it's called *Xu Xu*—then for dessert, pressed fruit with cheese and coffee.

These different kinds of fruit—peaches, pears, guavas, apricots—are pressed into a large slab and can be sliced just as cheese. A little bit of fruit and white cheese, similar to cottage cheese, but drier, picked up with fork and eaten together, is very tasty.

In the hotels in smaller towns, the food is bountifully served on large platters and dishes, boarding house style, and one could make their own selections of food.

Everyone tried to see how nice they could be to us, including a Dutchman who wanted our Express checks at 42.0 cruzeros, when the American dollar was worth 40.0 the day before. Several men from the United States came in and ate, spoke to us, then rushed on in the night to Sao Paulo and the better hotels.

The next morning the hotel man cashed our travelers checks at 50.0 cruzeros. We gave up trying to find a tire for the car, so the only thing left to do was to drive slowly on in. Everyone had advised the road through Itapetininge was the better road, which proved true, and the small city was well worth seeing.

All of this country is very lovely with its rolling hills, its small villages in the valleys with the church spires pointing heavenward. Then there would be magnificent stretches of dense forests—many of the trees were in bloom, and scattered through all of the undergrowth were the umbrella pine trees standing straight and very tall.

There just can't be enough said about the lovely, freshly painted, pastel, gingerbread Victorian churches of these communities along the highway. It would have been a great stunt to have made colored film of these churches to put in an album to show the different, delicate shades, and the varied types of architecture, with never two just alike, but to be seen every few miles along the way.

There was an exceptionally good highway at Saracabo, and it was easy sailing into Sao Paulo by noon, without the least bit of difficulty other than to be stopped by the police several times to explain the bunged-up condition of the car.

At Porto Alegre the police had given us a card, giving permission to proceed to Rio and explaining the accident. If anyone had been hurt in this accident, or if we hadn't had the card, there's no telling just what they might have done—probably put us in jail.

The city of Sao Paulo was a complete surprise. We never realized it was so big and spectacular with its up and down hills, its bridges and different levels of business houses, its roar of traffic with so little regard for the pedestrian walking in every direction, disregarding lights and signals.

After spending about an hour going through the baffling network of one-way streets, we finally reached the Sao Paulo Hotel. It took a couple of hours to get baths and clean the mud off of shoes and clothes and put on our best summer suits—it was as hot as the summers in Texas.

Then had the car washed to get the mud off and make it drive lighter, and to give it a little better appearance—then drove out to General Motors.

We asked to be admitted at the gates and drove down to the general offices, where we were ushered into the office of the general manager. Asked if he would like to see a Cadillac car that had been driven 14,000 miles from Venezuela to Sao Paulo.

He said, "Wait a minute, I want our public relations man in on this." Knowing the condition of the South American roads, these men seemed amazed that a Cadillac could make it through these roads. They were most interested in hearing about some of the unusual experiences of the trip and took pictures of the car and us with Mr. Fouse, the public relations man, in one of the pictures. They were, indeed, very nice to us.

These officials wanted to entertain us on the 13th of November, and we should have liked to stay over, but the ship *Del Monte* had just left Santas and was expected in Rio for several days of taking on cargo, and we were hopeful of getting passage on it to New Orleans, if we rushed on to Rio.

Our experiences on the 11th of November were pretty sad. The hotel clerk, who spoke English, when asked to park the car for the night, said there were several parking places to choose from around the hotel. It sounded like he was indicating the large, open lots in front of the hotel.

So without taking the hotel porter along to show the way, we just drove on to one of these lots. The parking man, speaking only Portuguese, did not understand this parking was for the night.

Anyway, by morning there was just the one car left on the lot and a large rock had smashed a window. Overcoats, shoes, alligator bags and belts, ponchos and many smaller gifts from Peru, Chile, and Argentina had been taken.

The greatest loss of all were the many sketches made from highways and the snowcapped mountains of Chile, along with large assorted boxes of colors, canvas boards, and paper.

The first thought was to rush to the Consulate offices for help, but everything was closed up there due to the holiday, November 11, Armistice Day. Then we reported to the police, leaving name, hotel, and list of things taken. Since they had only a skeleton crew for the day, all they did was smile, grin and say, "Okay, okay, we see."

Tired and weary yet from the shock of the accident, homesick, by then getting a boat home was uppermost in our minds. The car was put in an inside and closed garage for the next night, and the following morning, after servicing the car, before starting to Rio, found the apron shield on rear left was gone; evidently it had been taken off in the garage during the night. There was an uneasy feeling that everything we had, including the car itself, would be stolen if we didn't get out of the place.

Some of the finest eating places to be found anywhere were at Sao Paulo. We tried out several of the most famous places, one on a roof overlooking the city and at night it was certainly a gorgeous sight. The pepper and cognac steaks were well worth the extra cost to see them so beautifully prepared on a grill by the table.

Under normal circumstances, Sao Paulo would be an interesting city to live in, was the consensus of opinion; but being numb with worry over losing so many things, it was difficult to enjoy the place, without thinking of the loss.

Many people had tried to forewarn us that we needed to watch money, car and luggage in Brazil. The warning certainly proved true. It seemed like every time change was needed, there would always be a short-change of from 10 to 50 cruzeros, and invariably we would have to call the people down.

Even the hotel clerk had advised us to be most careful about counting our money; and then the hotel bill, when presented, showed an error of 50 cruzeros. It was exasperating, but what could one do about it? When called to their attention, they would apologize, shrug shoulders, shell out the extra cruzeros, then go on about their work.

Arrived in Rio on the 13th, after being stopped by the police many times, but immediately on seeing the card, the police would give us clearance and wave us on.

Soon after entering the city, a motorcycle policeman was asked the way to the Embassy—he saluted and said to follow him. In a very short time, we arrived in front of this spectacular edifice with barely enough white stones to hold it together.

The straight up and down structure was mainly blue and green glass windows—glass completely predominated over the entire building, even the doors of the front are of glass.

The top floor is most interesting with round blue portholes effect on top and on top of that a sunshade painted dark blue. It's ultra modern and the last word in glass. It would be one jumbled mess if an earthquake should happen along.

Went out to Copacabana Beach to get hotel rooms—we just couldn't stand the noise of the city—and parking the car was a big problem in town. The plan had been to stay at the Copacabana Palace Hotel and really celebrate the arrival in Rio, if and when we should ever arrive there, but the hotel prices were staggering and nothing extra to speak of, so decided to try the California, a fairly new and smaller hotel, very near the finer hotels.

The General Motors people in Sao Paulo had already made reservations for us there. So things worked out very well. Our $4.50 room with bath was extra nice and included continental breakfast. It had beautifully toned walls with matching drawn drapes, and a lovely painting of the flower market place in the city. It was a good thing this was a back room, as the water pounding and rolling in on the beach was plenty noisy, even back there.

There's no other city in the world just like Rio with its peninsulas, beaches, mountains, and islands—and its Sugar Loaf and Corvado.

No exploring or sightseeing was on the agenda

the first day—thoughts and time were taken up trying to find reservations for home. At that time of the year and in Rio, reservations are booked solid.

Went first to Delta, but they had nothing sure until the 19th of December. That put a crimp in us—to think about being on the sea on Christmas Day.

Moor McCormick next said they would have to wire for reservations at Santos and possibly would have a place for us on the *More McDale*, which would arrive Monday, but there was so much red tape to go through, they were sure the papers for the car could not be fixed up in so short a time.

The reply was, "You get the reservations through and we'll show you that we do get the papers fixed up." The difficulty we were letting ourselves in for was never dreamed of.

Friday at noon they phoned that the reservations were okay. Went to the Touring Club to get the car papers fixed; got in the wrong place, but quickness there probably saved us from losing the rest of our trunks in the car. We were just in time to see two fellows opening up the car—we don't know how, as it was locked. We yelled for the police.

Guards and people crowded around. It would have been useless to file complaints, and there's no idea what these fellows said to the officers—the simples thing seemed to just drive away.

At the Auto Club they said they couldn't possibly get the papers fixed to leave Monday morning, as it was necessary to get the president of the Bank of Brazil to prepare the export license for the car and us.

Then the chief of police had to check records to see if tickets had been given for over-parking, wrecks, or injury to anyone—he was required to sign a statement saying we had a good record.

On top of all this, Saturday was a holiday. It sure looked hopeless. Such a frustrated, helpless feeling that Auto Club gave one—shrugging us off as though we had no rights whatsoever, they said it would be utterly impossible to get on that boat on Monday.

Then, exploding, we said everything had happened to us in Brazil—a wreck, loss of clothes, tires ruined, and not once had the Auto Club helped us out; and if they didn't get the papers fixed to get on that boat on Monday, they would sure hear from the international Automobile Club organization.

This emergency sent us hurrying to the Consulate where the Vice-Consul was told the trouble, and he acted just like an old sorehead. He turned us down flat, saying they were short of men and they couldn't furnish interpreters for Americans on pleasure jaunts in South America.

We asked what he was doing there, if not to help Americans in distress, then turned around and stalked out. A Marine from Georgia had heard this conversation and he, in turn, bawled the Consulate out.

"That's no way to talk to American citizens—they are just an old couple trying to get home by Christmas, and we should do everything to help them," he was heard to say as we stood outside the door and listened.

Then we decided to go to the Ambassador, having a clerk call up for an interview. They received us at once. Mr. James Kemper sent Mr. Van Fleet, a nice young man, out to ask what they could do for us.

He was told we were having trouble getting the papers fixed for the car to be brought back to the

States, and we felt sure they could break through the red tape somehow and get these papers fixed so the car could be put on the ship on Monday.

He, with his secretary, a cute Brazilian, started the ball rolling by phoning the president of the Auto Club, the president of the Bank of Brazil, and the chief of police, and they all said they would prepare the papers the following morning if we would be at the Auto Club at 8:30 to meet a Consulate employee, a Portuguese, who would go with us and act as interpreter.

Before noon the following day, the papers were in order and everything was all set for Monday embarkation. Then, and not until then, could we comfortably take in the city and drives. About that time it started raining, which dampened our spirits considerably.

It was foolish to drive the winding road up to Corcovado and other high points, unless the views could be seen. The beach roads were followed endlessly. Many churches were seen—the church Nossa Senhoro I Glorio de Outeiro, with its bible scenes in blue tile, was worth the time. Then we drove up and down one street after another, all over the city, in the rain, just to be sure not to miss anything in this most unusual city.

It's the darnedest place in all the world to drive—the wildest, loudest, and craziest! The pedestrian is sued if he gets run over—no kidding! Cars didn't miss us by a breath several times when crossing pedestrian walks.

Another thing that was provoking was the 700 cruzeros the Automobile Club required to get the papers fixed up. That was nothing but highway robbery. They made the excuse that it was to pay for dock work, but we had to pay 250 cruzeros extra for that upon arrival at the docks.

Of all the countries we've ever been in, this is the biggest highjacking spot on earth; 35% of the people work for the government—not for the small salaries, but for the grafting on the side, so they say.

It rained all day Sunday, but we kept right on exploring in the car; the parks are wonderful with thousands of tropical plants from all over. We visited unique residential sections of ultra modern designs, where there were flowers overhanging fences and trees, of every description, bloom in patios and open yards. There was one tree that attracted our attention—the bloom looked like honeysuckle and the odor was like honeysuckle, but it was so much larger than the vine honeysuckle in the States.

At Sears and Roebuck we milled around, bought several gold items much more reasonable than could be found elsewhere.

Hoping the rain would clear before sailing, so some of the high drives could be made, kept us exploring all the day in the low places. Some of the most unusual shops, with every kind of trinket in the world—gems, geegaws, novelties and such filled the shops—jewelry is worn in gobs on arms and fingers—large cut stones of amber and amethyst seem the most worn.

On Saturday lunched at the Excelsior Hotel where the food was wonderful and the service excellent. On Sunday we put on our best clothes and had dinner at the Copacabana Palace, supposed to be the most outstanding and exclusive eating place in the city. It was good food, but cost plenty, and the flies were having a celebration, too; no screens—it's surprising.

A letter of credit from the American Express Company of the United States had been held in reserve for passage home. The American Express Company of Brazil refused to cash it, saying there were only two banks in Rio who could handle the money.

Now, these banks would cash it okay, but not at the exchange rate of the regular money exchange shop (*cambios*) 50 cruzeros to the dollar, so there was another gyp in this gyp land.

Early Monday morning this exchange was made of as small amount as possible, and the Ships Company was paid for the tickets. The car had to be turned over to the Ships Company that day, to be checked by officials when the emigration or exit papers were filled out and signed, and the passports stamped.

Then the passage home looked sure enough that one could relax. Then and only then did we feel fancy free to gawk around and see the rest of the city. We tried going on the *lotacao* (taxis) to see the city, but they were so fast and we so slow to read the signs showing where they were going that we finally gave them up and took a regular taxi about town and to Sugar Loaf.

There were some qualms about going up on top of Sugar Loaf in the cable car, but no sooner had the cable started, then all fears vanished. In olden days, sometimes the owner would go off and the people would be stranded in midair for a period of time—sometimes hours.

The view on Sugar Loaf was spectacular, giving a commanding view of the many beaches, the racetracks, the military installations, the city across the bay, and many islands and inlets surrounding this fantastic city built of skyscrapers adjoining tremendous mountains of granite—sometimes so close to the mountain, one could reach out of the window and touch the mountain.

A wonderful boiled fish dinner was enjoyed down at Alba Mar near the fish market, wharf and airfield. There we sat and watched cargo ships, ferries, and airplanes come in. That's the only time one could envy an air traveler, when the airplane comes in on a beautiful day and they get the panorama of so wonderful a harbor, with the granite rocks jutting out all over the harbor, like whales playing leapfrog, or dinosaurs suddenly petrified to granite.

Later in the afternoon, taxied to the cog trains to go up to Corcovado, on the famous high point of which stands the statue of Christ Redeemer. There were marvelous views of the city as the train wound around the mountain, but a drifting cloud had closed in as the top was reached. The long way was rewarded and we finally saw this tremendous statue of Jesus, with arms outstretched—a benign countenance seemed to diffuse itself through the mist.

The clouds played peek-a-boo for a time, but when they did open up in circles, there were these porthole views of the city below, which was well worth the wait, as the first train back down had gone.

As the sun went down, all the clouds seemed to draw away. The stars came out early above, and the twinkling lights of the city, from beach to mountaintops, gave the impression of being in the middle of a tremendous exploding sparkler. Rio was seen at its best!

By night we had walked the serpentine, mosaic walks, so famous the world over; by day we had driven miles upon miles of beaches populated by serious swimmers, wave jumpers, sand diggers, sunbathers, lollers, parasol parasites, readers, walkers, beachcombers.

Every kind of human being, every color and creed on the face of the earth seemed to be mixing together on these beaches, which, with a deep Down South complex, made one sick, in a way. It was hard to face the fact that what looked to be an all white girl was in happy communication and close relationship with a big, strapping black, and vice versa.

One couldn't help but ask questions as to how, when and where all this came about. This was the first part of a country in all of South America where more than half the population seemed to have the color and dominant characteristics of the mixed negro combination. This had not been true of the cities and villages in the south of Brazil, but the farther north one came, the greater the percentage.

On board ship is a fellow passenger, an Irishman from New York, who has lived in this country off and on for the past 30 years. He had a book, which has been translated into English—it's well worth reading and clears up a lot of questions in one's mind—"The Masters and The Slaves: A Study in Brazilian Civilization." If it hadn't been such a long and repetitious sort of essay, it would have been easier to read, but the more one got into it, the harder it was to put down.

It deals with the early Portuguese settlers and the South African negro slaves brought over for them to use in all kinds of export harvesting; also tells of propagating a mixed race of people with Indian natives used for the reproduction of humans for sale as slaves.

These Indian women were used as hatching machines, the masters taking the white Portuguese as wife and the Indian woman concubine or slave at will, all used for the same purpose of breeding. The priests fostered such goings on and the monks were the worst of all in breeding more people into being, and encouraged the worshipping of a pregnant woman—Our Lady of Expectancy.

The long and short of it is that there is such a conglomeration of bloods in the average Brazilian, it's hard to tell what he really is and probably accounts for his being such a forward sort of a person. There's not the least bit of shyness or inhibition in his makeup, due to color; in fact, he's as bold as any completely white person could be.

The percentage of all white is so limited here that one would not risk native born and reared here to be completely all white. It gives one a creepy feeling to see all this; this is a sample of what the whole world could be like a hundred years from now if they don't watch out.

On Wednesday went out in a launch to the ship in the bay—the ship was secured and on its way by midnight, to the good old USA. It sure felt good as the boat took on motion, enough had been seen to last a lifetime, and home was in the offing.

It had been stifling hot as the boat sat there and they were loading coffee from barges—it seemed like enough coffee for the whole world—A&P's name was on most of the sacks. The ship's officers and crewmen were extra nice, giving us the main stateroom where the south and east breezes flowed through the portholes all the way home.

Next morning they anchored at Ilhens to pick

up scads of coco beans. This little village was very artistic from the ship and we would have liked to visit it, and could have, but it would have been necessary to stay all day, not returning until four o'clock when the inspectors would come out again to check the cargo.

It was so beastly hot and the last days in Rio we had walked so much, that we decided the best thing to do was to stay on board ship and rest.

One of the men on the ship lent us his binoculars and we sat or stood on the cool side of the ship and watched the village and bay for hours. There were very few people stirring on the streets, which proves they, too, were respectful of the heat.

What kept our attention most of the time was the launching of these fishing craft from the beaches. These craft are called "Jesus boats" because the fishermen looked to be walking on the water.

Usually, there were three men in close proximity of each other, who would shove these erect poles along in the water, then they looked as though they were treading water at first, and finally there were glimpses of these logs showing they were standing on them.

The logs were laced together with rope, eventually a center pole would go up, on this a sail was hoisted, and then they were gliding smoothly along the water. The large ships sometimes find these men 40 miles out at sea fishing from such craft.

The sharks are supposed to be plentiful in these waters; however, all that could be seen was the playful porpoise in his leapfrog jump up and down; sometimes they would come along the bow of the ship and seem to scratch their sides against it.

The heat was stifling on the ship—it was a relief when, near midnight, they secured everything and got into motion again. Next morning we awakened to find the boat in the Bay of Bahia.

We were so thankful this historic city was on the ship's port of call. One of its main reasons for existence was and is its excellent harbor, but its history is compelling. Regardless of heat, this town must be explored the two days the ship was in port.

It had been said there was a church for every day of the year. Some time was spent trying to count the spires that lifted their points heavenward. The city, lower and upper, was found to be fascinating as the streams of traffic, going by car, elevator, or cable, kept up a constant flow.

The Moor McCormick manager offered his car and chauffeur to drive us over the city. The markets were not busy, as it was Sunday. We did see the market in its dirt and unkempt manner, the local people in flashy garb, carrying baskets full of bread, fruits, or toys on their heads, while walking down streets.

The lovely old buildings dating back hundreds of years were beautiful in Spanish architecture, with much filigree work. The outside of many of the old churches was impressive—the church, San Francisco, is one of the most outstanding of all seen inside. The gold leaf covering the scrollwork throughout is in a wonderful state of preservation, and the lifelike figures, with velvety flesh tones, of angels, and the larger figures of men and women seeming to hold up columns, was most impressive.

Then there was wall after wall of beautiful blue tile in scrollwork design bordering scenes of the bible, seen from iron grill gates leading to an enclosed cloister. When we asked to go behind these locked iron gates and fences to examine these designs more closely, the monk in attendance said no women were allowed. The monk said there were only 149 churches in the city.

When on the way to the beach road, there drove in front of us a green jeep with a broken window. Suddenly, it dawned on us that we had seen it before. The driver was asked to stop that jeep, but another car kept between us for miles.

At last, after much honking, the car and jeep stopped and the Constantines, whom we had seen in Chile, got out right there in the middle of the road and, with the surf pounding away nearby, we had a confab relating to our experiences since last seeing them.

They insisted we go on with them to a party given by the US Consulate people who were in the extra car. It seemed like the thing to do, so the Moor McCormick man returned to the ship, and we continued on with them.

The party was fun—they had good drinks, good food, good company, good conversation. One story the Constantines told us was of how the Dealy boys got their jackets burned. The Constantines had heated bricks to put in their sleeping bags, as they had felt sorry for the boys having to sleep on the ground, when they slept comfortably in the jeep. Suddenly, the boys were out of the bags and beating their coats on the ground. The coats were ablaze, and the coats were more important than the sleeping bags, which were also ablaze.

The party was on a plantation outside the city, where banana trees and cashew nut trees were grown in groves, with nuts and fruit springing from the trees in abundance. Horses were stabled for the guests to ride, and the cozy, comfortable living was appreciated.

There was an American negro from Chicago in the group of guests, who was down there to organize labor. He had been a teacher at Barnard College. The Consulate was giving him all the respect and consideration they gave others.

Another colored man from a family of well-educated people from Chicago, who has a sister who is a successful doctor there, was also a member of the Consulate. He did not like the bridge between the white and colored people in the United States and had applied for foreign service. He seems to fill an important niche here and is well respected.

They all came back to the ship with the Constantine party, where the festivities continued for several hours more. These people in their conversation and manner, behavior and dress held the respect of everyone.

It was nostalgic to see the Constantines again and swap experiences with them. They had gone over the same road conditions we had encountered and they, with their fifth gear, had had to be pulled out several times; so having assistance in getting through seemed not so bad for a Cadillac.

They never believed we would make it through some of these deep streams of water and deep rutted roads; and each time they would cross a dangerous place, they would think about us and wonder what we were going to do, or if we would get through!

They, as well as we, learned to use a Brazilian saying: *Deus-a-Proteccion*—God is a Protector!

If you are craving a dangerous adventure, under extreme difficulties, by all means, take a special, high wheel car and go the Pan American Highway this summer to the enchanted lands of South America. You will see sights and find experiences not to be found anywhere on the face of this old earth.

If you love comfortable adventure—wait five years. Then we would advise you to take a good supply of canned foods, drinking water containers, canned heat, extra cans for gasoline and, by all means, a high, off-the-ground car with narrow wheels for your travels down "South of the Equator."

If comfort means more to you than adventure—a comfortable car, comfortable roads, comfortable hotel rooms, good food each day—then please wait at least ten years for your trip below the Equator in a car; otherwise, you will find yourself stuck in the deep ruts or riding the dangerous ridges of the road. One small mishap might keep you from being as lucky as we.

Biographies

Lucretia Ayers Donnell was born in a covered wagon near Blanket, Texas in 1893 to Anna and Reverend William L. Ayers, a Baptist minister from Villa Rica, Georgia. In 1910 she attended Baylor Female College (University of Mary Hardin Baylor) in Belton, Texas on a Fine Arts Scholarship and won the Gold Medal Award for her original designs in china painting. She served as the assistant to the art professor and upon graduating in 1912 she was named a full professor of the Art Department.

Lucretia married Earl Roe Donnell in 1913 and they had two children, the future artist Lucretia Donnell Newman Coke and Earl Roe Donnell, Jr.

When the family moved to Dallas in 1924, Lucretia studied art under John Knott, Frank Klepper, Martha Simpkins and Frank Reaugh. She also studied under Oscar Berninghaus, Ernest L. Blumenschein and Frederick W. Becker in Taos and at the Art Institute of Chicago and with Robert Wood in California. She hand carved French provincial furniture and sewed designer clothing which she sold to fine department stores. Lucretia continued her studies in china painting in Europe in 1951, driving the roads in her car with her husband Earl for six months, even venturing behind the Iron Curtain to visit the fine porcelain plants.

For forty-five years, Lucretia taught oil painting and fine china painting in her large University Park studio. She was instrumental in forming the China Painting Teachers of Texas and served as its first president from 1958 to 1960. She also was a founder of the National China Painting Teacher's Organization that became the International Porcelain Artists and Teachers Organization. For her efforts the N.C.P.T.O. honored her with a gold medallion and a life membership.

Lucretia was awarded a Certificate of Merit from the US Navy for helping US servicemen during World War II. In this way, she memorialized her son, Earl Jr. who was killed in service to his country, completing a dive-bombing mission off the USS Enterprise, February 1, 1942.

Grand Angel to her three grand children, she could do anything. The word *can't* was not in her vocabulary. She had an infectious smile, quick wit, and street smarts and put the most delicious Thanksgiving dinners and other special treats on the table. Lucretia Donnell lovingly and graciously exemplified the meaning of the term, "true grit."

Earl Roe Donnell was born in 1889 in Wellborn, Texas. His father served in the Texas House of Representatives and owned the Donnell Creamery in Temple where young Earl worked. Upon graduation from the University of Texas, Earl married the "angel" he saw singing in the Mary Hardin Baylor choir in 1913. After working in the oil business, he founded the Donnell Ice Cream Company in Dallas. He was a member and officer of the Dallas Lions Club, Gilbraltar Blue Lodge and the Hella Temple Shrine. After retiring from Borden's, which had bought the Donnell Ice Cream Company, Earl raised and exhibited cattle and founded the Donnell Farm Implement Company.

Earl's only son, Earl Donnell Jr., was lost in World War II while serving as a naval aviator on the aircraft carrier Enterprise. Earl Sr. and Lucretia Donnell made it their passion to "adopt" the men of the US Donnell Flying Squadron and the destroyer escort (DE-56), USS Donnell and wrote a monthly clearinghouse type newsletter for them and also entertained "their boys" in their Dallas home whenever possible. Earl had an outgoing personality, loved people and they loved him.

Lucretia Donnell Newman Coke, Lucretia Ayers Donnell's daughter, was a recognized pastel artist, having been a student and protégé of the legendary Frank Reaugh. She excelled at portraiture and landscapes and exhibited throughout Texas, with her work featured in several books. Her mother also a student of Frank Reaugh and accompanied her daughter on many of the Reaugh sketch trips in the 1930s to west Texas as chaperone.

During the Pan American Highway trip, her mother mailed letters home to the family in Dallas. "Little Lucretia," as she was called, then typed the letters and painted the beautiful images in this book in India ink and watercolor using the postcards the Donnells sent to their three grandchildren as guides.

www.ingramcontent.com/pod-product-compliance
Lightning Source LLC
Chambersburg PA
CBHW081210170426
43198CB00018B/2905